Latin America's New Historical Novel

The Texas Pan American Series

Latin

America's

New

Historical

Novel

by SEYMOUR MENTON

 University of Texas Press   Austin

First Paperback Edition, 2011

Requests for permission to reproduce material from this work should be sent to
Permissions, University of Texas Press, Box 7819, Austin, TX 78713-7819.

∞ The paper used in this publication meets the minimum requirements of
American National Standard for Information Sciences—Permanence of Paper
for Printed Library Materials, ANSI Z39.48-1984.

Grateful acknowledgment is made for permission to reprint previously published
material from the journals *Cuadernos Americanos* ("La guerra de Mario Vargas
Llosa contra el fanatismo," vol. 4, no. 28, 1991), *Hispania* ("Christopher Columbus and the New Historical Novel," October 1992), and *Universidad de México* ("La campaña: Crónica de una guerra denunciada," vol. 46, 1991), and from
the chapter "*Noticias del imperio* y la nueva novela histórica" in Seymour Menton,
Narrativa mexicana desde "Los de abajo" hasta "Noticias del imperio" (Tlaxcala:
Universidad Autónoma de Tlaxcala, 1991).

LIBRARY OF CONGRESS CATALOGING-IN-PUBLICATION DATA

Menton, Seymour.
 Latin America's new historical novel / by Seymour Menton. — 1st ed.
  p. cm. — (The Texas Pan American series)
 Includes bibliographical references and index.
 ISBN: 978-0-292-72918-6
 1. Historical fiction, Latin American—History and criticism. 2. Latin American fiction—20th century—History and criticism. I. Title. II. Series.
PQ7082.N7M477 1993
863'.08109—dc20   93-787

A los miopes del mundo: literally, figuratively, . . .
and dialogically

Contents

Acknowledgments

I am deeply grateful to several friends for bringing to my attention recent historical novels from their own countries or from those in whose literature they have specialized. Without their cooperation, the following chronological lists could not possibly be as complete as they are.

Argentina: Malva Filer, Myron Lichtblau, Naomi Lindstrom, and Leonardo Senkman

Bolivia: Adolfo Cáceres Romero, Evelio Echevarría, and José Ortega

Brazil: Regina Igel, Wilson Martins, Malcolm Silverman, and Marijose Tartt

Chile: Juan Gabriel Araya, Evelio Echevarría, Lucía Guerra Cunningham, José Promis, and Juan Villegas

Colombia: Otto Morales Benítez, Alvaro Pineda Botero, and Jonathan Tittler

Ecuador: Jimmy Chica and Lola Proaño

Guadeloupe, Haiti, and Martinique: Aliko Songolo

Guatemala: Francisco Albizúrez Palma and Juan Fernando Cifuentes

Honduras: Ramón Luis Acevedo

Mexico: Francisco Alvarez, John S. Brushwood, Marcela del Río, Aurora M. Ocampo, Federico Patán, and Raymond D. Souza

Nicaragua: Jorge Eduardo Arellano

Panama: Enrique Jaramillo Leví and Donald Lindenau
Peru: Carlos Thorne and Julio Ortega
Uruguay: Fernando Aínsa and Jorge Ruffinelli
Venezuela: José Balza and Alexis Márquez Rodríguez

I am especially indebted to my old friend Myron Lichtblau (we were classmates at the City College of New York in the late 1940s) for having read with a critical eye an early draft of Chapter 1 and to my young friend Richard Barrutia (we go back only as far as the opening of the University of California, Irvine in the fall of 1965) for his constant encouragement.

I am also most appreciative of the superb copyediting by Liz Gold; of the efficient coordination of the publication process by University of Texas Press Managing Editor Carolyn Cates Wylie; and of the strong support of this project from its inception by Executive Editor and Assistant Director Theresa J. May.

Latin America's New Historical Novel

Prepenðix

Chronology of the Latin American Historical Novel,
1949–1992

The following lists of 367 new and not-so-new Latin American historical novels published between 1949 and 1992 normally would appear in
an appendix. However, by locating them in the prependix, I am foregrounding my preference for empirically rather than theoretically based
scholarship. More specifically, the subgenre of the Latin American New
Historical Novel of 1979 to the present did not emerge as the result of
a literary manifesto, nor did I become interested in it by reading some
theoretical text on hegemonic versus marginalized culture. In the course
of keeping up with the contemporary Latin American novel, I gleefully
discovered such high-quality works as Alejo Carpentier's *El arpa y la
sombra* 'The Harp and the Shadow' (1979), Antonio Benítez Rojo's *El
mar de las lentejas* 'Sea of Lentils' (1979), Mario Vargas Llosa's *La
guerra del fin del mundo* 'The War of the End of the World' (1981),
Abel Posse's *Los perros del Paraíso* 'The Dogs of Paradise' (1983), and
Fernando del Paso's *Noticias del imperio* 'News from the Empire'
(1987). At the same time, I began to perceive similarities that distin-
guished these five and a host of other post-1979 novels from their predecessors. After reading every New Historical Novel and as many not-
so-new historical novels as I could, postulating theories about the
nature of the phenomenon, and consulting the relatively few critical

studies available, I prepared a number of conference papers in 1989 and launched them tricontinentally in 1990[1] with the hope of expanding them into a full-blown book that would be ready for publication by October 12, 1992 ... or 1993.

(In the following lists, countries are abbreviated as follows: ARG–Argentina, BOL–Bolivia, BR–Brazil, CH–Chile, COL–Colombia, CR–Costa Rica, CU–Cuba, DR–Dominican Republic, EC–Ecuador, GDP–Guadeloupe, GUA–Guatemala, GYN–French Guiana, HT–Haiti, HON–Honduras, MTQ–Martinique, MX–Mexico, NIC–Nicaragua, PAN–Panama, PAR–Paraguay, PER–Peru, PR–Puerto Rico, SAL–Salvador, UR–Uruguay, VZ–Venezuela.)

Latin America's New Historical Novel, 1949–1992

1949   Alejo Carpentier, *El reino de este mundo*, CU
1962   Alejo Carpentier, *El siglo de las luces*, CU
1969   Reinaldo Arenas, *El mundo alucinante*, CU
1972   Angelina Muñiz, *Morada interior*, MX
1974   Alejo Carpentier, *Concierto barroco*, CU
   Augusto Roa Bastos, *Yo el Supremo*, PAR
   Edgardo Rodríguez Juliá, *La renuncia del héroe Baltasar*, PR
1975   César Aira, *Moreira*, ARG
   Carlos Fuentes, *Terra nostra*, MX
1976   Márcio Souza, *Gálvez imperador do Acre*, BR
1977   Pedro Orgambide, *Aventuras de Edmund Ziller en tierras del nuevo mundo*, ARG
1978   Abel Posse, *Daimón*, ARG
1979   Antonio Benítez Rojo, *El mar de las lentejas*, CU
   Alejo Carpentier, *El arpa y la sombra*, CU
1980   Antonio Larreta, *Volavérunt*, UR
   Martha Mercader, *Juanamanuela, mucha mujer*, ARG
   Alejandro Paternain, *Crónica del descubrimiento*, UR
   Ricardo Piglia, *Respiración artificial*, ARG
   Márcio Souza, *Mad Maria*, BR
1981   Silviano Santiago, *Em liberdade*, BR
   Mario Vargas Llosa, *La guerra del fin del mundo*, PER
1982   Germán Espinosa, *La tejedora de coronas*, COL
1983   Pedro Orgambide, *El arrabal del mundo*, ARG
   Abel Posse, *Los perros del Paraíso*, ARG

Denzil Romero, *La tragedia del generalísimo,* VZ
Juan José Saer, *El entenado,* ARG
1984   Martín Caparrós, *Ansay ó los infortunios de la gloria,* ARG
Edgardo Rodríguez Juliá, *La noche oscura del Niño Avilés,* PR
João Ubaldo Ribeiro, *Viva o povo brasileiro,* BR
1985   Carlos Fuentes, *Gringo viejo,* MX
Francisco Simón, *Martes tristes,* CH
1986   Márcio Souza, *O brasileiro voador,* BR
1987   Reinaldo Arenas, *La loma del ángel,* CU
Fernando del Paso, *Noticias del imperio,* MX
Denzil Romero, *Gran tour,* VZ
1988   Tomás de Mattos, *Bernabé, Bernabé,* UR
Juan Carlos Legido, *Los papeles de los Ayarza,* UR
Sergio Ramírez, *Castigo divino,* NIC
Denzil Romero, *La esposa del doctor Thorne,* VZ
1989   Arturo Arias, *Jaguar en llamas,* GUA
Napoleón Baccino Ponce de León, *Maluco,* UR
Saúl Ibargoyen, *Noche de espadas,* UR
Ignacio Solares, *Madero, el otro,* MX
José J. Veiga, *A casca da serpente,* BR
1990   Carlos Fuentes, *La campaña,* MX
Herminio Martínez, *Diario maldito de Nuño de Guzmán,* MX
1991   Antonio Elio Brailovsky, *Esta maldita lujuria,* ARG
Haroldo Maranhão, *Memorial do fim (A Morte de Machado de Assis),* BR
Julián Meza, *La huella del conejo,* MX
1992   Herminio Martínez, *Las puertas del mundo: Una autobiografía hipócrita del Almirante,* MX
Abel Posse, *El largo atardecer del caminante,* ARG
Augusto Roa Bastos, *Vigilia del Almirante,* PAR
Paco Ignacio Taibo II, *La lejanía del tesoro,* MX

The continued predominance of the New Historical Novel throughout 1992 and possibly beyond seems guaranteed by the public and private news that the following authors are in the process of writing other historical novels: Antonio Benítez Rojo (CU), Joaquín Armando Chacón (MX), Gerardo Cornejo (MX), Carlos Fuentes (MX), Gabriel García Márquez (COL), Fernando del Paso (MX), Sergio Ramírez (NIC), Denzil Romero (VZ), Benhur Sánchez (COL), Carlos Thorne (PER), and Mario Vargas Llosa (PER).

Latin America's Not-So-New Historical Novel, 1949–1992

The differences between the New Historical Novels and the traditional or not-so-new historical novels are explored in Chapter 1. Although the latter outnumber the former, in aesthetic quality most of the latter (but not all) are far less significant. The reason for including them here is to demonstrate the proliferation of all kinds of historical novels from the late 1970s to the present. The vast majority of the not-so-new historical novels are clearly distinguishable from the New Historical Novels, but in a few cases the categorization may be open to debate.

1949   Enrique Laguerre, *La resaca*, PR
Manuel Mujica Láinez, *Aquí vivieron: Historia de una quinta de San Isidro,1583–1924*, ARG
Erico Verissimo, *O continente*,[2] BR

1950   Luciano Alcalde, *Felipe II, Rey y Emperador de las Españas*, CH
Josefina Cruz, *El viento sobre el río*, ARG
Argentina Díaz Lozano, *Mayapán*, HON
Emmeline Carriès Lemaire, *Coeur de héros, coeur d'amant*, HTI
Tristán Marof (pseudonym of Gustavo A. Navarro), *La ilustre ciudad*, BOL
Pedro Niño, *El conquistador*, CH
Benjamín Subercaseaux, *Jemmy Button*, CH

1951   Ermilo Abreu Gómez, *Naufragio de indios*, MX
Joaquín Aguirre Lavayen, *Más allá del horizonte*, BOL
Manuel Gálvez, *Han tocado a degüello*, ARG
——, *Tiempo de odio y de angustia*, ARG
Alfredo Sanjinés G., *El Quijote mestizo*, BOL
Fernando Santiván (pseudonym of Fernando Santibáñez), *El mulato Riquelme*, CH

1952   J. M. García Rodríguez, *Princesa de Francia en Castilla*, DR
J. Fernando Juárez Muñoz, *El hijo del bucanero*, GUA
Ramón Jurado, *Desertores*, PAN

1953   Luisita Aguilera Patiño, *El secreto de Antatura*, PAN
Manuel Gálvez, *Bajo la garra anglo-francesa*, ARG
Edmundo Márquez, *Guerrillero*, CH
Francisco Méndez, *Hijo de virrey*, CH

1954   Jorge Carneiro, *A visão dos quatro séculos*, BR
Manuel Gálvez, *Y así cayó don Juan Manuel*, ARG
Renée Pereira Olazábal, *El perjuro*, ARG
Dinah Silveira de Queiroz, *A muralha*, BR

1955 David Viñas, *Cayó sobre su rostro*, ARG
1956 Rolmes Barbosa, *Réquiem para os vivos*, BR
      Antonio Di Benedetto, *Zama*, ARG
1957 Hernâni Donato, *Chão bruto: Romance mural, a conquista do
      extremo sudoeste paulista*, BR
      Agripa de Vasconcelos, *A vida em flor de Dona Bêja*, BR
1958 Ramón Amaya Amador, *Los brujos de Ilamatepeque*, HON
      Rodolfo Falcioni, *El hombre olvidado*, ARG
      Alejandro Magnet, *La espada y el canelo*, CH
      Roberto Otaegui, *Donde se pone el sol*, CH
      Nazario Pardo Valle, *Cien años atrás*, BOL
1959 Fernando Benítez, *El rey viejo*, MX
      Paulo Dantas, *O Capitão Jagunço*, BR
      Luis Hernández Aquino, *La muerte anduvo por el Guasio*, PR
      Francisco Vegas Seminario, *Cuando los mariscales combatían*,
      PER
1960 José A. Alcaide, *Víctor Rojas, salvador de doscientas vidas*, PR
      Leónidas Barletta, *Primer cielo de Buenos Aires*, ARG
      Josefina Cruz, *Doña Mencía la adelantada*, ARG
      Carlos Fuenzalida, *Don Helmuth, el colono*, CH
      Jorge Inostrosa, *El corregidor de Calicanto*, CH
      Alberto Reyna Almandos, *Episodios de la colonia; Relato no-
      vela de las invasiones inglesas*, ARG
      Hernando Sanabria Fernández, *Cañoto*, BOL
      João Felício dos Santos, *Major Calabar*, BR
      Francisco Vegas Seminario, *Bajo el signo de la mariscala*, PER
      Marcio Veloz Maggiolo, *El buen ladrón*, DR
      María Viancos de Jara, *Un violín en la calle*, CH
1961 Almiro Caldeira, *Rocamaranha*, BR
      Luis Enrique Délano, *El viento del rencor*, CH
      Carlos Droguett, *Cien gotas de sangre y doscientas de sudor*, CH
      Antonio Estrada, *Rescoldo*, MX
      Ramón Emilio Reyes, *El testimonio*, DR
      Francisco I. Schauman, *A lanza y cuchillo*, ARG
      Francisco Vegas Seminario, *La gesta del caudillo*, PER
1962 Jorge García Granados, *El deán turbulento*, GUA
      Pedro Motta Lima, *Fábrica da pedra*, BR
      Manuel Mujica Láinez, *Bomarzo*, ARG
      Manuel Muñoz, *Guarionex, la historia de un indio rebelde*, PR
      Acracia Sarasqueta de Smyth, *El guerrero*, PAN
      Gil Blas Tejeira, *Pueblos perdidos*, PAN

Marcio Veloz Maggiolo, *Judas*, DR
Armando Venegas Harbín, *La caja de Sándalo*, CH
1963 Valerio Ferreyra, *Rebelión en Babilonia*, ARG
Elena Garro, *Recuerdos del porvenir*, MX
Fernando Ortiz Sanz, *La barricada*, BOL
Eliseo Salvador Porta, *Intemperie*, UR
Fernando Santiván (pseudonym of Fernando Santibáñez), *Bárbara*, CH
1964 Demetrio Aguilera Malta, *La caballeresa del sol*, EC
————, *El Quijote de El Dorado: Orellana y el río de las Amazonas*, EC
Juan Francisco Ballon, *Tahuantinsuyo: Historia de un inca desconocido*, PER
Arturo Berenguer Carisomo, *El doctor Diego de Torres Villarroel: El pícaro universitario*, ARG
Carlos Esteban Deive, *Magdalena*, DR
Porfirio Díaz Machicao, *Tupac Catari, la Sierpe*, BOL
Wilson Lins, *Os cabras do coronel*, BR
Reinaldo Lomboy, *Puerto del hambre*, CH
Ibiapaba Martins, *Bocainas do vento sul*, BR
Luis Marcondes Rocha, *Café e polenta*, BR
João Felício dos Santos, *Cristo de lama*, BR
Guido Wilmar Sassi, *Geração do deserto*, BR
Luis Spota, *La pequeña edad*, MX
Virgínia G. Tamanini, *Karina*, BR
1965 Demetrio Aguilera Malta, *Un nuevo mar para el rey: Balboa, Anayansi y el Océano Pacífico*, EC
Irma Cairoli, *Eulalia Ares*, ARG
Jorge Inostrosa, *Los húsares trágicos*, CH
Pedro Leopoldo, *O drama de uma época*, BR
Wilson Lins, *O reduto*, BR
José López Portillo y Pacheco, *Quetzalcóatl*, MX
Manuel Mujica Láinez, *El unicornio*, ARG
Nazario Pardo Valle, *Peores que Judas*, BOL
Camilo Pérez de Arce, *La plaza de las cuatro calles*, CH
Dinah Silveira de Queiroz, *Os invasores*, BR
José Fausto Rieffolo Bessone, *Manco Capac, el profeta del sol*, ARG
Francisco I. Schauman, *Entre caudillos y montoneros*, ARG
1966 João Alves Borges, *O inconfidente*, BR

Almiro Caldeira, *Ao encontro da manhã,* BR
Argentina Díaz Lozano, *Fuego en la ciudad,* HON
Dyonélio Machado, *Deuses econômicos,* BR
Mario Monteforte Toledo, *Llegaron del mar,* GUA
Daniel Riquelme, *La revolución del 20 de abril de 1851,* CH
José Román Orozco, *Los conquistadores,* NIC
Mauricio Rosenthal, *Las cenizas de Dios,* ARG
Agripa Vasconcelos, *Gongo-Sôco,* BR
Carlos Vega López, *Así nacieron dos pueblos: Novela de la independencia,* CH
David Viñas, *En la semana trágica,* ARG
1967 Octavio Mello Alvarenga, *Judeu Nuquim,* BR
Maria Alice Barroso, *Um nome para matar,* BR
Carlos Droguett, *Supay, el cristiano,* CH
René León Echaiz, *Mientras corre el río,* CH
Wilson Lins, *Remanso da valentia,* BR
Acracia Sarasqueta de Smyth, *Valentín Corrales, el panameño,* PAN
Edmundo Vega Miguel, *42 prisioneros,* CH
1968 Josefina Cruz, *Los caballos de don Pedro de Mendoza,* ARG
———, *La Condoresa* (2nd edition, *Inés Suárez la Condoresa,* 1974), ARG
Ibiapaba Martins, *Noites do relâmpago,* BR
João Felício dos Santos, *Carlota Joaquina, a rainha devassa,* BR
Francisco I. Schauman, *Las montoneras de López Jordán: Historia novelada de las rebeliones jordanistas en Entre Ríos y las de los "blancos" en el Uruguay desde el asesinato del general Urquiza al de López Jordán,1870–1889,* ARG
1969 Miguel Angel Asturias, *Maladrón,* GUA
Jorge Inostrosa, *Bajo las banderas del Libertador,* CH
Fernando Ortiz Sanz, *La Cruz del Sur,* BOL
1970 Germán Espinosa, *Los cortejos del diablo,* COL
Sergio Ramírez, *Tiempo de fulgor,* NIC
Rafael Reygadas and Cecilia Soler, *Dos virreyes para la leyenda,* ARG
1971 Abelardo Arias, *Polvo y espanto,* ARG
Roberto Pérez Paniagua, *Los trece cielos,* GUA
Ricardo A. R. Ríos Ortiz, *Indios de Leoncito atacan Resistencia,* ARG
Maslowa Gomes Venturi, *Trilha perdida,* BR

1972 José Enrique Ardón Fernández, *Monseñor y Josefina*, GUA
Hernâni Donato, *O rio do tempo: O romance do Aleijadinho*, BR
Francisco Herrera Luque, *Boves el urogallo*, VZ
Alix Mathon, *La fin des baionettes*, HTI
Serge Patient, *Le nègre du gouverneur: Chronique coloniale*, GYN
Lautaro Yankas (pseudonym of Manuel Soto Morales), *Doña Catalina: Un reino para la Quintrala*, CH

1973 Josefina Cruz, *El conquistador conquistado: Juan de Garay*, ARG
Enrique Molina, *Una sombra donde sueña Camila O'Gorman*, ARG
Mario Luis Pereyra (M. L. Beney, pseudonym), *La brújula rota*, ARG
Valentin Romelle, *Djanga: Sous le ciel des Antilles*, HTI

1974 Jorge Inostrosa, *Combate de la Concepción*, CH
———, *El ministro Portales*, CH
Alix Mathon, *Le drapeau en berne*, HTI
Manuel Mujica Láinez, *El laberinto*, ARG

1975 Félix Courtois, *Scènes de la vie port-au-princienne*, HTI
Josué Montello, *Os tambores de São Luis*, BR

1976 Joaquín Aguirre Lavayén, *Guano maldito*, BOL
Jorge Dávila Andrade, *María Joaquina en la vida y en la muerte*, EC
Iván Egüez, *La Linares*, EC
Pedro Gómez Valderrama, *La otra raya del tigre*, COL
César Leante, *Los guerrilleros negros*, or *Capitán de cimarrones* (1982), CU

1977 Mario Bahamondes, *El caudillo de Copiapó*, CH
Mario Cortés Flores, *Conrado Menzel: Novela de la historia del nitrato de sodio de Chile, la guerra del Pacífico y la Revolución de 1891*, CH
Félix Courtois, *Durin Belmour: Roman ou conte fantastique*, HTI
José Daza Valverde, *El demonio de los Andes*, BOL
Luis Gasulla, *El solitario de Santa Ana*, ARG
Angelina Muñiz, *Tierra adentro*, MX
Moacyr Scliar, *O ciclo das águas*, BR
Néstor Taboada Terán, *El Manchaypuito*, BOL

1978 Baltazar Castro, *¿Ha almorzado la gente?* CH
Francisco Herrera Luque, *En la casa del pez que escupe el agua,*
VZ

1979 Eliécer Cárdenas, *Polvo y ceniza,* EC
Carlos Esteban Deive, *Las devastaciones,* DR
Alfredo Antonio Fernández, *El candidato,* CU
Francisco Herrera Luque, *Los amos del valle,* VZ
Cyro Martins, *Sombras na correnteza,* BR
Miguel Otero Silva, *Lope de Aguirre, príncipe de la libertad,* VZ
Ernesto Schóó, *El baile de los Guerreros,* ARG

1980 Eugenio Aguirre, *Gonzalo Guerrero,* MX
Josefina Cruz, *Saavedra, el hombre de Mayo,* ARG
Hernâni Donato, *O caçador de esmeraldas,* BR
Carlos de Oliveira Gomes, *A solidão segundo Solano López,* BR
José Luis González, *La llegada,* PR
Dyonélio Machado, *Prodígios,* BR
Carlos Valenzuela, *Santiago Bueras, huaso, soldado, héroe,* CH

1981 Marcos Aguinis, *El combate perpetuo,* ARG
César Aira, *Ema, la cautiva,* ARG
Libertad Demitrópulos, *Río de las congojas,* ARG
Dyonélio Machado, *O sol subterrâneo,* BR
Daniel Maximin, *L'isolé soleil,* GDP
Silvia Molina, *Ascensión Tun,* MX
Domingo Alberto Rangel, *Junto al lecho del caudillo,* VZ
Arturo Uslar Pietri, *La isla de Robinson,* VZ
Mauricio Wacquez, *Frente a un hombre armado (cacerías de 1848),* CH

1982 Jorge Eduardo Arellano, *Timbucos y calandracas,* NIC
Renato Castelo Branco, *Rio da liberdade,* BR
Júlio José Chiavenato, *Coronéis e carcamanos,* BR
Otto-Raúl González, *Diario de Leona Vicario,* GUA
Ramón González Paredes, *Simón Bolívar, la angustia del sueño,*
VZ
Jorge Ibargüengoitia, *Los pasos de López,* MX
Marila Lander de Pantín, *Añil,* VZ
Haroldo Maranhão, *O tetraneto del-Rei (o Torto, suas idas e venidas),* BR
Josué Montello, *Aleluia,* BR
Estela Saenz de Méndez, *María de las islas,* ARG
Michel Tauriac, *La catastrophe,* MTQ

Rafael Zárraga, *Las rondas del obispo,* VZ
1983   Enrique Campos Menéndez, *Los pioneros,* CH
Renato Castelo Branco, *A conquista dos sertões de dentro,* BR
————, *Senhores e escravos: A balada,* BR
María I. Clucellas, *La última brasa,* ARG
Francisco Herrera Luque, *La luna de Fausto,* VZ
Daniel E. Larrigueta, *Gracias a Pavón,* ARG
Angelina Muñiz, *La guerra del unicornio,* MX
Lisandro Otero, *Temporada de ángeles,* CU
Agustín Pérez Pardella, *Camila,* ARG
————, *El ocaso del guerrero,* ARG
Julio Travieso, *Cuando la noche muera,* CU
Manuel Trujillo, *El gran dispensador,* VZ
1984   Juan Ahuerma Salazar, *Alias Cara de Caballo,* ARG
César Aira, *Canto castrato,* ARG
Jorge Amado, *Tocáia Grande: A face obscura,* BR
Almiro Caldeira, *Arca açoriana,* BR
Cyro Martins, *Gaúchos no obelisco,* BR
Alix Mathon, *La relève de Charlemagne: Les cacos de la plume,*
    chronique romancée, HTI
Martha Mercader, *Belisario en son de guerra,* ARG
María Esther de Miguel, *Jaque a Paysandú,* ARG
Rui Nedel, *Esta terra teve dono,* BR
Pedro Orgambide, *Hacer la América,* ARG
Miguel Otero Silva, *La piedra que era Cristo,* VZ
Nélida Piñón, *A república dos sonhos,* BR
Andrés Rivera, *En esta dulce tierra,* ARG
1985   Homero Aridjis, *1492: Vida y tiempos de Juan Cabezón de Cas-*
    tilla, MX
Chermont de Britto, *Villegaignon, Rei do Brasil,* BR
Renato Castelo Branco, *O planalto: O romance de São Paulo,*
    BR
Alcy José de Vargas Cheuiche, *A guerra dos farrapos,* BR
Gabriel García Márquez, *El amor en los tiempos del cólera,* COL
Hugo Giovanetti, *Morir con Aparicio,* UR
Gastão de Holanda, *A breve jornada de D. Cristóbal,* BR
Tabajara Ruas, *Os varões assinalados: O romance da Guerra*
    dos Farrapos, BR
Adão Voloch, *O colono judeu-açu: O romance da colônia Qua-*
    tro Irmãos–Rio Grande do Sul, BR

1986 Enrique Campos Menéndez, *Aguilas y cóndores*, CH
Maryse Condé, *Moi, Tituba sorcière*, GDP
Rosario Ferré, *Maldito amor*, PR
Carlos de Oliveira Gomes, *Caminho Santiago*, BR
Próspero Morales Pradilla, *Los pecados de Inés de Hinojosa*, COL
Gonzalo Otero, *Las máscaras del rey sobre la tierra*, BOL
Caupolicán Ovalles, *Yo Bolívar Rey*, VZ
Agustín Pérez Pardella, *La caída de Buenos Aires*, ARG
José León Sánchez, *Tenochtitlán*, CR
Manuel Zapata Olivella, *El fusilamiento del diablo*, COL

1987 Gilfredo Carrasco Ribera, *El desierto de ceniza*, BOL
Fernando Cruz Kronfly, *La ceniza del libertador*, COL
Ricardo Elizondo Elizondo, *Setenta veces siete*, MX
Germán Espinosa, *El signo del pez*, COL
Francisco Herrera Luque, *Manuel Piar, caudillo de dos colores*, VZ
Eloy Lacava, *Vinho amargo*, BR
Gerardo Laveaga, *Valeria*, MX
Carlos A. Montaner, *Trama*, CU
Mauricio del Pinal, *3-Cabán*, GUA
Maria José de Queiroz, *Joaquina, filha de Tiradentes*, BR
Andrés Rivera, *La revolución es un sueño eterno*, ARG
Horacio Saldona, *El último virrey*, ARG
Alberto Ruy Sánchez, *Los nombres del aire*, MX

1988 Homero Aridjis, *Memorias del Nuevo Mundo*, MX
Rolando Rodríguez, *República angelical*, CU
Pedro Rubio, *Las lámparas de fuego: Novela pensando en Sor Teresa de los Andes*, CH
Juan José Saer, *La ocasión*, ARG
Milton Schinca, *Hombre a la orilla del mundo*, UR
Augusto Tamayo Vargas, *Amarilis de dos mundos*, PER

1989 Alfonso Balderrama Maldonado, *Oro dormido: Choquecamata*, BOL
Guillermo Blanco, *Camisa limpia*, CH
José Antonio Bravo, *Cuando la gloria agoniza*, PER
Carlos María Domínguez, *Pozo de Vargas*, ARG
Gabriel García Márquez, *El general en su laberinto*, COL
Andrés Hoyos, *Por el sendero de los ángeles caídos*, COL
Ana Miranda, *Boca do inferno*, BR

Félix A. Posada, *La guerra de la compañía Landínez*, COL
Marco Vinicio Prieto Reyes, *La Bogotá señorial*, COL
Gilberto Ramírez Santacruz, *Esa hierba que nunca muere*, PAR
Gonzalo Ramírez Cubilán, *Pequeña Venecia*, VZ
José León Sánchez, *Campanas para llamar al viento*, CR
Marcos Yauri Montero, *No preguntes quién ha muerto*, PER
Nicomedes Zuloaga Pocaterra, *Epitafio para un filibustero*, VZ

1990　Paulo Amador, *Rei Branco Rainha Negra*, BR
Laura Antillano, *Solitaria solidaria*, VZ
Juan Gabriel Araya, *1891: Entre el fulgor y la agonía*, CH
Armando Ayala Anguiano, *Cómo conquisté a los aztecas*, MX
Assis Brasil, *Nassau: Sangue e amor nos trópicos*, BR
Brianda Domecq, *La insólita historia de la Santa de Cabora*, MX
Autran Dourado, *Monte da Alegria*, BR
Germán Espinosa, *Sinfonía desde el nuevo mundo*, COL
Jean-Claude Fignolé, *Aube tranquille*, HTI
David Martín del Campo, *Alas de ángel*, MX
Próspero Morales Pradilla, *La mujer doble*, COL
José Luis Ontivero, *Cíbola*, MX
Denzil Romero, *La carujada*, VZ
Ricardo Rosillo Melo, *El virrey*, COL
Francisco Sandoval, *Bartolomé sin compañía*, GUA
Arturo Uslar Pietri, *La visita en el tiempo*, VZ
Juan Valdano, *Mientras llega el día*, EC

1991　Raúl Agudo Freites, *Miguel de Buría*, VZ
Marcos Aguinis, *La gesta del marrano*, ARG
Azriel Bibliowicz, *El rumor del astracán*, COL
Carmen Boullosa, *Son vacas, somos puercos*, MX
Luis Antonio de Assis Brasil, *Videiras de cristal*, BR
Horacio Bustamante, *La corona hecha pedazos*, PAN
Eduardo Casanova, *La noche de Abel*, VZ
Francisco Cuevas Cancino, *La pradera sangrienta*, MX
Leopoldo Garza González, *La fundación de Nuevo Laredo*, MX
Francisco Herrera Luque, *Los cuatro reyes de la baraja*, VZ
Gregorio Martínez, *Crónica de músicos y diablos*, PER
Mario Moya Palencia, *El México de Egerton, 1831–1842*, MX
Agustín Pérez Pardella, *Cristo, los judíos y el César*, ARG
———, *Ojos paganos, corazón cristiano*, ARG
Andrés Rivera, *El amigo de Baudelaire*, ARG
Mario Romano and Guillermo A. Koffman, *¿Quién conoció a Martin Bresler?* ARG

Javier Sicilia, *El Bautista*, MX
Ignacio Solares, *La noche de Angeles*, MX
Bernardo Valderrama Andrade, *El gran jaguar*, COL
Mercedes Valdivieso, *Maldita yo entre las mujeres*, CH

1992   Mario Anteo, *El reino en celo*, MX
Rosa Boldori, *La morada de los cuatro vientos*, ARG
Francisco Cuevas Cancino, *La pradera sangrienta*, MX
Julio Escoto, *El general Morazán marcha a batallar desde la muerte*, HON
Germán Espinosa, *Los ojos del basilisco*, COL
Andrés Hoyos, *Conviene a los felices permanecer en casa*, COL
Jorge Mejía Prieto, *Yo, Pancho Villa*, MX
Alvaro Miranda, *La risa del cuervo*, COL
Elena Poniatowska, *Tinísima*, MX

1 Latin America's New Historical Novel

Definitions and Origins

While some critics have prematurely hailed the demise of the "Boom" novelists and have touted the emergence of a new generation of "post-Boom" novelists,[1] the empirical evidence suggests that since 1979 the dominant trend in Latin American fiction has been the proliferation of New Historical Novels,[2] the most canonical of which share with the Boom novels of the 1960s muralistic scope, exuberant eroticism, and complex, neo-baroque (albeit less hermetic) structural and linguistic experimentation. The so-called postmodern collapse of the *"grandes narrativas"*[3] is unquestionably belied by such works as Alejo Carpentier's *El arpa y la sombra* 'The Harp and the Shadow' (1979), Antonio Benítez Rojo's *El mar de las lentejas* 'Sea of Lentils' (1979), Mario Vargas Llosa's *La guerra del fin del mundo* 'The War of the End of the World' (1981), Germán Espinosa's *La tejedora de coronas* 'The Weaver of Crowns' (1982), Abel Posse's *Los perros del Paraíso* 'The Dogs of Paradise' (1983), Fernando del Paso's *Noticias del imperio* 'News from the Empire' (1987), and Carlos Fuentes's *La campaña* 'The Campaign' (1990). García Márquez's *El general en su laberinto* 'The General in His Labyrinth' (1989) may not qualify as a New Historical Novel because of its re-creation of a very specific historical period with relatively few characters, and its conscious avoidance of exuberant experimentation. Nonetheless, it is clearly a superior historical novel, which, along

with many others—including such popular best-sellers as Morales Pradilla's *Los pecados de Inés de Hinojosa* 'The Sins of Inés de Hinojosa'
(1986) and Carlos Montaner's *Trama* 'Plot' (1987)—has enriched this
genre in the past more or less fifteen years. In other words, the emergence of the elitist, potentially canonical New Historical Novel as the
dominant subgenre since the late 1970s has been paralleled by the proliferation of the popular traditional historical novel.

Although I have chosen the 1979 date as the starting point for the
flourishing of the New Historical Novel in order to highlight Alejo Carpentier's contributions, two other outstanding novels that meet all the
criteria were actually published a few years earlier: Augusto Roa Bastos's *Yo el Supremo* 'I, the Supreme' (1974) and Carlos Fuentes's *Terra
nostra* (1975). In fact, they could even be labeled as paradigmatic, representing the opposite ends of the spectrum of New Historical Novels
from history-dominant to fiction-dominant. The case for 1975 could
also be argued on the basis of the rarely mentioned 81-page *Moreira*,
by the young Argentine César Aira (born in 1949), which is a carnivalesque treatment of the historical/legendary/literary Argentine bandit of
the 1870s replete with deliberate anachronisms, metafiction, and a variety of discourses.

Definitions of the New Historical Novel

Before proceeding any further, however, the term *historical novel*
must be defined, and then the *new* historical novel must be differenti-
ated from the old one. In the broadest sense, every novel is historical
since, in varying degrees, it portrays or captures the social environment
of its characters, even the most introspective ones.[4] Léon-François Hoffmann's observation that "history is an obsession with Haitian novelists"
(143) would certainly be true of all of Latin America, but Hoffmann's
definition is too broad and his percentage estimate is too low: "If we
define the historical novel as a novel in which the precise events taken
from history determine or influence the development of the plot and
provide it to a great extent with the referential background, about
20% of Haitian novels can be considered historical novels" (151–152).
Georg Lukács, in *The Historical Novel* (written in 1936–1937 but not
published until 1954, in German), actually objects to the classification
of novels and prose fiction into subgenres and stresses the similarities
between the realistic and the historical novels of both Dickens and Tolstoy (Part 3, Chapter 5). Nevertheless, in order to analyze the recent
proliferation of the Latin American historical novel, the category must

be reserved for those novels whose action takes place completely (in some cases, predominantly) in the *past*—arbitrarily defined here as a past not directly experienced by the author. Avrom Fleishman, in *The English Historical Novel* (1971), is even more arbitrary, excluding those novels that are set fewer than two generations back in time. On the other hand, David Cowart opts for an excessively broad definition— "fiction in which the past figures with some prominence" (6)—and structures his study on four different categories, including fictions of the future in which the future is shown to be growing out of the past and present (9, 76–119), such as George Orwell's *1984*. Raymond Souza, in *La historia en la novela hispanoamericana moderna* (1988), shares Cowart's broader view and emphasizes the philosophical and stylistic differences between history and fiction without distinguishing the historical novel as a special genre. Joseph W. Turner argues convincingly that it would be preferable for the sake of definition to discuss three different types of historical novels: documented, disguised, and invented. However, he also suggests the possibility of a fourth category, the comic historical novel, and mentions as its practitioners John Barth and Ishmael Reed. In view of the fact that Latin America's New Historical Novel is a combination of the comic, the documented, and the invented historical novel, these discrete categories are not very helpful in describing and analyzing the phenomenon.

Since the principal purpose of this book is to demonstrate the predominance since 1979 of the New Historical Novel rather than the telluric, psychological, magic realist, or nonfiction novel, Enrique Anderson Imbert's (1951) clear, straightforward definition is the most appropriate one: "We call 'historical novels' those whose action occurs in a period previous to the author's" (3).

According to this definition, the following well-known novels are excluded from this study because, in spite of their significant historical dimensions, they all encompass, at least partially, the author's own time frame: Carlos Fuentes's *La muerte de Artemio Cruz* 'The Death of Artemio Cruz' (1962), Ernesto Sábato's *Sobre héroes y tumbas* 'On Heroes and Tombs' (1962), Mario Vargas Llosa's *Conversación en la catedral* 'Conversation in the Cathedral' (1969), Alejo Carpentier's *El recurso del método* 'Reasons of State' (1974), and Tomás Eloy Martínez's *La novela de Perón* 'The Novel of Perón' (1985). Family sagas such as Gabriel García Márquez's *Cien años de soledad* 'One Hundred Years of Solitude' (1967), Panamanian Yolanda Camarano de Sucre's *Los Capelli* (1967), and Martinican Edouard Glissant's *Le quatrième siècle* 'The Fourth Century' (1964) and *La case du commandeur* 'The

Foreman's Cabin' (1981) are also excluded because the characters of the youngest generation are contemporaries of the authors.

More difficult to exclude from the historical category are those novels in which the narrator(s) or characters are anchored in the present or in the recent past, but whose principal theme is the re-creation of the life and times of a clearly distant historical character. In Venezuelan Francisco Herrera Luque's *Los cuatro reyes de la baraja* 'The Four Kings of the Deck' (1991), the protagonist is the late-nineteenth-century Francophile dictator Antonio Guzmán Blanco, but the narration is periodically interrupted by remarks from a group of intellectuals who in 1957 gather every Thursday in the Plaza del Panteón to discuss politics. Guzmán Blanco is portrayed as one of the four men who have controlled the destiny of Venezuela, along with José Antonio Páez, Juan Vicente Gómez, and Rómulo Betancourt. However, despite the title, Guzmán Blanco is the sole protagonist, and the novel is definitely historical.

In four different Mexican novels, a narrator or character anchored in the present is obsessed with exploring a period in the past. In Brianda Domecq's *La insólita historia de la Santa de Cabora* 'The Unusual Story of the Saint of Cabora' (1990) and Mario Moya Palencia's *El México de Egerton, 1831–1842* (1991), the vast majority of the novelistic material, as in *Los cuatro reyes de la baraja*, is historical, and therefore it would be splitting hairs to deny them the title of historical novels. On the other hand, in Silvia Molina's *La familia vino del norte* 'The Family Came from the North' (1987) and Luis Arturo Ramos's *Este era un gato . . .* 'Once Upon a Time There Was a Cat' (1987), the events of the present are at least equal in importance to the discovery of the past, and therefore they really should not be classified as historical novels— which, of course, has absolutely nothing at all to do with the appraisal of their quality. In other cases, the relative importance of the narrators' present circumstances and the objects of their investigations may be more difficult to determine categorically, as in Brazilian Moacyr Scliar's *A estranha nação de Rafael Mendes* 'The Strange Nation of Rafael Mendes' (1983), and Venezuelan Laura Antillano's *Solitaria solidaria* 'Alone and Committed' (1990).

Latin America's Traditional Historical Novel, 1826–1949

Given the working definition of the historical novel, how does the New Historical Novel differ from its predecessors? The traditional historical novel dates back to the early nineteenth century and is primarily identified with romanticism, although it subsequently evolved in the twentieth century within the aesthetics of modernism, *criollismo,* and even existentialism, as in the unique case of Antonio Di Benedetto's *Zama* (1956). The Latin American romantic historical novel, inspired not only by Sir Walter Scott but also by the colonial chronicles and, in some cases, by Golden Age drama, begins with the anonymous *Jico-téncal* (1826), the story of the "Encounter of Two Worlds" in which the Tlaxcalans are exalted and the Spaniards excoriated. However, it was not until the 1840s that the romantic historical novel assumed a pioneering role in the development of the genre, and then only in a small number of Latin American countries: in Mexico, with Justo Sierra's *La hija del judío* 'The Daughter of the Jew' (1848–1850); in Argentina, with Vicente Fidel López's *La novia del hereje* 'The Heretic's Fiancée' (1845–1850); in Colombia, with Juan José Nieto's *Ingermina* (1844) and Juan Francisco Ortiz's *El oidor Cortés de Meza* 'The judge Cortés de Meza' (1845); and in Cuba, with *Guatimozín* (1846), by one of the few Latin American women novelists of the nineteenth century, Gertrudis Gómez de Avellaneda.[5] In Brazil, in spite of the country's relatively tranquil transition from colonial to independent status, the romantic historical novel did not appear until the following decades, as represented by José de Alencar's *O Guarani* (1857) and *Iracema* (1865).

Although the romantic novel was replaced in Europe by the realistic novels of Dickens and Balzac in the 1830s and 1840s, and in Spanish America by the realistic novels of Chilean Alberto Blest Gana in the 1860s,[6] the romantic historical novel continued to be cultivated right up through the end of the century and even into the first decade of the twentieth century. Perhaps the most amazing example of the romantic historical novel's longevity is the publication in 1897 of *Durante la reconquista* by the "Spanish American Balzac," Alberto Blest Gana, who three decades earlier had published the first Spanish American realistic novels.

In addition to entertaining several generations of readers with their thrilling episodes and their heroic and angelical protagonists pitted against fiendish, diabolical villains, the goals of most of these novelists were to contribute to the creation of a national consciousness by familiarizing their readers with characters and events of the past, and to bolster the Liberal cause in the struggle against the Conservatives, who identified with the political, economic, and religious institutions of the colonial period.

Since nineteenth-century realism, almost by definition, concentrated on contemporary problems, with a strong emphasis on pictur-esque customs and regionalist speech, there was no realistic historical novel—at least not until 1928, when Tomás Carrasquilla published his still relatively little-known *La marquesa de Yolombó*. Paradoxically, however, the single best Latin American historical fiction writer of the nineteenth century was Ricardo Palma, whose six series of *Tradiciones peruanas*, dating from 1872 to 1883, are cast much more within the realistic than the romantic mold.[7]

In contrast to the romantic historical novelists, the authors of his-torical novels written during the modernist period (1882–1915) were less concerned about engendering a national consciousness and sup-porting the Liberals than they were about finding alternatives to *cos-tumbrista* realism, positivistic naturalism, bourgeois materialism, and, in the case of Mexico, to revolutionary turbulence. The main goal of these novels was the more or less faithful re-creation, albeit artistically embellished, of the historical setting, whether it was the Spain of Philip II in Argentinean Enrique Larreta's *La gloria de don Ramiro* (1908), the New Spain in the texts of the Mexican *colonialistas* Francisco Mon-terde (*El madrigal de Cetina y el secreto de la escala* 'Cetina's Madrigal and the Secret of the Staircase', 1918) and Julio Jiménez Rueda (*Sor Adoración del Divino Verbo*, 1923), the Holy Land in *Phineés* (1909) by Colombian Emilio Cuervo Márquez, or fourteenth-century Byzan-tium in *El evangelio del amor* 'The Gospel of Love' (1922) by Guate-malan Enrique Gómez Carrillo.

During the thirty-year period from 1915 to 1945 in which *crio-llismo* was the dominant trend in the novel and short story, the search for national identity once again became a major preoccupation, but with emphasis on contemporary problems: the struggle between urban civilization and the barbarism of the hinterland, socioeconomic exploi-tation, and racism. In this period, the number of historical novels was relatively small, but those that were published continued in the mimetic vein, re-creating the historical setting with fictitious protagonists: *Ma-talaché* (1924) by the Peruvian *indigenista* Enrique López Albújar, and two novels by a pair of prolific Venezuelan author-statesmen: *Las lan-zas coloradas* 'The Red Lances' (1931) by Arturo Uslar Pietri and *Pobre negro* (1937) by Rómulo Gallegos. Probably the most outstanding Latin American *criollista* historical novel is Brazilian Erico Verissimo's *O continente* 'The Continent' (1949), the first volume of the well-known trilogy *O tempo e o vento* 'Time and the Wind', a monumental national epic from a Rio Grande do Sul perspective that traces Brazilian history up through the 1930s and 1940s.

Carpentier and the New Historical Novel

The first real New Historical Novel, Alejo Carpentier's *El reino de este mundo* 'The Kingdom of This World', was published in 1949, the same year as *O continente,* and a full thirty years before the New Historical Novel became the dominant trend. Although it is a composite history of the struggle for Haitian independence from the middle of the eighteenth century through the first third of the nineteenth century, loosely united by the mythical or composite historical figure of Ti Noel,[8] the novel subordinates Haitian history to the philosophical question of why human beings continue to struggle for freedom and social justice in the face of insurmountable odds. However, the ideological message is simultaneously pro- and antirevolutionary—that is to say, dialogic. As it is *the* pioneering New Historical Novel, all the protagonists, except possibly for Ti Noel, are historical figures, albeit minor ones (Mackandal, Bouckman, Pauline Bonaparte), with the exception of Henri Christophe. Also in keeping with the New Historical Novel is the distortion of history through the absence of such important Haitian historical figures of the period as Toussaint l'Ouverture,[9] Jean Jacques Dessalines, and Alexandre Pétion.

Carpentier's claim to the scepter as Latin America's first new historical novelist does not depend exclusively on *El reino de este mundo.* The concept of the cyclical nature of history forms the basis of his two long short stories "Semejante a la noche" 'Like the Night' (1952), in which a soldier bids farewell to his beloved on the eve of his departure for war in six different chronological periods, from the Trojan War to World Wars I and II; and "El camino de Santiago" 'The Highroad of St. James' (1954), in which the soldier Juan of Antwerp goes on a pilgrimage to Santiago de Compostela to atone for his sins, changing his name to Juan the Pilgrim. He later sails for Havana and commits other sins before returning to Spain, where his name becomes Juan the West Indian. In the fair at Burgos, Juan the West Indian meets another repentant Juan who is on the way to Compostela—his double—and persuades him to sail for America, thus indicating that the cycle will continue.

Furthermore, between 1949 and 1979, the publication dates of *El reino de este mundo* and *El arpa y la sombra,* Carpentier published two other New Historical Novels: *El siglo de las luces* 'Explosion in a Cathedral' (1962), in which certain parallelisms may be drawn between the French Revolution of 1789 and the Cuban Revolution of 1959,[10] and *Concierto barroco* 'Baroque concert' (1974), in which all the arts are fused, chronological lines are blurred, distinctions between elite and popular culture disappear, three historical composers (Vivaldi, Handel, and Scarlatti) are strong supporting actors, Stravinsky and Louis Armstrong make anachronistic cameo appearances, and overall a carnivalesque atmosphere prevails.[11] Although Carpentier's synthetic-composite-dictator novel *El recurso del método* 'Reasons of State' (1974) and his socialist epic *La consagración de la primavera* 'The Rites of Spring' (1978) do not conform to our definition of the historical novel because they present events concurrent with the author's own life, they do further illustrate Carpentier's obsession with history.

Nevertheless, *El arpa y la sombra* (1979) is Carpentier's first and only historical novel in which the undisputed protagonist is a famous historical personage, Christopher Columbus. Not only that, but its three parts illustrate three very different approaches taken by other practitioners of the New Historical Novel. Part 1, like Roa Bastos's *Yo el Supremo* and Antonio Benítez's *El mar de las lentejas*, is a completely realistic, mimetic re-creation of two chronotopes: (1) a specific, unidentified day—possibly in the early 1870s—in Rome, where Pope Pius IX has just finished preparing the written proposal for the beatification of Christopher Columbus, and (2) a trip by Giovanni María Mastai (the future Pius IX) in 1823–1824 to Argentina and Chile in search of a Spanish American saint, in which he interacts with both literature and history: the slaughterhouse of Esteban Echeverría's famous short story and the historical conflicts between the liberal dictator Bernardo O'Higgins and the ambitious general Ramón Freire, between the Conservative *pelucones* 'bigwigs' and the Liberal *pipiolos* 'novices'.

Part 2 of the novel, like Herminio Martínez's *Diario maldito de Nuño de Guzmán* 'Nuño de Guzmán's Cursed Diary' (1990), is a first-person narration of a famous historical figure, Christopher Columbus. Entitled "*La mano*" 'The Hand' in deference to the "Gran Almirante's" legerdemain and his skill in lying (the eighth capital sin), this part presents Columbus's distorted death-bed confession in which Carpentier himself is not above "lying"—he has Columbus reveal to the reader that he would call Queen Isabella "Columba" in their nights of intimacy (91). In fact, the ailing Carpentier identifies with the dying Columbus and provides the reader with an accurate description of his own style, in an example of the self-referential, metafictional quality of many of the New Historical Novels:

> Since it's easy to keep on talking once you get started, I gradually became inspired by my own words, enlarging my gestures, stepping

back to allow my voice to resound, listening to myself as I would to somebody else, and the names of the most splendid lands, both real and fabled, began to roll off my tongue. Every gleaming, glistening, glittering, dizzying, dazzling, exciting, inviting image in the hallucinatory vision of a prophet came unbidden to my mouth as if impelled by a diabolical interior energy.[12]

The demythifying aspect of Columbus's confession is also typical of such recent historical novels as Jorge Ibargüengoitia's *Los pasos de López* (1982; about Mexico's Padre Miguel Hidalgo) and Martín Caparrós's *Anzay* (1984; about Argentina's Mariano Moreno). In 1983, Fernando del Paso called for Spanish American novelists to "assault" the official versions of history, thus establishing a link to the official version of the banana strike in *Cien años de soledad* and to the Argentine movie *Official Story*, about the 1976–1983 military dictatorship.

Part 3 of *El arpa y la sombra*, like *Los perros del Paraíso*, *Noticias del imperio*, and so many other New Historical Novels, is predominantly carnivalesque. The uproarious debate over the beatification of Columbus is witnessed by the latter's ghost; a variety of nineteenth-century authors as well as the early sixteenth-century defender of the Indians Fray Bartolomé de las Casas intervene; and Carpentier establishes a linkage with the presently impending Quincentennial by setting the debate not long before *1892*: "And the best proof is that a prize of thirty thousand pesetas has just been created to be awarded to the best biography—solidly documented, credible, modern—in an open contest intended as a general commemoration of the quadricentennial of the Discovery of America, which will take place shortly" (142).

Characteristics of the New Historical Novel

Whether the actual year of birth of the New Historical Novel is designated as 1949, 1974, 1975, or 1979, there is no question that it was primarily engendered by Carpentier, with strong support from Jorge Luis Borges, Fuentes, and Roa Bastos, and that it is clearly distinguishable from the previous historical novel by the following set of six traits that are evident in a large number of novels from Argentina to Puerto Rico (although all six are not necessarily found in each novel):

1. The subordination, in varying degrees, of the mimetic recreation of a given historical period to the illustration of three philosophical ideas, popularized by Borges[13] and applicable to all periods of the past, present, and future. As they appear in "Tema del traidor y del

héroe" 'Theme of the Traitor and the Hero' (*Ficciones,* 1944) and "Historia del guerrero y la cautiva" 'Story of the Warrior and the Captive' (*El aleph,* 1949)—and, even as early as 1935, in some of the stories in *Historia universal de la infamia*—these ideas are (a) the impossibility of ascertaining the true nature of reality or history; (b) the cyclical nature of history; and (c) the unpredictability of history—that although history tends to repeat itself, occasionally the most unexpected and amazing events may and do occur.

2. The conscious distortion of history through omissions, exaggerations, and anachronisms.

3. The utilization of famous historical characters as protagonists, which differs markedly from the Walter Scott formula—endorsed by Lukács—of fictitious protagonists. Indeed, the protagonists of some of the better historical novels of the past decade are Christopher Columbus, Magellan, Felipe II, Goya, Francisco de Miranda, Maximilian and Carlota, and Santos Dumont. Couched in other terms, while nineteenth-century historians subscribed to the "great man" theory of history, nineteenth-century novelists molded their own fictitious protagonists from among ordinary people who had no history. Conversely, while late-twentieth-century social historians focus on the particular in order to enlarge our understanding of the general society and culture (e.g., Warren Goldstein's 1989 *Playing for Keeps: A History of Early Baseball* and Donald Reid's 1991 *Down and Dirty: Paris Sewers and Sewermen*), late-twentieth-century novelists delight in portraying sui generis history's outstanding men and women.

4. *Metafiction,* or the narrator's referring to the creative process of his own text. Although Robert Alter in *Partial Magic: The Novel as a Self-Conscious Genre* (1975) identifies this trait with some of the world's most esteemed novels, from *Don Quijote* and *Tristram Shandy* on, the influence of Borges is also clearly observable in several of the New Historical Novels in the narrator's questioning of his own discourse by parenthetical phrases and the use of the word *perhaps* and its synonyms, as well as in the sometimes apocryphal footnotes.

5. *Intertextuality.* Since García Márquez surprised the readers of *Cien años de soledad* with the insertion in his novel of characters from novels by Carpentier, Fuentes, and Julio Cortázar, intertextuality has become increasingly fashionable among the theorists as well as among the majority of the novelists. Although the theoretical notion was first introduced by Bakhtin, it was "popularized" by Gérard Genette and Julia Kristeva. The latter writes that "any text is constructed as a mosaic of quotations; any text is the absorption and transformation of another.

The notion of *intertextuality* replaces that of intersubjectivity, and poetic language is read as at least *double*" (37). Allusions to other works, often explicit, are frequently made in jest, as in Abel Posse's *Los perros del Paraíso*. The extreme example of intertextuality is *palimpsest*, or the rewriting of another text, such as Vargas Llosa's *La guerra del fin del mundo*, a rewriting in part of Euclides da Cunha's *Os sertões* 'Rebellion in the Backlands' (1902); or Reinaldo Arenas's *El mundo alucinante* 'Hallucinations' (1969), a rewriting of the *Memorias* ([ca. 1820] 1917) of Fray Servando Teresa de Mier; or Silviano Santiago's *Em liberdade* 'Freed' (1981), an apocryphal continuation of Graciliano Ramos's *Memórias do cárcere* 'Prison Memoirs' (1953); or Haroldo Maranhão's 1991 *Memorial do Fim (A Morte de Machado de Assis)* 'Memorial of the End (The Death of Machado de Assis)', a parodic re-creation of the real and fictitious world of Brazil's greatest author at the time of his death in 1908.

6. The Bakhtinian concepts of the *dialogic*, the *carnivalesque*, parody, and *heteroglossia*. First, in keeping with the Borgesian idea that reality and historical truth are unknowable, several of the New Historical Novels follow Bakhtin's interpretation of Dostoyevsky's novels as being dialogic—that is, as containing two or more often conflicting presentations of events, characters, and world views.

Bakhtin's notion of the carnivalesque, which he developed in his studies on Rabelais, is prevalent in several of the New Historical Novels, in their humorous exaggerations and their emphasis on bodily functions, from sex to elimination. It should be noted, however, that the credit for popularizing Rabelais belongs to García Márquez, who in *Cien años de soledad* (1967) not only graphically describes scenes of exaggerated eating and sexual prowess but explicitly acknowledges his debt to Rabelais when the character Gabriel leaves Macondo for Paris "with two changes of clothing, a pair of shoes, and the complete works of Rabelais" (409). Bakhtin began to influence Latin American literature a few years later: perhaps the first direct mention of his work was Severo Sarduy's 1969 *Escrito sobre un cuerpo* 'Written on a Body' (72); it was not until the 1970s that his works were published in Spanish; and one of the first critical studies in a Hispanic professional journal, Emir Rodríguez Monegal's *"Carnaval/Antropofagia/Parodia,"* did not appear until 1979.

The humorous aspects of the carnivalesque are also reflected in the New Historical Novel's frequent use of parody, which Bakhtin considers "one of the most ancient and widespread forms for representing the direct word of another" (51).

The fourth of the Bakhtinian concepts that often appears in the New Historical Novels is heteroglossia: the multiplicity of discourses, or the conscious use of different types of speech.

In addition to these six characteristics, the New Historical Novel differs markedly from the traditional romantic historical novel in its far greater variety of modalities. The high degree of historicity in *Yo el Supremo*, *El mar de las lentejas*, and *Noticias del imperio* distinguishes these three New Historical Novels from others within the genre, such as the much more fanciful and pseudo-historical *Terra nostra* and *Los perros del Paraíso*, and the totally apocryphal *La renuncia del héroe Baltasar* 'The Resignation of Baltasar the Hero' (1974) and *La noche oscura del Niño Avilés* 'The Dark Night of the Boy Avilés' (1984) by Edgardo Rodríguez Juliá. The alternation between two rather widely separated time periods in *El arpa y la sombra*, *La tejedora de coronas*, Martha Mercader's *Juanamanuela, mucha mujer* 'Juanamanuela, Quite a Woman' (1980), and Napoleón Baccino Ponce de León's *Maluco* (1989) contrasts with the concentration on a very specific and limited historical period in *La guerra del fin del mundo*, on the one hand, and, on the other, the unabashed anachronism of *Los perros del Paraíso*. Yet all are New Historical Novels. In some cases, the representation of the past masks comments on the present (*La guerra del fin del mundo* and Juan Carlos Legido's *Los papeles de los Ayarza* 'Ayarza's Papers' [1988]) while in others the evocation of the past bears very little or no relationship to the present (*Noticias del imperio* and *Maluco*). The historical detective stories *Volavérunt* 'They Flew' by Antonio Larreta (1980) and *Castigo divino* 'Divine Punishment' by Sergio Ramirez (1988), with their relatively limited numbers of characters, are quite different from the panoramic, muralistic, or encyclopedic novels exemplified by *Terra nostra*, *La tejedora de coronas*, and *Noticias del imperio*. In addition to Christopher Columbus in *El arpa y la sombra*, the protagonists of the apocryphal autobiographical novels range from Santa Teresa in Angelina Muñiz's *Morada interior* 'Interior Dwelling' (1972) to the ferocious conquistador in *Diario maldito de Nuño de Guzmán*.

Reasons for the Flourishing of the New Historical Novel

Now that the phenomenon of the New Historical Novel has been duly observed and defined, the next logical step is to theorize about why it began to flourish in the late 1970s. Literary historians invariably theorize or speculate about the emergence or predominance of certain movements, styles, or genres in a given period of time or in a given country or countries. As far as the New Historical Novel (NHN) is concerned, it is obvious that the historical novel in general has assumed far greater significance since 1979 than it did during the *criollista* period of 1915–1945. In fact, although Carpentier's 1949 *El reino de este mundo* has been identified as the first NHN, the number of historical novels in general published in the past thirteen years (1979–1992) was 194, which outstrips the 173 historical novels published in the preceding twenty-nine years (1949–1978). Furthermore, with the exception of Carpentier's *El reino de este mundo, El siglo de las luces,* and *Concierto barroco,* only nine other novels published in the 1949–1978 period can be considered New Historical Novels, seven of which were published in 1974–1978. Therefore, the only pre-1974 New Historical Novels, aside from those of Carpentier, are Reinaldo Arenas's *El mundo alucinante* (1969) and Angelina Muñiz's *Morada interior* (1972).

Another indication of the predominance of the New Historical Novel since 1979 is that it has been cultivated by the major novelists from four distinct literary generations, who represent most of the Latin American countries: first, Cuban Alejo Carpentier (1904–1980); second, Mexican Carlos Fuentes (b. 1929), Peruvian Mario Vargas Llosa (b. 1936), and Brazilian Silviano Santiago (b. 1936); third, Nicaraguan Sergio Ramírez (b. 1942), Cuban Reinaldo Arenas (1943–1990), Puerto Rican Edgardo Rodríguez Juliá (b. 1946), Mexican Herminio Martínez (b. 1949), and Guatemalan Arturo Arias (b. 1950); and, most recently, Argentinean Martín Caparrós (b. 1957).

The most notable exception to this trend appears to be Chile, where Francisco Simón's *Martes tristes* (1985) is perhaps the only example of the New Historical Novel. The explanation may lie in recent Chilean novelists' greater concern with the immediate past: the military coup against the Allende government in 1973, the Pinochet dictatorship, and the exile experiences many of them shared. On the other hand, the scarcity of the New Historical Novel in Chile may also be attributed to the traditional preference of its novelists for realistic, contemporary settings. In 1949 José Zamudio Zamora observed that "our country, a country of historians as it has been called, is not outstanding in this genre in which history and fiction are combined" (9).

Since both the new and the traditional historical novels published from 1979 to 1992 vary so greatly, it is impossible to attribute the proliferation of the entire genre to one or more specific causes. A more judicious approach is to propose and discuss as many factors as possible, not all of which will be equally applicable to all works.

Probably the single most important factor in stimulating the publication of so many historical novels in the past fifteen years or so has been the awareness since the late 1970s of the approaching Quincentennial of the discovery of America. In fact, the paradigmatic New Historical Novel of 1979, *El arpa y la sombra,* features Christopher Columbus as its protagonist, and one of the four alternating threads of *El mar de las lentejas,* also published in 1979, has as its protagonist one of the soldiers in Columbus's second voyage. Actually, the earliest appearance of Columbus in the post-1949 novel, albeit a cameo one, was in García Márquez's 1975 *El otoño del patriarca* 'The Autumn of the Patriarch'. In the same year, Carlos Fuentes published *Terra nostra,* in which America is discovered not by Columbus but by the archetypal old and young sailors. In 1980, which was already considered by Jorge Ruffinelli to be "at the threshold of the Quincentennial" (my translation, 51), Uruguayan Alejandro Paternain published *Crónica del descubrimiento* 'Chronicle of the Discovery', which narrates the apocryphal discovery of Europe in 1492 by a group of Indians. A highly fictionalized Columbus co-stars with Queen Isabella in Abel Posse's 1983 novel *Los perros del Paraíso.*

In a more recent novel, Homero Aridjis's *Memorias del Nuevo Mundo* (1988), the figure of Columbus is subordinated to a fictitious sailor, Juan Cabezón—the protagonist of Aridjis's previous novel, *1492: Vida y tiempos de Juan Cabezón de Castilla* (1985). Moreover, after only thirty-five pages of *Memorias del Nuevo Mundo,* the focus shifts from the discovery of the New World to the Conquest of Mexico, and Columbus abruptly disappears from the novel. The significance of the Quincentennial for Latin American writers is further highlighted, paradoxically, by Carlos Fuentes's futuristic novel *Cristóbal Nonato* (1987), based on the anticipated birth of the putative protagonist on October 12, 1992. Finally, among the latest New Historical Novels published are Herminio Martínez's 1992 *Las puertas del mundo (una autobiografía hipócrita del Almirante)* 'The Doors of the World (The Admiral's Hypocritical Autobiography)' and Augusto Roa Bastos's *Vigilia del Almirante* 'The Admiral's Vigil' (October 1992!).

If the recent novelistic appearances of Columbus date from 1975 (*El otoño del patriarca*), his philatelic presence, also occasioned by the approaching Quincentennial, began in the Dominican Republic with the Spanish Heritage Series from 1976 to 1978 and continued with the country's 1982 series in commemoration of the 490th anniversary of the discovery of the New World, the 1983–1986 Casa de España Annual Regatta Series, and the 1987 Discovery of America Series. Undoubtedly many more series followed in the years 1987 to 1992.[14] President Joaquín Balaguer also decided to honor Columbus with the construction of a fifty-million-dollar pyramid-shaped lighthouse at the entrance to the Santo Domingo harbor to house Columbus's bones. The lighthouse is designed to project on the water a gigantic laser beam in the form of a 3,000-foot-long cross to symbolize the evangelical aspect of the Conquest. Columbus and the discovery of America have also been honored philatelically in the past decade throughout Latin America.

However, the significance of the Quincentennial is not limited to remembering Columbus and the discovery of the New World. It has also generated a greater awareness of the historical bonds shared by the Spanish American countries, as well as a questioning of the continent's official history. In 1987 and 1989, Cuba issued a total of eight strips of five stamps each devoted to Latin American history. The 1987 ones featured heroic Indians who fought bravely against the *conquistadores,* such as the Cuban Hatuey, the Mexican Cuauhtémoc, and the Chilean Lautaro. The 1989 issue paid tribute to a broad range of authors, from the relatively early nineteenth-century *pensadores* 'intellectuals' José Cecilio del Valle and Sarmiento to the mid-twentieth-century novelists Rómulo Gallegos, Miguel Angel Asturias, and Alejo Carpentier.

As was to be expected, the celebration of the Quincentennial has also sparked a renewal of the long-standing dispute between critics and defenders of the Spanish Conquest. On July 9–12, 1984, at a meeting in Santo Domingo of several national committees for the Quincentennial of the "discovery" of America, the term *"Encuentro de Dos Mundos"* 'Encounter of Two Worlds' was officially proposed by the Mexican delegation headed by Miguel León-Portilla, who had coined the phrase.[15] In Mexico City, on October 12, 1986, groups of Indians celebrated the *"Día de la Dignidad del Indio"* by marching down the Paseo de la Reforma past the Columbus statue, shouting *"Cristóbal Colón al paredón"* 'Christopher Columbus to the firing squad' (Ortega y Medina, 162). In Ecuador, the Confederación de Nacionalidades Indígenas protested against commemorating the "Spanish invasion" (*Casa de las Américas,* 29, no. 174 [May–June 1989], 118), and Ecuador planned a convocation to celebrate 500 years of indigenous resistance. Jorge Ruffinelli, in his appraisal of Alejandro Paternain's *Crónica del descubrimiento,* expressed his current political concerns: "Naturally, as we draw near to the year of celebration, 1992, a story that inverts the cultural relations in which we have lived for five hundred years without challenging their legitimacy had to become attractive. . . . Paternain's novel is only a source of amusement, but it points unequivocally toward a present-day Latin American consciousness of decolonization" (52). The official Cuban cultural journal *Casa de las Américas,* without taking a strong position on the merits of the Conquest, related it to current political conflicts: "And we are not talking about evaluating only that event that is contradictory in itself but also its interpretation in the light of today's conflicts, many of which are seen as reflections of the positions that dignitaries, institutions, and governments assume vis-à-vis the Quincentennial" (*Casa de las Américas,* 29, no. 174 [May–June 1989], 103).

In July of 1991, Venezuelan President Carlos Andrés Pérez convened in Caracas a group of outstanding Latin American authors and politicians to prepare an agenda for a future meeting aimed at preparing a joint Latin American statement on the discovery of America. In keeping with the greater emphasis on pluralism and compromise since 1989, a variety of political views were represented by ex-presidents Raúl Alfonsín of Argentina, Julio Sanguinetti of Uruguay, and José Sarney of Brazil, and an impressive array of writers including Gabriel García Márquez, Sergio Ramírez, Mario Monteforte Toledo, Leopoldo Zea, Arturo Uslar Pietri, and David Escobar Galindo.

Although all the planning of conferences and celebrations of the Quincentennial have undoubtedly stimulated both the resurgence of the historical novel and the questioning of the role of Latin America in the world after five hundred years of contact with Western civilization, a more somber theory is that the increasingly grim situation throughout Latin America in the 1970s and 1980s is responsible for the popularity of what is essentially an escapist subgenre. In 1898, Spain's defeat at the hands of the United States and its subsequent loss of Cuba and Puerto Rico, symbolizing the end of its role as an imperial power, caused the young intellectuals of the period to examine their nation's past in search of a raison d'être for the modern era, the twentieth century. The Generation of 1898's obsession with *Don Quijote,* and with Spain's cultural heritage in general, represented an attempt to bolster national pride, but also an unwillingness to face reality. Although Latin America's current crisis cannot be identified with any single event, the following occurrences in the 1970s and 1980s, as well as the long-range outlook, constitute a very bleak picture from which the authors of the New Historical Novels may be turning away, either as an escape from reality or as a search for national or continental ingredients that might offer a glimmer of hope in coping with the future. In the 1970s, the military dictatorships in Argentina, Uruguay, Chile, and Brazil were guilty of inordinate abuse of human rights, and many intellectuals took refuge in the United States and Europe. Although the revolutionary Sandinista movement triumphed in Nicaragua in 1979, other revolutionary guerrillas have not succeeded in taking power, and only in Peru have the guerrillas maintained a significant presence up until 1992. The Revolution of 1989—that is, the collapse of the Eastern European communist governments and the subsequent dissolution of the Soviet Union—the defeat of the Sandinistas at the polls, and the decreasing significance of Cuba as a revolutionary role model have caused despair among those Latin American intellectuals who since the 1920s had looked to socialism as the ultimate solution for the tremendous inequities suffered by their compatriots.

In the 1980s, the gradual collapse of the military dictatorships in the Southern Cone countries and the elections of civilian Christian Democrat Vinicio Cerezo in Guatemala and of *Aprista* Alan García in Peru brought a short-lived hope for democracy and a general improvement of the situation. However, that hope has disappeared as political democracy has been undermined by the ineptness of these two young presidents; the decline in world oil prices and the subsequent economic crises in Mexico and Venezuela; and the insurmountable foreign debt, runaway inflation, and unemployment in almost all Latin American countries from Puerto Rico to Argentina.

The end of the Cold War and the democratization and consequent privatization of Eastern Europe may well have negative consequences for Latin America. Foreign aid from the wealthier nations is likely to be channeled more to Eastern Europe than to Latin America. Furthermore, many political commentators are now predicting that the international conflicts of the future will be between the developed countries of the northern hemisphere and the underdeveloped and developing countries of the southern hemisphere—the Third World countries—with the latter succumbing to hunger, disease, and political violence.

The fascination with history on the part of novelists and readers in the past two decades has also been paralleled by the publication of scholarly biographies and collages of historical vignettes. Ira Bruce Nadel, in his 1984 *Biography: Fiction, Fact and Form*, stated categorically that "in the twentieth century, biography has reasserted experimentation, linking itself to fiction rather than history" (185). In 1982 Octavio Paz published his 670-page study of the life and times of Mexico's greatest colonial poet with a title reminiscent of the nineteenth-century romantic historical novels: *Sor Juana Inés de la Cruz o Las trampas de la fe.* In 1990 literary scholar José Luis Martínez published an objective, 1009-page study of the life and times of Hernán Cortés, simply titled *Hernán Cortés*—an undertaking all the more extraordinary in view of Mexico's long-standing official as well as popular repudiation of Cortés: there are no statues of Cortés in Mexico, nor are any streets named after him.[16]

Devoid of scholarly pretensions, overtly political, and somewhat novelistic in tone are three historical collages that have gone back beyond the Conquest period to the pre-Columbian civilizations in order to present panoramic murals of five hundred years of suffering and exploitation: Guillermo Cabrera Infante's *Vista del amanecer en el trópico* 'View of Dawn in the Tropics' (1974), Roque Dalton's *Las historias prohibidas del Pulgarcito* 'The Banned Stories of Tom Thumb' (1974), and Eduardo Galeano's *Memoria del fuego* 'Memory of Fire' (1982–1986). The last two in particular differ ideologically from many of the New Historical Novels in that they are monologic denunciations of the national hegemonic sectors and of their Spanish and, later, U.S. imperialist allies.

Another manifestation in the past decade of an increasing interest in history has been a rediscovery by academicians of colonial literature, which in some cases has been studied concomitantly with the historical novel. The 1987 conference of the Instituto Internacional de Literatura Iberoamericana at the City College of New York was entitled *"La historia en la literatura iberoamericana,"* and most of the papers were devoted to colonial literature. The April 1991 Congreso de Mexicanistas at the Universidad Nacional Autónoma de México was devoted to the *crónica* in its broadest sense, with papers presented on the colonial chronicle, the social chronicle of the late nineteenth-century modernists, the historical novel in general, and the contemporary testimonial chronicle of Elena Poniatowska and Carlos Monsiváis.[17]

The various definitions of the word *chronicle* evidenced above, plus the use by postmodern literary critics of the umbrella term *historical discourse* to cover a variety of literary genres, reflect the blurring of lines between literary genres that is typical of the postmodern period. This phenomenon also coincides with the questioning of the distinction between history and fiction. It is no accident that it was in 1973, on the eve of the flourishing of the New Historical Novel, that Hayden White published his frequently cited *Metahistory,* which, by analyzing the narrative discourse of nineteenth-century historians, challenged history's claim to be a science and stressed its fictive character. The following year, critical theorist Murray Krieger also observed that the historian is always an interpreter, and therefore history is close to fiction (339). During the 1970s and 1980s history professors became increasingly receptive to the idea of incorporating novels into their syllabi, and in 1982, to cite only one example, Professor Brad Burns of U.C.L.A. published an article in the *Inter-American Review of Bibliography* entitled "Bartolomé Mitre: The Historian as Novelist, the Novel as History."

At the same time, literary scholars felt no compunction about writing historical texts. In 1982, the oft-quoted, Parisian-based Bulgarian semiotician Tzvetan Todorov, writing as a moralist and semi-novelist more than as an historian, published *The Conquest of America: The Question of the Other.* He condemns Columbus for considering the Indians as inferior, for his obsession to convert them to Christianity, and for his obsessive search for gold. Likewise, Todorov faults Cortés for thinking in an egocentric way and for not considering Indians as human beings. Todorov also emphasizes the importance of language and of the interpreters in the Conquest of Mexico, refers to Cortés's "semiotic conduct" (121), and plays semiotically and gratuitously with the distinction between subject and object (132). In the text's epilogue, Todorov extends Fray Bartolomé de las Casas's prophecy that Spain will be punished for its criminal deeds to all imperialist European powers.[18] Somewhat pretentiously, Todorov states that he wrote the book to prevent the genocide of the Conquest from being forgotten: "For the other remains to be discovered" (247).

The New Historical Novel in Europe and the United States

Whatever the specific historical and cultural features that have engendered the New Historical Novel and a variety of other historical discourses in the past two decades in Latin America, a natural question is to what extent the NHN also makes an appearance in Europe, the United States, and other parts of the world. In *History and the Contemporary Novel* (1989), David Cowart observes the "increasing prominence of historical themes in current fiction" (1) in Europe and the United States and attributes it to our age of anxiety: "we look to history now to provide clues for understanding, gauging, addressing the more absolute instability of our nuclear present" (29). Marc Bertrand notes the return of the historical novel in France around 1975 after the decline of the *Nouveau Roman,* at least in quantitative terms. Although the Latin American New Historical Novel is not derived from European or U.S. historical novels, it is interesting to observe that a rather similar phenomenon has developed in certain other Western countries—although clearly not with the same intensity as in Latin America. In fact, there is no question that many of the U.S. and European NHNs have been influenced by Latin American writers, particularly Borges and García Márquez.

Although Carpentier's *El reino de este mundo* (1949) is clearly the first of the Latin American New Historical Novels, it is antedated in Europe by Virginia Woolf's *Orlando* (1928), subtitled *A Biography.* Dedicated to Vita Sackville-West, *Orlando* is a delightful parody of nineteenth-century biographies and a satire of English society from the sixteenth to the twentieth centuries. While it is true that the protagonist's life is traced right up to the present of 1928, an exception should be made here in the definition of what is or is not an historical novel since roughly 90 percent of the novel transpires in preceding centuries. What identifies it most as a precursor—if not actually the first New Historical Novel—is its carnivalesque nature, with the protagonist changing sex midway in the novel, its intertextuality, and its metafiction. The biographical implausibility is heightened by the inclusion, as in a traditional biography, of photographs of Orlando in different stages of his/her approximately 350-year life, as well as a complete index. Although the Latin American New Historical Novel can hardly be said to have originated from *Orlando,* it should be noted that the Virginia Woolf novel was praised and translated in 1936–1937 by Jorge Luis Borges, and that Orlando actually appears as a character in two Latin American NHNs. In Reinaldo Arenas's *El mundo alucinante* (1969), Orlando's name is always accompanied by the epithet *"rara mujer"* 'strange woman' (Chapter 27). In Denzil Romero's *Grand tour* (1987), he serves as Francisco de Miranda's guide in a tour of London, and on board *The Mayflower* explains their mutual attraction in terms of Platonic love.

Despite the importance of *Orlando,* similar New Historical Novels did not make their appearance outside Latin America until the 1960s, and it was probably not until the 1980s that they constituted a trend. The first reason for the gap is also applicable to Latin America: novelists' predominant concern between 1930 and 1945 with contemporary social problems. The second reason is more particularly applicable to the United States and, to a certain extent, to Europe: the traditional exclusion of the best-selling historical novels,[19] or historical romances, from the canon, as exemplified by the attitude taken toward Margaret Mitchell's *Gone with the Wind* (1936). In a 1974 book on the U.S. historical novel, Harry B. Henderson III stated, "The historical novel, as a genre, has never won the place it deserves in literary history and critical esteem because it possesses two salient faults in the eyes of most students of literature: impurity and vulgarity" (xv). David Cowart chastises second-rate historical fiction on aesthetic grounds for failing "to transmute mere facts into something of ideational consequence. . . . The inferior historical novel is positively gravid with information; the inferior historical novelist fails to subordinate raw history to art" (20). French critic Marc Bertrand states that in France "the historical novel has scarcely ever occupied the foreground of the literary stage" (77).

After *Orlando*, the most important of the non–Latin American NHNs, and the first chronologically, is *The Sot-Weed Factor* (1960) by U.S. writer John Barth (b. 1930), a staunch admirer of both Borges and García Márquez, and a contemporary of the major Boom writers. An over-800-page mock epic of the settlement of Maryland in the late seventeenth and early eighteenth centuries, the novel is similar to some of the later Latin American novels in that it is a linguistic tour de force with a strong carnivalesque tone and large doses of metafiction and intertextuality. The intercalated apocryphal, secret journal of Captain John Smith provides a Rabelaisian account of the Captain's relations with Pocahontas. Historical "truth" is obviously sacrificed for novelistic fantasy. The innumerable disguises in the novel project a dialogic vision of reality—or, in Borgesian terms, you can't tell who's the hero and who's the traitor. The Candide-like fictitious protagonist Ebenezer Cooke, now turned cynic, shocks his roguish, picaresque valet with the following words:

> "And this war to the death 'twixt Baltimore and Coode! . . . How do we know who's right and who's wrong, or whether 'tis a war at all? What's to keep me from declaring they're in collusion, and all this show of insurrection's but a cloak to hide some dreadful partnership? . . . What is't but childish innocence keeps the mass o' men persuaded that the church is not supported by the brothel, or that God and Satan do not hold hands in the selfsame cookie-jar." (555)

Nor can one tell the difference between "civilization" and "barbarism" (a frequent theme in Latin American literature from *Facundo* and *Doña Bárbara* to NHNs *Noticias del imperio* and *La campaña*), as indicated in the title of Part 3, Chapter 11: ". . . Mary Mungummory Poses the Question, Does Essential Savagery Lurk beneath the Skin of Civilization, or Does Essential Civilization Lurk beneath the Skin of Savagery?—But Does Not Answer It" (649). The same Bakhtinian/Borgesian attitude, couched in typically exuberant Latin American style, is applied to the philosophy of history in the title of Part 3, Chapter 18: "The Poet Wonders Whether the Course of Human History Is a Progress, a Drama, a Retrogression, a Cycle, an Undulation, a Vortex, a Right- or Left-Handed Spiral, a Mere Continuum, or What Have You. Certain Evidence Is Brought Forward, but of an Ambiguous and Inconclusive Nature" (734).

Continuing in the same ludic vein but with a strong note of social protest, Ishmael Reed's *Mumbo Jumbo* (1972) is a loosely knit view of the 1920s through the Black Power, anti–Vietnam War perspective of the late 1960s and early 1970s. The apocryphal "Jes Grew" movement is feared by the white establishment; the 20-year Marine occupation of Haiti is criticized; the Harding administration is mocked; Black musicians and entertainers Scott Joplin, Bert Williams, Cab Calloway, Bessie Smith, Josephine Baker, and others are interspersed with the fictitious characters; and a significant number of pages are devoted to voodoo and the ancient Egyptian cults of Isis and Osiris. A highly original work, *Mumbo Jumbo* is devoid of traditional plot and characterization and, like jazz, features thematic improvisation.

British writers Anthony Burgess and Robert Nye contributed to the New Historical Novel in the 1970s with *Napoleon Symphony* (1974) and *Falstaff* (1976), respectively. As the title indicates, Burgess's novel is based on Beethoven's *Eroica* Symphony and presupposes a knowledge of the Napoleonic period. Another linguistic tour de force, the novel ends with a series of parodies of nineteenth-century authors. *Falstaff*, also primarily ludic, is a 450-page monologue by the Shakespearean archetypal liar, set in the fifteenth century but, unlike *The Sot-Weed Factor*, written in modern vernacular. As an example of the author's liberties with history and literature, Falstaff's cook is named Macbeth, and his pet rat, Desdemona.

Despite the above antecedents, it may be said that outside Latin America the New Historical Novel did not really flourish until the 1980s, when it was heralded by a very different type of NHN: Italian Umberto Eco's *The Name of the Rose* (1980). A 600-page murder mystery set in an Italian Franciscan abbey in 1327, *The Name of the Rose* is not a linguistic tour de force, nor is it primarily ludic, nor does it distort history. What makes it a New Historical Novel is that, as a murder mystery, it is in part a parody of Sherlock Holmes, and it contains many other examples of intertextuality. Furthermore, in addition to recreating fourteenth-century monastic life and the political conflicts involving the Papacy and the religious orders (with dates and all), Eco, like Borges, uses history to project philosophical ideas applicable to all periods of time. He also uses many of Borges's metafictional devices. The presence of Borges in the novel (Jorge of Burgos[20] is the oldest man in the monastery) is hardly disguised, and Eco in his 1984 *Postscript* explicitly acknowledged his debt to the Argentine writer: "Everyone asks me why my Jorge, with his name, suggests Borges, and why Borges is so wicked. But I cannot say. I wanted a blind man who guarded a library (it seemed a good narrative idea to me), and library plus blind man can only equal Borges, also because debts must be paid" (27).

Terry Eagleton, the British Marxist literary theorist, followed Eco's New Historical Novel with the high-quality *Saints and Scholars* (1987). Opening in Dublin precisely on May 12, 1916, the novel intertwines the Irish Easter Rebellion led by James Connolly (1868–1916) with anachronistic philosophical conversations between Ludwig Wittgenstein (1889–1951) and Mikhail Bakhtin's elder brother Nikolai, and with an intertextual appearance by James Joyce's Leopold Bloom, who bemoans Molly's eloping with Stephen. The revolutionary conditions in Ireland are juxtaposed with those in Russia on the eve of the Bolshevik triumph and the twilight of bourgeois life in the Vienna of aged Emperor Franz Josef. Given Eagleton's ideology in his theoretical books, the most surprising aspects of the novel are the dialogic attitude toward revolution and the carnivalesque tone.

Although there are other works outside Latin America that qualify as New Historical Novels, the best example to close this section is, for obvious reasons, Brooklyn-born Stephen Marlowe's *The Memoirs of Christopher Columbus* (1987). A very dense but highly enjoyable fictitious autobiography, Marlowe's novel subverts all the known and unknown details of Columbus's life through the narrator's philosophical questioning:

> What's the purpose of history?
> According to the father of all historians, Herodotus of Halicarnassus (c. 480–425 B.C.), it's to perpetuate the memory of "great and wonderful deeds." I guess history's become a lot more sophisticated since then, because its practitioners are equally inclined to perpetuate the memory of mean and awful deeds. Not that they seem to get any closer to the truth, whatever truth is. (462)

As in Posse's *Los perros del Paraíso*, intertextuality and metafiction abound, with strong doses of anachronism. Columbus's first voyage of discovery is compared in Chapter 8 to *The Odyssey*, the story of Noah's ark, *Moby Dick*, Joseph Conrad, *Mutiny on the Bounty,* and *The Caine Mutiny.* The author notes that the first landing is not witnessed by a "half-billion T.V. viewers around the world" in spite of "beating Neil Armstrong by almost 500 years" (199).

The carnivalesque tone prevails throughout, with racy erotic episodes between Columbus and a series of women including Tristram, who is really Isolde in disguise, and Beatriz, whose parents were burned at the stake by the Inquisition, and who is constantly referred to as the lovely Petenera, a reference to the opera *Carmen*. Not only does *The Memoirs of Christopher Columbus* have all six traits of the New Historical Novel, but it is also a delightful linguistic tour de force, with Columbus speaking primarily in the vernacular of the 1980s. And, in true 1980s style, it questions the religious justification for the Conquest. The Indian Guacanagarí asks Columbus in sign language: "'If your Father God and Son God and Ghost God came down from Heaven to kill you, would you defend yourself?'" (358).

As in Latin America, the precisely but narrowly defined New Historical Novels in the U.S. and Europe constitute only a minority of the large number of historical novels in general that have been published in the past two decades. They cover a very broad spectrum ranging from what Linda Hutcheon calls the postmodern "historiographic metafiction, obsessed with the question of how we can come to know the past today" (47), to what Biruté Ciplijauskaité calls the "new feminine historical novel" (128), to the popular historical romances on sale in airports and supermarkets. Hutcheon cites Roa Bastos's *Yo el Supremo* as a paradigmatic postmodern historical novel, but also includes some that really do not qualify as New Historical Novels, like the well-known *Ragtime* (1975) by E. L. Doctorow. This book is basically a mimetic social history of the United States in the first two decades of the twentieth century with fictitious protagonists, although such historical figures as J. P. Morgan and Houdini play relatively important minor roles. Hutcheon also does not distinguish between novels that take place in the past and those that deal with contemporary history, such as Robert Coover's *The Public Burning* (1977) about the Richard Nixon era and Salman Rushdie's *Midnight's Children* (1981) about India's struggle for independence. On the other hand, she does comment on a variety of postmodern, authentic historical novels that do attest to the recent popularity of the historical novel in general: John Banville's *Doctor Copernicus* (1976) and *Kepler* (1981), Natalie Z. Davis's *The Return of Martin Guerre* (1983), and John Fowles's *The French Lieutenant's Woman* (1969) and *A Maggot* (1985).

Biruté Ciplijauskaité, in her book on the contemporary European feminine novel, *La novela femenina contemporánea (1970–1985): Ha-*

cia una tipología de la narración en primera persona, sets out to prove that the women historical novelists,[21] beginning with Marguerite Your-cenar in *The Memoirs of Hadrian* (1951), write in a more emotional and more lyric style than the men and often aim at revising the image of famous men, as in Jeanne Bourin's *Très sage Héloïse* 'Most Wise Héloïse' (1966) about Pierre Abélard and Françoise Chandernagor's memoirs of Mme de Maintenon *L'allée du roi* 'The King's Path'(1981) about Louis XIV. Although most of the French, German, Portuguese, and Spanish (not Latin American) novels that she discusses were published in the 1980s, only *Urraca* (1982) by Spaniard Lourdes Ortiz has several traits of the New Historical Novel.

This survey would be incomplete if, in addition to the U.S. and European historical novels already mentioned, it did not include some of the better-known popular novelists: in Britain, Mary Renault, with eight novels about ancient Greece from *The Last of the Wine* (1956) and *The King Must Die* (1958) to *Funeral Games* (1981); in France, Julien Green, with two massive novels about the U.S. pre–Civil War South, *Les pays lointains* 'The Far-off Countries' (1987) and *Les étoiles du Sud* 'The Stars of the South' (1989); in Germany, Patrick Süskind, with *Perfume: The Story of a Murderer* (1985), which is just that and, although it takes place in eighteenth-century France, is only very marginally historical; and in the U.S., James A. Michener, with *The Source* (1965), and Gore Vidal, with *Burr* (1973), *Lincoln* (1984), and *Hollywood: A Novel of America in the 1920s* (1990).

Manos a la(s) obra(s): Let's Get to (the) Work(s)

Regardless of the plausibility of the above theorizing about its origins, what is much more important is that the New Historical Novel, since the late 1970s, has become the dominant trend in the already consecrated Latin American novel and has already produced some truly outstanding works that deserve to be on everybody's canonical list in 1992, and will perhaps continue to be on everybody's canonical list in 2092.

2 Mario Vargas Llosa's War on Fanaticism

La guerra del fin del mundo, with a Coda on
José J. Veiga's *A casca da serpente*

Everything becomes easy if one is capable of identifying the good or the evil behind each and every thing that happens.—*La guerra del fin del mundo,* 378

La guerra del fin del mundo (1981), Peruvian Mario Vargas Llosa's best novel, ends with the words "I saw them" (568).[1] Since these words, spoken by an emaciated old hag, refer to the archangels that carry the ex-bandit João Abade up to heaven, she is obviously seeing what she wants to see: an example of the blind faith engendered in the poor, the maimed, and the repentant bandits by the fanatic prophet Antônio Conselheiro, leader of the historic Canudos rebellion against the government in the hinterlands of northeastern Brazil at the end of the nineteenth century. The old hag's words are intertextually reminiscent of the Haitian black slaves in Carpentier's *El reino de este mundo* who see their executed mystic leader Mackandal transformed into a "buzzing mosquito" (51), and of Remedios la Bella's family in *Cien años de soledad* who see her ascend to heaven. Similarly, even the "civilized" urban correspondents assigned to cover the Canudos rebellion see what they want to see: "'They could see and yet they didn't see. All they saw was what they'd come to see. Even if there was no such thing there. It wasn't just one or two of them. They all found glaring proof of a British-monarchist conspiracy. How to explain that?' " (415). Since the hero of Vargas Llosa's novel is an anonymous nearsighted journalist, the leitmotif of sight also reflects the Weltanschauung projected throughout the novel: that there is no one absolute truth, no single true interpretation of history or reality—a Weltanschauung in keeping with the magic realism of Borges and García Márquez,[2] in keeping with the tenets of postmodernism, and in keeping with Mikhail Bakhtin's concepts of the dialogic and the polyphonic.

If there is no one true interpretation of history or reality in the postmodern world of the 1980s, then fanaticism can hardly be justified, whether it be the fanaticism of the Iranian ayatollah, of Joseph Stalin, or of the Brazilian prophet Antonio Consejero (as Vargas Llosa spells his name). Therefore, the principal theme of *La guerra del fin del mundo* is not the condemnation of Antonio Consejero and his fanatical followers but the condemnation of fanaticism, wherever it may be found.

In his 1989 response to Ayatollah Khomeini's call for the death of Salman Rushdie because of his novel *The Satanic Verses*, Vargas Llosa explicitly restates the theme of his 1981 novel:

> I've been thinking about you very much and what has happened to you. I am in total solidarity with your book, and I would like to share with you this assault on rationalism, reason and freedom. Writers should unite forces in this most crucial moment in creative freedom. We thought this war was won a long time ago, but it wasn't. In the past, it was the Christian Inquisition, Fascism, Stalinism; now it's Muslim fundamentalism, and there will probably be others. The forces of fanaticism will always be there. The spirit of freedom will always be menaced by un-rationality and intolerance, which are apparently deeply rooted in the human heart. (*New York Times Book Review*, March 12, 1989, 1)

On a more personal level, Vargas Llosa's condemnation of fanaticism in late nineteenth-century Brazil is also aimed at the left-wing extremists who have excoriated him, particularly since 1971, for his criticism of the Cuban government's curtailment of freedom of artistic expression.[3] Although the Peruvian Shining Path guerrillas have also been a target of Vargas Llosa's campaign against fanaticism,[4] they did not emerge until 1980, and therefore it is unlikely that they directly influenced the writing of the novel published in 1981. Vargas Llosa's presidential candidacy in the fall of 1988, as the representative of a coalition of centrist parties that defend private property, makes the ties between the Brazilian past and the Peruvian present even more apparent.

The condemnation of fanaticism in the novel, the importance of which has been ignored by most of the critics,[5] is paralleled by the undermining of certain stereotypes and complemented by praise for flexibility, change, objectivity, and relativity. In contrast to the four principal fanatics, who are identified with fire, the flexible, compromising Barón de Cañabrava is symbolized by the chameleon—but without its usually negative connotations.

The Prophet has "incandescent eyes" (4), "eyes afire" (21), and quotes the following lines from the Bible: *"Vine para atizar un incendio!"* (91) 'I bring not peace, but a sword!' (84), or literally, 'I came to stoke a fire!' Later he warns that "this place will be destroyed by fire" (151) and that "there will be four fires" (152). The Canudos rebellion against the republican government starts with the Prophet's burning of the 1889 secularization decrees. The fire leitmotif is reinforced by the periodic regional droughts and by the frequent bonfires, as well as by the literal and metaphoric use of a great variety of "inflammatory" words, such as *"se enardecieron"* (57) 'became so inflamed' (48); *"como si se carbonizaran"* (267) 'as though they were being burned to cinders' (277); *"chispeaban estrellas"* (253) 'the stars were already out' (262), or literally, 'the stars were sparkling'; *"pelos flamígeros"* (152) 'fiery-red locks' (151); and many others.

The Prophet's bitter enemy is the equally fanatic Colonel Moreira César, ardent defender of the Republic, who is sent by the government to defeat the Canudos rebels. Earlier in the book he suppresses, with an iron hand, the several revolts that break out in the first years of the Republic. With a zeal reminiscent of the Jacobin Robespierre (240), he argues in favor of a dictatorial republic, without parliament and without political parties, "in *O Jacobino,* that incendiary paper" (145). He assumes command of the troops in *"la atmósfera ardiente"* (147) 'the stifling heat' (146), or literally, 'the burning atmosphere', of the appropriately named city of Queimadas (from the verb *queimar* 'to burn'). The narrator emphasizes César's fiery eyes: *"unos ojitos que echan chispas"* (146) 'little eyes that flash' (144), or literally, 'little eyes that project sparks', and he speaks *"en un tono encendido"* (147) 'in an impassioned tone' (146), or literally, 'in an inflamed tone'. To complete the picture, he rides a white horse and the rebels call him *"Cortapescueço"* 'Throatslitter.' In a scene reminiscent of Rodolfo Fierro's lying down to sleep in a manger after personally shooting three hundred prisoners in Martín Luis Guzmán's *"La fiesta de las balas,"* the Colonel orders his soldiers to slit the throats of two prisoners and "then appears to put the execution entirely out of his mind. With nervous, rapid strides, he starts off across the clearing toward the hut where a hammock has been put up for him" (193). Even after he is mortally wounded, he almost literally rises from the dead—the doctor doubts that he will recover consciousness (319)—to insist on having the nearsighted journalist write down his opposition to his officers' decision to retreat.

In order to identify the two opposing fanatical forces with each other—in accord with the underlying Jungian, Borgesian philosophy that all human beings, even enemies, are one—the author highlights the similarities between them[6] with the phrase *"el Can contra Canudos"* (177) 'the *Can* against Canudos' (179), where *"Can"* means 'Dog', symbol for Hell, and represents the epithet bestowed on the government by the rebels. The wooden whistles, sounded throughout the novel as an integral part of the rebels' tactics, are also echoed by the government troops. At the beginning of Part 3, Chapter 6, the nearsighted journalist equates "the symphony of whistles" (284) with Moreira César's "call to charge and slit throats" (284). The very first sentence of Part 3, announcing the arrival of Colonel Moreira César, emphasizes the sound of the whistle: *"El tren entra pitando en la estación de Queimadas"* (143) 'The train whistles as it enters the Queimadas station' (141). Some time later, the nearsighted journalist lies awake thinking of the government sentinels on duty who *"se comunicarán mediante silbatos"* (250) 'who will signal to each other all night long by blowing whistles' (258).

On a larger scale, the differences between the republican government and the Canudos rebels, as representatives of the struggle between urban civilization and rural barbarism, are also blurred. The rioting in Rio de Janeiro and São Paulo in response to the defeat of Colonel Moreira César, which culminated in the murder of the gentle, politically naive monarchist Gentil de Castro, is, in the eyes of the Baron, as absurd as any of the rural violence. In reply to the reporter's statement that what happened in the cities was logical and rational, the Baron exclaims: "—Logical and rational that the mob should pour out into the streets to destroy newspaper offices, to attack private houses, to murder people unable to point out on a map where Canudos is located, because a handful of fanatics thousands of kilometers away defeated an expeditionary force? That's logical and rational?" (379–380).

The novel's third fanatical protagonist is the Scottish phrenologist and anarchist Galileo Gall. Although he is portrayed in a more favorable light than the Prophet and the Colonel because he is faced with some dilemmas, he too is a fanatic who is identified with fire. It is no accident that the author bestows on him "fiery-red hair" (8) and a small, reddish beard. Gall served time in jail after being convicted of having set fire to a church. He fought in the 1871 Paris Commune and, like Moreira César, contributed articles to a radical newspaper, *L'Etincelle de la révolte* 'Spark of Revolt', published in Lyons, France. According to his own memoirs, read by the Barón de Cañabrava and his fellow landowner Gumúcio, Gall may also have been involved in more than one murder: "'I'm inclined to believe that the story is true', Gumúcio said. 'Because of the natural way in which he tells of all those extraordinary things—the escapes, the murders, his voyages as a freebooter, his sexual abstinence'" (310). As a result of his experience as a revolutionary and because he is *"fogueado en las luchas políticas"* (74) 'a battle-hardened veteran of political struggles' (67), or literally, 'molded by fire in political struggles', Gall hopes to help the Canudos rebels in spite of their religious fanaticism. Faced with a difficult choice, Gall prefers to forgo his dogmatic anticlericalism in order to fight on the side of freedom from government.

As part of his fanatic revolutionary idealism, Gall is convinced that sex distracts men from their revolutionary goals. When, after ten years of abstinence, he allows himself to be aroused by the physically unattractive Jurema, he has difficulty explaining his actions and rationalizes, with another fiery image, that *"la ciencia es todavía un candil que parpadea en una gran caverna en tinieblas"* (108) 'science is still only a candle faintly glimmering in a great pitch-dark cavern' (103).

Just as the opposing fanatical forces of the Canudos rebels are paired off in Part 3 of the novel against fanatical Colonel Moreira César's third expedition, the fanatical anarchist Galileo Gall is paired off against Jurema's husband, the guide Rufino, who is the novel's fourth leading fanatic. Whereas the first and third sections of each chapter (which I will designate here as A and C) are devoted respectively to Moreira César and the Prophet and his followers, the second (B) and fourth (D) sections of Part 3 are devoted respectively to Gall and Rufino. In both conflicts, the opponents gradually draw closer and closer to each other, and when they finally do meet, the two prolonged struggles are enveloped first in gunpowder and then in mud, in order to blur the differences between the bitter enemies. Again in keeping with the archetypal concept that all human beings are one, and in almost a mirror image of the mortal struggle between Arturo Cova and

Narciso Barrera in José Eustasio Rivera's *La vorágine* (1924), Gall and Rufino actually "lie dying in each other's arms, gazing into each other's eyes" (307).

Rufino, however, differs somewhat from his three fellow fanatics in that Vargas Llosa, like García Márquez in *Crónica de una muerte anunciada* 'Chronicle of a Death Foretold' (1981) is condemning not the fanatical individual but rather the fanatical Latin American matrimonial code. Rufino feels obligated by group pressure to cleanse his honor both by killing his wife Jurema because she was raped by Gall and by slapping the latter's face before or while killing him. Rufino's friend Caifás[7] tells him, "'Death isn't enough. It doesn't remove the stain. But a slap, a whiplash, square in the face, does. Because a man's face is as sacred as his mother or his wife'" (186). Caifás even refuses to carry out Epaminondas's orders to kill Gall because, according to the code of honor, the offended husband himself must kill the rapist as well as the "unfaithful" wife. Only in the eventuality that the offended husband should die would the friend be obligated to kill the offending parties. Rufino's mother, in spite of being a "gaunt grim-faced old woman with hard eyes" (159), also feels dishonored to the point of abandoning her shop of candles and religious objects in Queimadas in order to make the long trek to Canudos.

Rufino sets fire to his sullied home, and when he finally catches up with Gall, "his eyes were gleaming like burning coals" (291). Gall defends himself with a club, but his own blind faith in anarchism prevents him from comprehending Rufino's fanaticism. Instead of killing his enemy, he tries to reason with him: "'You blind, selfish, petty traitor to your class—can't you see beyond your vainglorious little world? Men's honor doesn't lie in faces or in women's cunts, you idiot. There are thousands of innocents in Canudos. The fate of your brothers is at stake: can't you understand?'" (292). Of course, Rufino is incapable of understanding Gall's words just as Gall is incapable of comprehending Rufino's code of honor. Similarly the victim, Jurema, even though she is aware of the local code of honor, directs the following words to her dead husband: "You struck him in the face, Rufino. . . . What did you gain by that, Rufino? What use was there in getting your revenge if you've died, if you've left me all alone in the world, Rufino?" (307).

In opposition to the four principal fanatics, the chameleon-like Barón de Cañabrava—wealthy landowner, political cacique, ex-minister under the Empire, and ex-ambassador to Great Britain—actually becomes the co-protagonist of the novel (second only to the myopic journalist) and Vargas Llosa's ideological spokesman. He is also the prime example of the novel's challenge to certain Latin American stereotypes. For Vargas Llosa, the belief in stereotypes—the belief that all members of a certain social class, a certain profession, or a certain religious, ethnic, or national group have an invariable set of characteristics—is akin to fanaticism in its various manifestations in the novel. In Part 3, while the opposing pairs of fanatics kill each other in Sections A, B, C, and D of each chapter, a fifth section (E) is created (not found in Parts 1 and 2) to highlight the Baron's rational self-control even in the face of provocative encounters with each of the four fanatics: Moreira César, Gall, Rufino, and the Prophet's representative, Pajeú, he of the fiery scar: "Pajeú's scar seems to become incandescent emitting red-hot waves that reach his brain" (393). Earlier, upon returning from Europe, the Baron listened somewhat inattentively to the bad political news from his cohorts because he was more concerned about locating his pet chameleon: "an animal that he had grown fond of as others conceive an affection for dogs or cats" (165). Later, the Baron, referring to Colonel Moreira César, categorically expresses his dislike for all fanatics: "He was a fanatic and, like all fanatics, dangerous" (166). The Baron then proceeds to surprise his supporters by declaring calmly his willingness to compromise with the fanatical Colonel, offering him the backing of their Partido Autonomista. He justifies his decision with one of the first of all political axioms: "in order to defend Bahia's interests we must remain in power and in order to remain in power we must change our policy, at least for the moment" (167).

However, it is not so much his political astuteness but rather his human compassion and his own suffering that contribute to the Baron's breaking out of the Latin American stereotype of the wealthy, heartless landowner. As the wedding godfather of the guide Rufino and Jurema, the former servant of his own wife, the Baron feels compelled to grant Rufino permission to kill Jurema because of her putative infidelity with Galileo Gall. From what Rufino tells him, the Baron becomes aware of his political enemy Epaminondas's trick to kill Gall in order to "prove" that the British government was supporting the Canudos rebellion because it wanted to restore the Brazilian monarchy. In spite of this discovery, the Baron is more concerned about Jurema's plight and the effect on his wife. The following lines, which close out the chapter, further demonstrate the author's determination to question the validity of the stereotype: "But despite the extraordinary discovery he had made, he was not thinking about Epaminondas Gonçalves, but about Jurema, the young woman whom Rufino was going to kill, and about how sorrow-stricken Estela would be if she learned of this" (191–192).

The Baron's character as a compassionate human being is further developed—again at the very end of a chapter—during Colonel Moreira César's visit to his hacienda. In spite of the fact that the Baron allows the doctor to treat the fanatical Colonel for his epileptic convulsions in the Baron's own home, the Colonel shows no appreciation: "You and I are mortal enemies, the war between us is without quarter, and we have nothing to say to each other" (217). The Baron's ability to maintain his composure in the face of this provocation—he calmly replies, "I thank you for your frankness" (217)—clearly enhances his stature. Earlier, the Baron's wife pointed out to the Colonel that the Baron had freed his slaves five years before slavery was officially abolished in the whole nation.

In the next chapter, in somewhat parallel situations, the Baron has encounters with two other fanatics: Galileo Gall and the ex-bandit Pajeú. The latter informs the Baron that he has been instructed to burn the hacienda but without harming the Baron and his wife. Recognizing that resistance would be futile, the Baron laments the world's being taken over by the fanatics: "No, he would never understand. It was as useless to try to reason with him as it was to argue with Moreira César or Gall. The Baron felt a shiver down his spine; it was as if the world had taken leave of its reason and blind, irrational beliefs had taken over" (246). Then, because of his great concern for his wife Estela, the Baron sacrifices his own political career by permitting Gall to leave his home and continue his trek to Canudos. Realizing the tremendous fanaticism of the people of Canudos, the Baron tries to come to an agreement with the Republicans (272). He even offers to support Epaminondas's candidacy for the governorship of the state of Bahia with only one condition: the protection of rural and urban private property. The Baron's attempt to convince Epaminondas to accept the pact alludes implicitly to Vargas Llosa's Peru of the 1970s and 1980s.

> We must make our peace, Epaminondas. Forget your shrill Jacobin rhetoric, . . . Jacobinism died with Moreira César. Assume the governorship and let us defend civil order together amid this hecatomb. Let us keep our Republic from turning into what so many other Latin American republics have [become]: "a grotesque witches' sabbath where all is chaos, military uprisings, corruption, demagogy. . . ." (349)

In Part 4 of the novel, the Baron's importance is foregrounded by his occupying for the first time the first rather than the last section of each chapter. Retired from politics and embittered by his wife's insanity—"'Those flames are still burning here inside me. . . . It was as though the children I lost when they were born were being burned to cinders'" (277)—the Baron continues to identify with the chameleon: "'Beloved chameleon, elusive little creature, my good friend. I thank you with all my heart for having made my wife laugh'" (355). Because of the chameleon, he accepts the nearsighted reporter's request to work for the Baron's newspaper once again, forgiving him for having resigned to work on Epaminondas's rival newspaper.

The final step in the destruction of the stereotype of the all-powerful, heartless landowner is consummated, paradoxically as it may seem, by his raping his wife's loyal lesbian[8] servant Sebastiana, in the former's presence—in the Baron's final appearance in the novel. In order to win the ultimate victory in his war against fanaticism, Vargas Llosa daringly chooses one of the most common and reprehensible abuses of the typical landowner, and *in this particular situation,* transforms it. Although from the point of view of the servant, it is a plain and simple case of rape, since all the Baron's sweet words and erotic caresses are incapable of making her fear and resistance vanish, Vargas Llosa appears to justify this rape. From the beginning of the scene, the Baron's love for his insane wife is emphasized. When Estela unexpectedly steps into the room and observes what is happening, "she did not appear to be frightened, enraged, horrified—merely mildly intrigued" (539). In fact, "this turning outward, this interest in something outside herself" (539) may indicate for her the beginning of a return to the world of reality. Grateful for his wife's attitude, the Baron kisses her hands and feet. When Estela actually seems to condone the rape by placing her hand on the Baron's head—"he felt it alight on his hair and remain there, its touch soft and conciliatory, a contact for which he felt the most heartfelt gratitude because there was nothing hostile or reproving about it; on the contrary, it was loving, affectionate, tolerant" (540)—he regains his erection, and consummates the rape of the servant while the wife, seated on the edge of the bed, "was still holding Sebastiana's face between her two hands, gazing at her with pity and tenderness" (540). The episode ends with the Baron in total ecstasy, *almost:* he wakes up in Sebastiana's bed; he observes Sebastiana and Estela asleep in the latter's bed with a feeling of tenderness, melancholy, gratitude, and a touch of anxiety; he contemplates the bay illuminated by the rising sun; but, with his wife's binoculars, he observes how, in the final sentence of the section, "the people in the boats were not fishing but tossing flowers into the sea . . . and though he could not hear them—his heart was pounding—he was certain that those people were also praying and perhaps singing" (541–542). The fishermen had miraculously discovered the spot in the bay where the government had secretly buried Consejero's head. Since the rape scene is immediately preceded by a relatively lengthy description of the "feast of vultures" (535) after the fall of Canudos, the implication is that the Baron will never be able to erase Canudos from his mind.

Regardless of the ending, this generally positive interpretation of the rape episode is further reinforced by the Baron's relations with other characters. At the beginning of the episode, the Baron recalls the fanatic anarchist Gall's chastity vow: "I have been as stupid as he was, he thought. Without ever having sworn to do so, he had kept a similar vow for a very long time, renouncing pleasure, happiness, in favor of that base occupation that had brought misfortune to the person he loved most dearly in this world" (536). The Baron then proceeds to reject the sexual abstinence model of the fanatic Gall in order to follow the example of the nearsighted journalist who had spoken to him a few moments earlier "of love, of pleasure in a fervent voice: the greatest thing in all this world, Baron, the one and only thing whereby man can discover a measure of happiness, can learn what the word happiness means" (535). However, the significant distinction between the two acts of love and pleasure is that the newspaperman's experience with Jurema is reciprocal—the only real example in the novel of a woman's experiencing sexual pleasure: "His terror turned to joy as he embraced this woman as desperately as she was embracing him. A pair of lips met his, clung to his, returned his kisses" (488). Whereas the focalizer (the person through whose point of view the action is presented)[9] in this quote is the man, Jurema's sentiments are validated when she is the focalizer at the very beginning of Section C of the following chapter:

> She opened her eyes and continued to feel happy, as she had all that night, the day before, and the day before that, a succession of days that were all confused in her mind, till the evening when, after believing that he'd been buried beneath the rubble of the store, she found the nearsighted journalist at the door of the sanctuary, threw herself into his arms, heard him say that he loved her, and told him that she loved him, too." (517)

A case could be made that the Baron, in raping Sebastiana, is making love to a surrogate for his wife: the Baron had earlier remarked that Sebastiana "was still a woman with a firm, beautiful, admirably preserved figure. 'Just like Estela' " (309). But in no way does Sebastiana or the wife experience any sexual pleasure at any time.

The rape scene must also be considered in the context of the fourth and final part of the novel, in which love as a humanizing factor—even in the midst of the most horrible, dehumanizing war—is an important theme.Just as the Baron's tender thoughts of his wife Estela are constantly uppermost in his mind, making him perceive reality through a kind of screen or filter, Pajeú cannot keep Jurema out of his mind throughout the long episode in which he leads the federal troops into an ambush. She is apparently his first love, and thanks to her, "he had discovered that he was not hard inside" (439). Two other variations of love and lust are uppermost in the minds of other characters in Part 4: João Abade's love for Catarina (whose parents he had killed in his bandit days), in spite of her inability to respond to his sexual desires, and Sergeant Fructuoso Medrado's abusive sexual affair with the wife of one of his soldiers.

Although fanaticism as the major theme of the novel may be partially upstaged by love in Part 4, it is at the same time reinforced, both directly and indirectly. No matter how strongly the fanaticism of the Canudos uprising is condemned throughout the novel, the periodic, systematic presentation of events through the eyes of the "underdogs" inevitably arouses sympathy and admiration in the reader.[10] In order to prevent this natural reaction from overwhelming the novel's ideological message, Vargas Llosa highlights in the final two chapters the extremes to which fanatics may be driven. In the Prophet's dying moments, the Beatito (the 'Little Pious One', one of the most devout of the disciples since early adolescence) convinces himself and the others of the holiness of the incontinent Prophet's urine and excrement and leads the group in a communion ceremony:

> There was something mysterious and sacred about that sudden, soft, prolonged breaking of wind, about those attacks that seemed never to end, always accompanied by the emission of that little trickle of water. He divined the secret meaning: "They are gifts, not excrement." He understood very clearly that the Father, or the Divine Holy Spirit, or the Blessed Jesus, or Our Lady, or the Counselor himself wanted to put them to the test. In a sudden happy inspiration, he came forward, stretched his hand out between the women, wet his fingers in the trickle and raised them to his mouth, intoning: "Is this how you wish your slave to take Communion, Father? Is this not dew to me?" All the women of the Sacred Choir also took Communion, in the same way. (510)

The death of the Prophet is followed by other examples of fanatic behavior. The León de Natuba (the 'Lion from Natuba') accedes to the wishes of a dying mother to prevent the rats from eating the corpse of her child by carrying it into a wall of flames: "'I'm taking him, I'm going with him. This fire has been awaiting me for twenty years now, Mother'" (550). After the Beatito requests a truce in order to save the old folk, the innocent children, and the pregnant women, João Abade arrives and, convinced that the soldiers will slit the people's throats, opens fire on them to protect them from being dishonored (554). The sequel to this episode is an even greater condemnation of fanaticism. When Antonio Vilanova's wife criticizes João Abade's actions, attributing them to a regression to his former self as João Satán, Antonio—probably the most normal of all the Prophet's followers—actually threatens to kill her: "'I don't ever want to hear you say that again. . . . You've been my wife for years, forever. We've gone through everything together. But if I ever hear you say that again, it's all over between us. And it will be the end of you, too'" (556).

In addition to these direct condemnations of the Canudos fanatics[11] in Part 4, two other fanatics in Part 3, Colonel Moreira César and Rufino, are made to appear even more fanatical in contrast with their respective counterparts, General Artur Oscar and the ex-bandit Pajeú. The fourth leader of a government expedition against the Canudos rebels, and the highest ranked (his predecessors were a lieutenant, a major, and a colonel), General Artur Oscar is portrayed as a more humanized version of a military officer. He is deeply concerned about the loss of human life among his troops. In contrast to the dying Colonel Moreira, who objects to retreating, General Oscar orders one of the final attacks on Canudos discontinued in spite of the angry protests of some of his officers: "But victory is within our reach, sir!" (490). He displays human understanding for the student doctor who confesses to having acceded to the request of the badly maimed Lieutenant Pires to kill him. General Oscar's fascination with fireworks and his taking possession of the former home of fireworks expert Antonio Fogueteiro are variations of the fire leitmotif which, as has been indicated, recurs throughout the novel as the symbol of fanaticism. In this case, however, the General's fascination with fireworks is linked to his childhood and contributes to his portrait as a humanized individual. Not all military officers conform to the stereotype, nor are all Catholics in the novel fanatics. General Oscar, a "devout believer who rigorously obeys the precepts of the Church" (492) and who has not advanced as rapidly as he should have in the Republican Army because he didn't renounce his Catholicism and become a Mason, is confused and grieved by the religious practices of the Consejero and his followers. However, his lack of fanaticism is perhaps best revealed after he listens to conflicting opinions among his officers about the causes of the Canudos rebellion: the barbarism of a race of "degenerate mestizos" or a monarchist conspiracy (469). His dissatisfaction with an absolute, positivistic, deterministic explanation is actually a questioning of the geographic and racial explanations of the rebellion offered by Euclides da Cunha in his Os sertões 'Rebellion in the Backlands' ([1902] 1973).

> General Oscar, who has followed this exchange with interest, is still perplexed and hesitates when they ask him his opinion. Yes, he finally says, ignorance allows aristocrats to turn these miserable wretches into fanatics and spur them on to attack what threatens the interests of the rich and powerful, for the Republic guarantees the equality of all men, thereby doing away with the privileges that are a right by birth under an aristocratic regime. But inwardly he is not at all convinced of what he is saying. When the others leave, he lies in his hammock thinking. What is the explanation of Canudos? Hereditary defects of people of mixed blood? Lack of education? A predisposition toward barbarism on the part of men who are accustomed to violence and who resist civilization out of atavism? Something to do with religion, with God? He finds none of these explanations satisfactory. (500)

At the other end of the social scale, Rufino's wife Jurema is intimately linked to different manifestations of fanaticism as well as of stereotypes and their debunking. She is unwittingly responsible for Gall's abandoning his fanatical chastity vow and for her husband Rufino's fanatical obsession with revenge. Jurema's (and the novel's) prizing of life over blind adherence to a fanatical code is further illustrated in the episode when she offers no resistance to the first of several soldiers who are about to rape her. In order to save her life, she actually cooperates with the soldier: "With her eyes half closed she sees him feel about inside his trousers, unbutton them, as he tries to lift her skirt up with the hand that has just let go of the rifle. She helps him as best she can, hunching up, stretching out one leg . . ." (304). She is miraculously saved by the arrival of Pajeú and other Canudos rebels who kill the soldier and comfort her. Little by little Pajeú falls in love with Jurema and actually asks her to marry him, supported by his Canudos cohorts. When Jurema rejects him because of her growing love for the nearsighted journalist, Pajeú, "'the most evil man in all the sertão'" (92), should have killed his rival according to the same social mores that made Rufino kill Gall. However, in this case, because Pajeú has been "touched" by the Consejero, he is able to repress his violent impulses as well as the fanatical code, thus strengthening the case against Rufino. Pajeú's hatred and contempt for the cowardly nearsighted journalist is expressed during his final instructions to the small group of survivors who have been designated to escape from Canudos while he draws the enemy's attention with a suicide attack: "'Sneeze now, . . . not then. Not when you're waiting for the whistles to blow. If you sneeze then, they'll plunge a knife in your heart. It wouldn't be right if they captured everyone on account of your sneezes'" (526). The importance of this episode is underlined by Pajeú's prominence in various sections of Chapters 3, 4, and 5 of Part 4.

In keeping with the magic realist view that the strangest and most unexpected events can and do occur and that fanaticism and stereotypes are therefore ridiculous, Pajeú is overwhelmed in hand-to-hand combat by the homosexual soldier Queluz. Just as General Oscar's compassion and his reluctance to come up with a dogmatic explanation of the Canudos rebellion represent a deviation from the military officer stereotype, the physical strength and courage of Queluz challenge the stereotype of the homosexual and contribute to Vargas Llosa's war against fanaticism. Accused of molesting a teenage bugler, Queluz accepts his punishment of thirty lashes without flinching and apparently gains the respect of some of his jeering companions. He does not reappear in the novel until the fourth section of the next-to-the-last chapter, which begins with a reaffirmation of his homosexuality and culminates in his being welcomed as a hero for having captured Pajeú: "Queluz receives a welcome that is an apotheosis. The news that he has killed one of the bandits who have attacked them and has captured Pajeú soon makes the rounds, and everyone comes out to have a look at him, to congratulate him, to pat him on the back and embrace him" (530). What makes this episode even more effective is its ambiguity.[12] Vargas Llosa avoids the danger of converting the homosexual soldier from a negative stereotype to a positive one: an unqualified hero. In fact, the element of chance in the capture and Queluz's cover-up of part of the story are in keeping with Borges's "Tema del traidor y del héroe." Pajeú and twenty or thirty of his men are able to slip into the government camp and kill many soldiers because Queluz has fallen asleep while on guard duty. When he wakes up and realizes what has happened, his feelings of guilt are coupled with fear of punishment. He furiously tries to fire his rifle, but the trigger does not budge. When it finally does, the bullet grazes his own nose. He discovers the corpse of his guard-duty companion and starts to carry it back to camp in order to prove to his commanding officer that he had spotted the bandits and had tried to stop them. At this point, two of the retreating bandits appear. Queluz reloads his rifle and kills one of them. When the trigger sticks again, he hits the other bandit with the rifle butt. They then engage in a hand-to-hand combat ("Queluz is good at fighting hand to hand, he has always shown up well in the tests of strength organized by Captain Oliveira," 529), and Queluz comes out on top. It is only at this point that Queluz realizes that his opponent is Pajeú. Would he have been intimidated if he had known that he was fighting against Pajeú?

In addition to the stereotypes of the ruthless landowner, the rigid, inhumane general, and the cowardly homosexual, *La guerra del fin del mundo* also challenges the stereotypes of the materialistic merchant or businessman, the lascivious priest, and the clever investigative reporter with acute peripheral vision. Although the latter is more an American than a Latin American stereotype, Vargas Llosa's myopic Brazilian war correspondent has also obviously been designed to challenge a stereotype.[13]

One of the Prophet's most trusted and capable followers is Antonio Vilanova, a former merchant. Even though he has revealed his talent and penchant for business ever since he was a child, and even though his energy and his resiliency seem to guarantee his commercial success in spite of the droughts, floods, pestilence, and violence of northeastern Brazil, Antonio Vilanova comes to realize that he has been destined to accept the Prophet and to join in his mission. Little by little, his energy is diverted from his business activities to the creation of the new town (his family name *Vilanova* is appropriate) of Canudos in a manner that is reminiscent of José Arcadio Buendía's founding of Macondo in *Cien años de soledad*.

> He was the one who had parceled out the land so that they could build their dwellings and put in their crops, advised them what to grow and what livestock to raise, and it was he who took charge of bartering in the villages round about, exchanging the things Canudos produced for the things it needed, and when donations began to come in, it was he who decided how much would be set aside for the Temple of the Blessed Jesus and how much would go for the purchase of arms and supplies. . . . The Health Houses for the old, the sick, and the disabled were his idea. . . . (179)

Antonio Vilanova, his brother Honorio, and their respective families remain loyal to the Prophet until the bitter end and participate in the actual fighting. Moments before dying, the Prophet calls for Anto-

nio and, despite the latter's desperate protestations, orders him to escape from Canudos and to continue his holy mission: "—Go out into
the world to bear witness, Antonio, and do not cross inside the circle
again. . . . You are a man who is acquainted with the world. Go, teach
those who have forgotten their lessons how to count" (511). The metaphorical use of the verb *to count* emphasizes Vilanova's former career
and recalls his first two encounters with the Prophet: when the latter
helps him bury his nephew and rejects his offer of a monetary reward,
"—You haven't learned to count, my son" (79); and about five years
later, in Canudos, when Vilanova turns pale at the sight of the Prophet
and falls to his knees after the Prophet asks, "—Have you learned to
count yet?" (81).

The conversion of the lascivious priest Padre Joaquim is another
example of Vargas Llosa's sophisticated challenges to typical Latin
American stereotypes. The characterization of Padre Joaquim, the last
of the Prophet's converts to be introduced in Part 1, differs from that
of the others in that his transformation is more gradual. Portrayed at
first as a Rabelaisian bon vivant guilty of all seven of the capital sins
except for greed, he is puzzled and intrigued but not convinced over a
period of months and even years by the Prophet's violent denunciations
of immoral priests. When the mother of his three children leaves him to
follow the Prophet, Padre Joaquim continues to exercise his priestly
duties in the town of Cumbe, but little by little he becomes more
involved in the Canudos rebellion. First, he defies the Archbishop of
Bahia's orders by saying mass in Canudos and administering to the
spiritual needs of the Prophet's followers. He subsequently travels to
different towns in order to gather medicine, provisions, explosives, and
news of troop movements for the Canudos rebels. However, when he is
captured by Colonel Moreira César, he is terrified of dying, confesses
everything, and is even willing to draw a street map of Canudos
showing its defenses in order to save his life. He tells the Colonel that
he envies the rebels' faith, but that he is different: "'They cause me
such uneasiness, such envy on account of that faith, that peace of mind
that I've never known. Don't kill me . . . I'm telling you everything I
know. I'm not like them. I don't want to be a martyr; don't kill me'"
(256–257). The fanatical Colonel's Machiavellian decision not to kill
Padre Joaquim in order to "prove" that the Church is hostile to the
Republic deflects some of the reader's repugnance toward Padre Joaquim for his cowardice. However, when he next appears in the novel,
he seems totally redeemed. During the clash between the Colonel's government troops and the Canudos rebels, Padre Joaquim escapes; he en-

counters the helpless Jurema, the Dwarf, and the nearsighted journalist on the battlefield and ultimately deposits them safely in Canudos. Ironically, it is the formerly terror-stricken Padre Joaquim to whom the terror-stricken nearsighted journalist turns after his glasses are broken. He is amazed at the priest's self-confidence and his skill at handling a rifle: "Was this the same elderly little man the nearsighted journalist had seen whimpering and sniveling before Colonel Moreira César, half dead with panic?" (484). When the reporter hysterically accuses the rebels of being fanatics and assassins, the priest, totally converted, calmly replies: " 'They're being killed by the dozens, by the hundreds. . . . And what for? For believing in God, for living their lives in accordance with God's law. It's the Massacre of the Innocents, all over again' " (485). In order to emphasize the extent of the priest's transformation, his earlier image is recalled by the incredulous Baron in his conversation with the nearsighted journalist: " 'That little curé who's fathered a whole pack of kids? That toper who regularly commits all the seven capital sins was in Canudos?' " (417). Rifle in hand, Padre Joaquim dies in battle.

To a certain extent, the characterization of Padre Joaquim is paralleled by that of the nearsighted journalist, who ultimately becomes the real hero of the novel. At first, he is portrayed as the antithesis of the heroic reporter. In his first physical description, he is likened explicitly to a scarecrow:

> Young, nearsighted, with thick eyeglasses. He does not take notes with a pencil but with a goose-quill pen. He is dressed in a pair of trousers coming apart at the seams, an off-white jacket, a cap with a visor, and all of his apparel seems fake, wrong, out of place on his awkward body. He is holding a clipboard with a number of sheets of paper and dips his goose-quill pen in an inkwell, with the cork of a wine bottle for a cap, that is fastened to the sleeve of his jacket. He looks more or less like a scarecrow. (25)

To top it off, he is subject to fits of sneezing, particularly in moments of danger. At the same time that he considers himself "a civilized person, an intellectual, a journalist" (477), he realizes, after reviewing his own life, that he is not very different from the Dwarf or from the León de Natuba: "He, too, was a monster, maimed, disabled, abnormal" (480). Therefore, he belonged in Canudos: "It was no accident that he had ended up where the cripples, the unfortunate, the abnormal, the long-suffering of this world had congregated. It was inevitable: he was one of them" (480).

The image of the nearsighted journalist as the improbable war correspondent is more sharply focused after his glasses break. A sudden, fear-induced sneeze at the sight of Moreira César's severed head sends the glasses flying. Upon hitting the ground, the lenses shatter[14] and the distraught myopic reporter becomes blind for all intents and purposes. Thus Vargas Llosa privileges the other senses. The reporter later tells the Baron that even though he didn't see what happened in Canudos, "—I felt, heard, smelled the things that happened. . . . And I intuitively sensed the rest" (357). Even before his glasses are broken, the reporter subverts his own sense of sight during Moreira César's campaign: "He feels strange, hypnotized, and the absurd idea passes through his mind that he is not really seeing what he is seeing" (314).

In contrast to the other subjective or venal newspapermen, the nearsighted journalist does change as a result of the Canudos experience, thus earning the somewhat skeptical respect of the chameleon-loving Baron: "'In other words, Canudos made a real journalist out of you'" (354). Before attaining that status, he has to face up to his true cowardly condition, belying his reputation among his colleagues as a daredevil: "he had won the reputation among them of being a fearless reporter, ever in search of new experiences" (367). Particularly after his glasses break, his human dignity is all but destroyed: "That little figure moving back and forth, tripping and falling and picking himself up again and peering at the ground with his outlandish monocle, was such a funny sight that the women finally began pointing at him and making fun of him" (403). Even his "guardian angel" Jurema is hard put to repress her laughter: "Was there anyone more helpless and terrified than her son? Everything frightened him: the people who brushed past him, cripples, madmen, and lepers who begged for alms, a rat running across the floor of the store. Everything made him give that little scream of his, made him turn deathly pale, made him search for her hand" (402).

In spite of everything, the nearsighted journalist and Jurema not only survive but, through love, attain the pinnacle of happiness and pleasure. That their sexual union should actually take place in Canudos at the moment "when the world began to fall apart and the horror had reached its height" (502)—and that it should be the most unlikely attraction between "a little mongrel bitch from the backlands" (504) and a relatively cultured, albeit physically unattractive, newspaperman—causes the amazed Baron to muse on the inscrutable, magic realist nature of the world:

Once again the Baron was overcome by the feeling that it was all unreal, a dream, a fiction, which always took possession of him at the very thought of Canudos. All these happenstances, coincidences, fortuitous encounters, made him feel as though he were on tenterhooks. Did the journalist know that Galileo Gall had raped Jurema? He didn't ask him, staggered as he was at the thought of the strange geography of chance, the secret order, the unfathomable law of the history of peoples and individuals that capriciously brought them together, separated them, made them enemies or allies. (502)

Thus, since the world of *La guerra del fin del mundo* is illogical—"'If there were any logic to this story, there are any number of times when I should have died in Canudos'" (506)[15]—the nearsighted coward not only survives but becomes the real hero of the novel.

Of all the characters in the novel, the nearsighted journalist is the one whose importance steadily increases, and the one who experiences the war from more perspectives than anyone else.[16] In Part 1, he makes only two brief appearances, in the B sections of Chapters 1 and 2: observed by Gall in the Salvador newspaper office and interviewing Lieutenant Pires Ferreira after the first defeat of the government troops. Part 2 consists primarily of the reporter's stylized account of the debate in the legislative assembly over the second defeat of a larger contingent of government troops, commanded by Major Febronio de Brito. The journalist actually views, throughout Part 3, the defeat of the third contingent of government troops beside their commander, the fanatic Colonel Moreira César. By contrast, with his glasses shattered and huddled with Jurema and the Dwarf in a desperate effort to survive, he *feels* rather than sees the ultimate defeat of the Canudos rebels in the fourth government campaign, from the low vantage point of the Prophet's saintly or repentant followers: Maria Quadrado, Padre Joaquim, Pajeú, the León de Natuba, and the Vilanova brothers and their respective wives.

Structurally speaking, the nearsighted journalist gets to occupy center stage in Part 4 by being the principal focalizer in Section C of each of the six chapters and by dialoguing with the Baron after the war has ended in Section A of each chapter. Although the chameleon-loving Baron is the author's constant spokesman because of his dislike and distrust for all fanatics, the nearsighted journalist upstages him because of his transformation. His "return from the dead" at the end of the war may be equated with the return from the descent into the underworld in the archetypal adventure of the hero. The reporter, aided by Jurema's

love, has finally vanquished his cowardly fear and selfishness. He self-
confidently expresses to the Baron his double mission of helping the
tubercular Dwarf, now hospitalized, and of preserving history in the
only way possible, by writing: "'I shall not allow them to forget. . . .
That's a promise I've made myself. . . . In the only way in which things
are preserved . . . by writing of them'" (357). The Baron, on the other
hand, because of the painful consequences of the Canudos rebellion,
would prefer to forget it. Whereas the nearsighted journalist considers
the Baron cynical, the latter considers the former naive, angelical, and
"a fanatic, perhaps" (416), by which Vargas Llosa may purposely in-
tend to question his own condemnation of fanaticism.[17] In his commitment to continue searching for the story of Canudos, the nearsighted
journalist actually rejects Epaminondas's offer to raise his salary on the
condition that he abandon his Canudos project. He has already begun
to check over all the newspapers in the Academy of History and is now
intent on interviewing the Baron.

Why does the nearsighted journalist remain anonymous throughout the novel when the other historical characters are specifically
named? In addition to the constant emphasis on his nearsightedness,
which reinforces the "seeing" leitmotif and the novel's Weltanschauung,
the character's anonymity may suggest that he is a fictitious version of
Euclides da Cunha, the Brazilian newspaperman who wrote the 1902
classic *Os sertões* about the Canudos War. The multiple-viewpoint account of the rebellion that the nearsighted journalist is in the process of
writing—and which is the Vargas Llosa novel—goes far beyond Da
Cunha's positivistic, sociological, and essayistic work of 1902.

The existence of another possible version of the Canudos story is
postulated by Vargas Llosa through the words of the grotesque but
highly intelligent León de Natuba: "—I wrote down the Counselor's
every word. . . . His thoughts, his evening counsels, his prayers, his
prophecies, his dreams. For posterity. So as to add another Gospel to
the Bible" (485). However, the Canudos scribe's notes are burned, just
as the myopic reporter's are lost, and the former's cannot be recon-
structed since he himself perishes in the flames. Still another written
version, albeit partial, is Gall's account of what happens to him after his
interview with Epaminondas, an account requested by the Baron.

In keeping with the postmodern, Bakhtinian world of the 1970s
and 1980s, *La guerra del fin del mundo* is a polyphonic novel: not only
are the historical events viewed from different perspectives, but ultimately history is viewed as imitating literature, as suggested by Borges
in "Tema del traidor y del héroe": "That history should have copied

history was already sufficiently astonishing; that history should copy literature was inconceivable . . ." (73–74). At the end of Part 2, the nearsighted journalist asks Epaminondas to let him cover the Moreira César campaign because seeing a real hero would be almost like reading a novel: "'Seeing a flesh-and-blood hero, being close to someone very famous is a very tempting prospect. It would be like seeing and touching a character in a novel'" (137). Also, from the point of view of the Prophet, many of the historical events that occur have their antecedents in the Bible: "The Counselor explained that the fact that the Throat-Slitter had a white horse came as no surprise to the believer, for wasn't it written in the Apocalypse that such a horse would come and that its rider would be carrying a bow and a crown so as to conquer and rule? But his conquests would end at the gates of Belo Monte through the intercession of Our Lady" (300). In fact, as the novel progresses, its essentially mimetic character is increasingly subjected to questioning. Despite having been present in the final days of Canudos, and despite having experienced the previous three military campaigns in different ways, and despite all his interviews with the Baron and all his painstaking research in the Academy of History, the myopic reporter's final version of what actually occurred can only be an approximation of the historical truth or—according to Vargas Llosa, following in the tradition of Borges—possibly a rewriting of the popular traditional tales handed down by rural storytellers from generation to generation.[18] Significantly, the storyteller in the novel, the Dwarf, becomes the nearsighted journalist's close friend. Moreover, the tales he tells are familiar to a variety of the principal characters, including João Abade and the Baron. João Abade, who has been fascinated since childhood with the story of Roberto el Diablo 'Robert the Devil', realizes how strange the world is when he reflects on his having accepted the Prophet in order to escape from his bloody past, only to find himself engaged in a much bloodier struggle: "Abbot João left the store thinking how strange things had turned out in his life, as they did in everyone's perhaps. —Like in the minstrels' stories—he thought" (180).

Not only do they have a basis in history, but João Abade and the novel's other repentant murderers are also reenacting the "Terrible and Exemplary Story of Robert the Devil" (355) that the Dwarf recounts along with stories about Charlemagne and the Twelve Peers of France. Some parts of Robert the Devil's story are narrated in Part 1, in João Abade's biographical sketch, but although there are several other allusions to it throughout the novel, it is not until the final pages that the story is completed, revealing the close parallelism with the repentant bandits. Robert's father was the Duke of Normandy; his mother was sterile and old, and she had to make a pact with the devil in order to conceive and give birth to Robert. The latter was born possessed by a destructive spirit which made him a suitable model for the Brazilian bandits: "Robert plunged his knife into the bellies of pregnant women or slit the throats of newborn babes . . . and impaled peasants and set fire to huts where families were sleeping" (557). After being redeemed by the Buen Jesús 'Good Jesus', he saved Emperor Charlemagne from the attack of the Moors, married the Queen of Brazil, and traveled all over the world in search of the relatives of his former victims, whose feet he would kiss while begging them to torture him. By the time he died, he was known as "Robert the Saint become a hermit" (557). The fact that Vargas Llosa, via the Baron, alludes to the scholarly preservation of these folktales gives them still greater weight in the novel: "The Baron was reminded of Profesor Tales de Azevedo, a scholar friend of his who had visited him in Calumbi many years before: he would spend hour after hour listening, in rapt fascination, to the minstrels at fairs, have them dictate to him the words that he heard them sing and recite, and assured him that they were medieval romances, brought to the New World by the first Portuguese and preserved in the oral tradition of the backlands" (355).

Whether the Prophet's followers in Canudos were reenacting legendary folktales and whether the historical accounts of the uprising are distorted are questions that may never be resolved. Brand new historical and novelized versions of the Canudos rebellion may present still other interpretations that will enrich our total appreciation of what did or did not happen. The 1989 novel *A casca da serpente* 'The Serpent's Skin', by Brazil's well-known magic realist José J. Veiga (b. 1915), actually continues the Prophet's story after his resurrection. What is (perhaps) noncontroversial is the outstanding quality of Vargas Llosa's "symphony of narrativity," to borrow a phrase from Roberto González Echevarría ("Sarduy," 70), in which all the musical notes, phrases, leitmotifs, and structures are directly related to the major theme: the condemnation of fanaticism.[19]

Coda: *A casca da serpente*

If Vargas Llosa's *La guerra del fin del mundo* is a "symphony of narrativity," the scant 155 pages of José J. Veiga's New Historical Novel *A casca da serpente* are a delightfully entertaining postmodern popular song with a similar anti-fanaticism message but with a different final "twist."

The historical protagonist Antônio Conselheiro does not die in Canudos but is spirited off by a few of his surviving followers, while another corpse is dressed in his tunic and buried in his grave. The ruse succeeds and the Prophet leads his followers to Itamundé, where they found a new settlement, the Nova Canudos—ironically named *Concorrência* 'Competition'—on a mountain top, even though *"água não gosta de subir morro"* 'water doesn't like to climb uphill' (77).

Whereas Vargas Llosa denounces fanaticism by mimetically portraying its consequences, Veiga subverts fanaticism through the Conselheiro's apocryphal transformation, or change of skin—any relationship to Carlos Fuentes's *Cambio de piel* 'Change of Skin' (1967) may not be coincidental. To the great amazement of his followers, the Conselheiro gradually sheds his saintliness by calling for a rest stop (13–15); by not wasting so much time in prayer (27); by bathing (28); by teaching his followers how to organize a democratic town meeting (46); and by shaving his beard and donning modern clothing made by a tailor (89). This last decision is accompanied by one of the many examples in the novel of popular sayings: *"Vida nova, cara e estampas novas"* 'A new life; a new face and a new image' (89).

Once the new Canudos is established, foreign visitors begin to arrive, and the Conselheiro expresses sincere interest in a series of modern inventions, an intertextual allusion to José Arcadio Buendía in *Cien años de soledad*. The first to appear is the camera, which truly amazes the Conselheiro: *"ficou com cara de cabra que vê girafa pela primeira vez"* 'he put on a face like that of a hillbilly who sees a giraffe for the first time' (115).

Not only is there intertextuality with *Cien años de soledad*, but also possibly with Posse's *Los perros del Paraíso*, since both Columbus and Antônio Conselheiro invoke Isaiah[20] in the creation of a new world: *"Isaías, eis que as coisas de antes já vieram, e as novas eu vos anuncio. Eu crio céus novos e nova terra"* 'Isaiah, behold the things of old have now returned, and the new ones I am announcing to you. I am creating new heavens and a new land' (54). Moreover, the novel clearly refers intertextually to Euclides da Cunha's original 1902 *Os sertões* and Vargas Llosa's *La guerra del fin del mundo*. However, in keeping with the Veiga novel's discreetly playful tone, Euclides da Cunha's full name is mentioned only once in its expanded form, Euclides Rodrigues Pimenta da Cunha (11), while on four other occasions the reporter is referred to as Pimenta da Cunha (47, 78, 118, 121). By not referring to him as Euclides da Cunha, Veiga demonstrates that he is striving for the autonomy of his text. By the same token, of the Conselheiro's fanatical followers who play such an important role in *La guerra del fin del mundo,* only Antônio Beatinho makes a brief appearance at the beginning of the novel (5–15), while João Abade (78) and Pajeú (79) are only mentioned in passing. Veiga further distances himself, on the other hand, by featuring Canudos survivors who do not appear in Vargas Llosa's novel: Bernabé José de Carvalho, Quero-Quero, Pedrão, the outspoken Marigarda, who turns out to be the Conselheiro's first cousin from Ceará, and the boy Dasdor, with his pet turtle and his burro who almost dies of asphyxiation for having tried to swallow a frog. The cast of characters is enhanced by a pair of Irish Sinn Fein patriots, an American geologist, and a charming Brazilian woman composer.

The appearance of Pedro the Russian anarchist (154) immediately evokes the image of Vargas Llosa's Scottish anarchist Gall, but Veiga uses his anarchist for a different ideological purpose. Pedro greatly admires the egalitarian society of Concorrência, which is serving as a model for countless others all over the world and which supports his own questioning of Darwin's theory of the survival of the fittest: *"—Vi na Ásia colônias de animais de espécies diferentes vivendo na harmonia, e não em luta feroz pela existência"* 'In Asia I saw colonies of different species of animals living in harmony, and not in a ferocious struggle for life' (142).

The narrator ends the novel with a rather explicit ideological statement which refers both to the new Canudos and to the formerly Communist Eastern European countries: "If from that dream and that effort, only ruins remain today, that does not mean that the dream was absurd" (154). This is a view that Vargas Llosa would find difficult to accept. In a mock illustration of how history repeats itself, in 1965 some unidentified invaders, who appear in earlier works by Veiga,[21] blow up the statue of Antônio Conselheiro and destroy the town of Concorrência, making room for a *"depósito de lixo atômico administrado por uma indústria química com sede fictícia no Principado de Mônaco"* 'deposit of atomic waste administered by a chemical firm with fictitious headquarters in the Principality of Monaco' (155). In its anachronistic fusion of the resurrected dissenting Prophet, the nuclear waste problem of the 1980s (and 1990s and succeeding decades), and the pop culture of the 1950s (movie-star Grace Kelly's 1956 marriage to the Prince of

Monaco), *A casca da serpente* is a more typical New Historical Novel than the more mimetic *La guerra del fin del mundo*. In fact, the two novels could be considered as representing two poles of the NHN: the light and breezy, albeit politically serious, popular song and the long, humorless, albeit spell-binding, symphony.

3 Abel Posse's Denunciation of Power

Los perros del Paraíso

Whereas *La guerra del fin del mundo* utilizes a primarily mimetic approach to denounce all forms of fanaticism, *Los perros del Paraíso* 'The Dogs of Paradise' by Argentinean Abel Posse utilizes a primarily ludic approach to denounce all forms of power.[1] With the discovery of the New World as its central theme, the text involves and alludes to a very broad galaxy of power. "The Tavern of the New Phalanx of Macedonia" (69), frequented by Christopher Columbus, evokes twentieth-century Fascist dictators Mussolini and Franco as well as Alexander the Great of ancient Greece; the fifteenth-century Turkish "curtain of scimitars" (7) evokes the Iron Curtain which separated eastern and western Europe for the past four decades of the twentieth century; and the ideological power of organized religions and of Marxism is denounced, as is the power of contemporary urban muggers whose victims lie "floating in a ditch; murdered because of the careless oversight of not carrying something to give the assailants" (70). For an Argentinean to write a novel about Christopher Columbus—who is usually more associated with Caribbean history—during a period when his compatriots were reexamining Argentine history in terms of the repressive military dictatorships of 1976–1983[2] is totally in keeping with the Bakhtinian dialogic, ironic, and carnivalesque nature of the text. In other words, the voices that are heard in the novel are often polemical and contradictory,

but what is indisputable is the denunciation of power: "the terrible re-
active force that emanates from all Power" (70).[3] Furthermore, just as
the events of 1896–1897 in northeastern Brazil reflect conditions in
Peru and Latin America in the 1970s in the Vargas Llosa novel, in this
work the unique fusion of the four Columbus voyages into one, along
with a whole spate of outrageous anachronisms, lead the reader to look
for possible parallelisms with political conditions in the Argentina of
the late 1970s and early 1980s. The chorus of Jewish mothers (147)
bemoaning their expulsion from Spain in 1492, along with the anachronistic czarist pogroms in Russia (153), cannot help but recall the
Argentine mothers of the Plaza de Mayo in Buenos Aires protesting
against the disappearance of their loved ones during the military government of the Proceso de Reorganización Nacional (1976–1983).

Perhaps the best starting point to illustrate this combination of the
apparently dialogic nature of the novel and its relatively clear denunciation of the Argentine military is the novel's title, *Los perros del Paraíso*.
The title in itself is ironic since dogs, like the mythological three-headed
Cerberus, are usually considered the guardians of the entrance to Ha-
des.[4] While Columbus identifies the mouth of the Orinoco River with
the Biblical Paradise, the arrival of the Spaniards represents for the Indians the loss of Paradise and the entrance into the Inferno. On the
other hand, while the Spaniards' ferocious hounds rip the Indians to
shreds, the next-to-the-last page of the novel describes the invasion/re-
volt of "an army of the diminutive dogs of Paradise" (299) that symbolizes the revolutionary potential of the masses of oppressed Indians and
mestizos. They are "unafraid of the fiercely barking mastiffs or the
shouts and musket fire of guards. . . . Insignificant, always denigrated,
now in numbers they formed a mammoth and formidable beast. Their
enormous, peaceful, silent presence was terrifying . . ." (299).[5]

However, the novel ends on a pessimistic note: the rebellious "diminutive dogs" hold the city for only one hour before retreating. A
possible interpretation of their brief, unsuccessful rebellion is that it refers to the many guerrilla movements that sprang up in Argentina and
all over Latin America during the 1960s and early 1970s, only to suc-
cumb to U.S.–supported counterinsurgency forces during the 1970s. In
the 1980s, these same little dogs "have wandered field and town, from
Mexico to Patagonia. Rarely, spurred by extreme hunger, they have attacked sheep and horses" (300). The passage ends on a humorous note,
unobtrusive and unexpected, but in keeping with the ironic and parodic
tone of the entire novel: "They are ubiquitous, these irrelevant creatures
no kennel club would register" (300).

The connection between the events in the novel and the Argentine military is established through direct allusions to Juan and Evita Perón, Borges, and Columbus's Italianate Buenos Aires dialect of Spanish. The organizer of the first brothel in the New World *(La Diabla)* and the leader of the first military coup (Francisco Roldán), with whom she is in cahoots, clearly suggest the Peróns. The reference to the edenic Eve as Evita leaves no room for doubt: *"La Diabla,* who was dolled up like a veritable Evita" (270).[6] The linkage between Roldán and Juan Perón is achieved through the reference to Italy and Germany (Perón's models were Mussolini and Hitler): "Boldly, he assigned himself the title of 'colonel' (an Italian denomination seldom used in the Spain of that day). Defiantly, he began wearing a frogged jacket and a spiked Prussian helmet" (261). Posse's anti-Peronist stance is clearly spelled out in both his earlier novel *Momento de morir* 'A Time to Die' (1979, signed "Venice 1975"), about the leftist guerrilla terrorism of the early 1970s, and his later novel *Los demonios ocultos* 'The Hidden Demons' (1987), about the Nazi refugees in Argentina and their ties to Perón and his military successors—the specific references to Evita and Juan Perón should not be interpreted too literally, to the point of excluding the right-wing generals of the late 1970s and early 1980s, popularly known as "gorillas": "The monkeys, almost simultaneously with Colonel Roldán, led the first American conspiracy" (278).

Although the presence of Borges is felt throughout the novel,[7] one specific Borgesian footnote is included from a nonexistent book to confirm Columbus's Argentine dialect: "'Colón said *piba* [sic] instead of *niño, bacán* for *bon vivant, mishiadura* instead of *miseria,* and *susheta* instead of *mujer,* words heard today only in tangos and the slang of *lunfardo* poetry. . . . (See Nahum Bromberg, *Semiología y Estructuralismo,* 4, *'El idioma de Cristoforo Colon'* [Manila: 1974])" (71).

Aside from the thinly veiled Argentine connection, *Los perros del Paraíso* places greater emphasis on equating the Spanish Conquest with twentieth-century American imperialism,[8] Nazism, and other forms of tyranny or exploitation. In the relatively few scenes involving the Indians, certain aspects of their pre-Columbian civilizations are also criticized, in defiance of Todorov and the other boosters of alterity ("otherness"),[9] but without condoning the genocidal invasion. Emanuel Swedenborg (1688–1772), the Swedish scientist and mystical religious leader who appears in the novel as one of three famous anachronistic landsknechts (the other two are Marx and Nietzsche), decries the actions of the Caribbean cannibals,[10] apparently accepting Columbus's questionable report to Ferdinand and Isabella, but also condones it somewhat by comparing it to Catholic communion:

> As for the cannibals who castrate, fatten, and feast upon the Tainos, who are their ideal of beauty, they aspire to be reincarnated in those perfect and envied bodies. They prefer the testicles, it is true; they roast and eat them as a special dish, because they sense in them the origin of the seed of perfection. Why does the Catholic partake of Christ in the host? Is it not to hold Him next to his heart, deep in his being? We have seen many Catholics who are revoltingly greedy for God! Is that not true? (249)

Referring specifically to the Spanish Conquest, the narrator states unequivocally: "The invasion was without doubt genocidal. The Spanish were the new cannibals,[11] capable of devouring the cannibals themselves" (280).

Rather than idealize the Aztecs and the Incas, Posse presents them through the same postmodern, dialogic lens that he uses to view all the novel's characters and events. As an extension of the Mexican reconceptualization of the "Discovery of America" as the "Encounter of Two Worlds," representatives of the Aztec and Inca empires meet in Tlatelolco in 1468–1469 to decide whether they should invade "the lands of the pale ones" (32). By beginning this section with the words "a final solution to their solar problem was really all the Aztecs wanted" (29), the narrator clearly evokes the Nazi plan to exterminate the Jews. The imperialistic Aztecs argue in favor of the invasion because with only "twenty or thirty thousand of the pale brutes" (32) they would be able to construct the Temple of Huitzilipochtli and resolve their problem of the gods' thirst for blood.

The Incas, however, seem to know the palefaces better, since one of their balloons got as far as Düsseldorf,[12] and their envoy is not very enthusiastic over the project. At the same time, Inca socialism, which has been mythified by José Carlos Mariátegui, Raúl Haya de la Torre, and the ideologues of the 1968 Peruvian military revolution, is ridiculed in the novel for its new mining law that provides for "six hours per day and four months of labor per year. Six hours" (31). All doubts about the narrator's attitude toward Inca socialism and socialism in general are clarified by the following short paragraph on the same page: "These Aztecs were open to grace and inexactitude. They tolerated free commerce and the lyric. The Incan world, in contrast, was geometrical, statistical, rational, two-dimensional, symmetrical. Socialist, in sum" (31).

In an example of metafiction, this dramatic encounter between Aztecs and Incas is immortalized when the characters step inside the Codex Vaticanus C, where the final banquet is portrayed. The chapter comes to a tragicomic close with the last attempt of the frustrated Aztec *tecuhtli,* expert practical politician that he was, to convince Huamán: " 'My lord, it would be best if we ate the white-faces for lunch, before they have us for supper' " (34).

The Aztec-Inca banquet also triggers a look forward to the 1980s with a lament over the destiny of the new mestizo race in a world dominated by U.S. culture, as exemplified by fast-food restaurants. Furthermore, the mention of Cambodian iconography links the remote Asian origins of the Aztecs to the growing international preeminence of Asians in the late twentieth century: "(How could anyone imagine that those adolescents and solemn princesses with large full lips like the goddesses of Cambodian iconography would one day be dishwashers and waitresses in the Nebraska Cafeteria, 'only fifty meters from the Plaza de las Tres Culturas. Reserved parking'?)" (62–63). Another poignant example of the tragic state of Aztec culture and power in the 1980s is the location of the Indian poetic lament over the Spanish invasion, part of the *Book of Ancestors* from Chilam Balam de Chumayel: "The text, recovered by Roldán's men, is to be found in the Vienna Museum of History, in the same case as the feather crown of the emperor Moctezuma" (285).

The dialogic approach used by Posse in his presentation of the pre-Columbian Indian civilizations may also be observed in his nonmimetic characterization of the novel's protagonist Christopher Columbus. As a child, Columbus is beaten up by his brother-in-law and his cousins for daring to be different. The cheesemakers and tailors resent "the subversive presence of the mutant, the poet" (15) and his desire to become a navigator. His mother realizes that because of his future greatness, he must endure the hatred and resentment of his mediocre peers: "She understood that the rite that was about to take place was an essential test born of the hatred and resentment felt by the mediocre, and that it served to measure, fortify, and temper the virtue of the great" (17). Nevertheless, Posse does not portray Columbus as the archetypal, mythical hero. In fact, the narrator refers to him as the "amoral genovés" (87) 'unscrupulous Genoese' (110), one of the four supermen—but not superhuman beings—who will propel Ferdinand and Isabella's "chariot of power": "The Chariot of Power had begun to roll. Isabel and Fernando were on their way to finding their heroes, their supermen (Gonzalo de Córdoba; the swineherd Pizarro; an unscrupulous Genoese; the adventurer Cortés. Supermen innocent of the least theory of supermanhood . . .)" (110).

No matter how astute (like Homer's Ulysses) and ambitious Columbus later seems, he is also driven by the totally irrational force emanating from his conviction that he is a "direct descendant of the prophet Isaiah."[13] The question of his family's Jewish origins is treated dialogically and humorously in the following passage. The three consecutive *esdrújulas* 'words accented on the antepenultimate syllable' *("escépticos, eclécticos, sincréticos")* and the metaphoric use of *navegaban* 'sailed the seas' at the end of the passage succinctly summarize his family's religious situation.

> The Colombos were prudently Catholic. They went to mass on Sundays, ostentatiously, obedient, with the rather constructive skepticism of the *petite bourgeoisie* before the All-Powerful.
>
> They were also known to have Hebrew blood. In the tailors' branch, they could boast here and there of a hooked nose, of a pointed ear or two. . . .
>
> They were skepticals, eclectic, syncretic, astute. They sailed the seas of opportunistic polytheism. (25)

Reinforcing the dialogic portrait of Columbus with postmodern humor, the narrator characterizes the admiral not only as "always ambiguous" (209) but also as biologically amphibian: "Between the second and third toes on each foot was a thin connective membrane like that of ducks and other aquatic-terrestrial creatures. The admiral was palmate, and—who could doubt it now—definitely amphibian by nature" (246). As the ultimate example of postmodern humor and ambiguity, Columbus in the 1470s plans to tell the Catholic Monarchs that the earth is flat and that sailors have been reluctant to sail westward for fear of falling off the spherical earth because, unlike the humble ant, "they do not have gum on the soles of their feet. . . . Only a man who knows that the earth is flat—even though the world is round—has the courage to sail toward the Indies! The king and queen must be so informed!" (81).

From a more historical point of view, the search for the most direct route to the Orient is presented in the novel as a completely commercial, 1980s-type enterprise, but Columbus's only real motivation, withheld from everyone, is to discover the terrestrial Paradise. In the second half of the fifteenth century, "the multinationals were suffocating, reduced to inter-city commerce" (7). When Columbus presents his plans at the court of the Catholic monarchs, he is supported by a group of high-ranking *conversos* (converted Jews) motivated both by the possibility of financial gain and the desire to find a New Israel for the Jews threatened by the "long-feared mass expulsion" (124). Royal Treasurer Santángel writes to Columbus that the year 1492 "is the year signaled by the Cabala, the year of redemption following persecution. 'You are the envoy! The Hebrews of Asia await you in order to resettle the promised land, for all of us'" (149). The port of Palos is also flooded, anachronistically, by all the Central European Jews, victims of the "czarist pogroms" (153).

Nevertheless, Columbus is far from being portrayed as a redeemer. His purpose is not to provide a haven for the persecuted Jews but rather to find the terrestrial Paradise "where that trap of consciousness, that net woven with the two threads of Space and Time, no longer ruled" (150). In other words, he is searching for eternal life for himself and others. In spite of his secret mystical mission, Columbus reveals human frailties when he has second thoughts—"the admiral felt the enormous weight of his terrible responsibility" (151)—and he feels the urge to "Leave everything behind! Flee with Beatriz and the boy, and in absolute anonymity begin the delights of a life without greatness. Open a pharmacy in Flanders, or a butcher shop in Porto. Flee from History!" (151).

More seriously, in order to save his own skin in Córdoba during Torquemada's stepped-up persecution of the Jews, Columbus earlier "expounded on the inarguable need to eliminate Jews. . . . He spoke of purity of blood, of responsibility to country, of focusing everything around One Kingdom, One People, One Faith" (123)—all in spite of the fact that he had moved in with Beatriz, the pharmacist's poor Jewish relative. Columbus has also previously exploited other women by "stealing insect-riddled maps from bureau drawers while the seduced widows of sailors less fortunate than he slept the exhausted sleep of pleasure and guilt" (79). He may even have married Felipa Moñiz in order to get his hands on "the famous secret chart the Florentine geographer and cosmographer Paolo Toscanelli had sent to the departed Perestrello with a clear X-marks-the-spot over the Antilles and Cipango" (87).

The ambivalent portrayal of Columbus continues during the voyage(s) to the New World. His leadership at sea is unquestionable—in fact, the narrator compares him to the R.A.F. heroes of World War II with a parody of Winston Churchill's famous speech: "Never will so many have owed so much to one man" (192). Yet the narrator also reports how Columbus, with some justification, deceives his men at sea:

"The admiral, conscious that they are disheartened and alarmed, enters false information. Each morning for the day's run, he reckons fewer leagues than they have made. You have to put blinders on a horse when you expect to confront fire or a savage bull" (195).

The four voyages are fused into one, and Columbus identifies the mouth of the Orinoco as the site of the terrestrial Paradise. He and his followers come across a huge black-and-yellow anaconda which they assume is the one that had spoken to Eve. The giant *ceiba* tree is identified as the Tree of Life. Totally convinced that they have found the pre-Adamite terrestrial Paradise, Columbus proclaims the Ordinances of Nudity and Idleness.

The Ordinance of Nudity restores the innocence of the Garden of Eden and outlaws lust, but without contradicting the subsequent Biblical mandate to reproduce and to multiply: "'Padre, let the men increase and multiply. But let them do so without shameful pleasure and without fancy capers. Here there is no urgency. Lust is an offshoot of frustration'" (249). What amazes and amuses the reader and reinforces the dialogic nature of the novel is that, before arriving in the New World, Columbus is portrayed as a champion of lust. He suspends his Portuguese wife Felipa from a ceiling beam by her ankle in order to explore her geographically: "He nibbled her fleshy parts. He studied the secretion and nature of her moistnesses. His tongue explored the expanse of that well-bred skin" (86). Soon after Felipa dies, Columbus falls in love with the Jewess Beatriz in Córdoba, reacting to the "stirring of a healthful animalism" (121). After he arrives at the Canary Islands with his three caravels, he succeeds in vanquishing the "sexual demonism" (167) of Beatriz Peraza Bobadilla, whose previous lovers concluded their nights of lovemaking by being "thrown into the sea from the north window of the tower" (167). In the face of Columbus's sexual prowess, "Beatriz de Bobadilla felt inclined to abandon her bloody sadism and yield instead to the joys of submission" (179). In a new version of the Ulysses-Circe episode, Columbus succeeds in continuing his voyage after three days of tremendous sexual pleasure: "He knew intuitively that she longed for death (erotic and figurative, that is) at his hands. He stepped up his phallic aggression to its highest power. (That was most probably the moment they reached level 8 of lechery on the Hite scale.)" (180).

The Ordinance of Idleness condemns not only work but all activity: "The paroxysms of activity the Caucasoid Europeans had set as a standard of conduct was, according to the Ordinance, a mark of damnation, of life after Paradise" (257). Although Western commercialism is criticized throughout the novel, in true dialogical form Columbus, enamored of the hammock—"His days were long and uneventful. Neither subsistence nor existence pried him from his hammock" (289)—is blamed by the narrator for having established the model for the negative image of the Spanish American mestizo:

> It was evident that the admiral had suffered a probably irreversible mutation. The rational consciousness characteristic of Occidental "men of reason" had forsaken him.
>
> Unconsciously, whether as self-punishment or self-acclaim, he had been transformed into the first complete South American. Although he had not been born of carnal union between races, he was the first mestizo. A mestizo without an umbilicus. Like Adam. (288)

In the face of Columbus's Edenic recommendations, the majority of his men resist, protest, and finally revolt, with an allusion to the Russian Revolution. Instead of delivering their tools, "the husbandmen, inveterate kulaks, buried their sickles and whetstones like dogs burying a disputed bone" (258). With a coup d'état—*"el primer bolivianazo"* (200) 'the first military takeover' (268)—Francisco Roldán, "the strongman" (261), establishes another typical trait of Latin America:[14] "This scandalous praetorian appropriation was to be the longest-continuing crime of *doing* in America" (271). Once "the disease of *doing*" (260) is reinstated, capitalism is condemned as much as or more than Columbus's Edenic idleness: "The years of entrepreneurial frenzy began" (274); the custom of smoking becomes prevalent in Europe because Dr. Nicot proves "that in addition to giving pleasure, nicotine cured cancer" (274). The priests become the accomplices of the entrepreneurs when they declare "the rape of Indian women a venial sin" (274) atoned for by only "a penance of three Our Fathers and three Ave Marias. . . . Those ecclesiastical clarifications were indispensable in orienting the attitude of the business community at the moment of an economic boom" (274).

When Columbus returns to the coast, in chains, he marvels at the profusion of signs: "Santángel Bank and Hawkins Ltd., Bologna Beauty Salon, Palace of the Inquisition (Semper Veritas), Cook Travel Agency, United Fruit Company, Castile Hotel, Sagardúa Buffet" (298). Although the modern reader can share Columbus's profound grief over the fact that "everyone, including his relatives, was busily sacking Paradise" (297), one cannot accept his exaltation of the Edenic idleness.

If Columbus is portrayed ambiguously—as being, on the one hand, idealistic and heroic, and on the other, amoral—Queen Isabella, as a more clear-cut representative of power, is portrayed more negatively. The parallelism in Part 1 between the childhood games of Columbus and Isabella (both born in 1451) and their precocious awareness of their future greatness establish Isabella as almost the novel's co-protagonist.[15] In the novel's very first episode, the ten-year-old "bossy" (12) Isabella leads her friends into the royal bedroom and, hooking the hem of "the sleeping king's nightshirt" (14) with a long reed, "exposes the impotence of King Enrique IV" (2), her half-brother, thus establishing her claim to the throne over that of Juana la Beltraneja. In order to enter the bedroom, Isabella first has had to conquer the aged lion, archetypically "stretched across the threshold" (13), by grabbing his mane, biting his ear, and punching him in the face—one of the novel's many displays of intertextuality, here with the *Poema de Mio Cid* and *Don Quijote*. Her rivalry for the royal succession of Castile with la Beltraneja culminates in the civil war precipitated by her seizing power only one day after the death of Enrique IV: "a true *Putsch*" (73). By calling it a *Putsch*, the author identifies Isabella with Hitler, an identification reinforced by the use of other words associated with Nazism such as *SS* and *swastika,* and especially by her persecution and expulsion of the Jews. In one of the novel's Borgesian footnotes, the narrator states "that Hitler expressed his unconditional admiration for Isabella of Castile to Göring" (54).

Isabella's premature self-coronation, without consulting her husband Ferdinand of Aragon, infuriates him and provides the narrator with the opportunity to question today's feminist view of history: "She had not put the horns on him through sex, but by seizing the short, hard sword of Power. Unacceptable behavior in that age of adamant phallocracy.[16]

It is also Isabella, rather than Tomás de Torquemada, the grand inquisitor, who is responsible for the heightened activity of the Inquisition: "'You, a monk; how can you live in the quiet world of the court! You must go out and seek sin in the streets, in bodies! You must save yourself saving others!'" (97). Isabella's fanatical Catholicism, in true dialogic fashion, is hardly consistent with her apparently uncontrollable lust. On the other hand, it could be argued that both sex and religion contribute to her quest for power. Upon seeing Ferdinand for the first time, Isabella is attracted to his physical power: "Isabel stared at the nape of the youth's neck. It was the neck of a bull in rut, a knot of power, the knee of a Roman gladiator" (36). Hard put to repress her lust for Ferdinand, Isabella, like Columbus, is characterized as animalistic: "She tried to find relief by galloping wildly over the rocky terrain.

She winded three horses in ten days' time. The chronicle records that she began to exude the strong—but not, of course, repulsive—odor of a large cat in heat" (45). In their first actual intercourse, Isabella is no less the aggressor than is Ferdinand:

> Probably she was possessed as she possessed him, and her maiden-head simply ripped, like the strong fine silk of the tent of the Great Turk surprised in his encampment by a summer storm. Rupture through internal convex pressure, not external concavizing action.
>
> In sum: at some moment during the tilling and toil of the night of October 15 and 16, the turgid gland of the Aragonese prince confronted—"man to man"[17]—the aggressive Isabeline hymen. (56–57)

The two lovers later meet in the Almagro Monastery disguised as a Franciscan monk and a Carmelite nun, which provokes strange dreams among the penitents: "The next morning in the refectory, following matins, the abbot heard evidence that by a surprising coincidence all the dreams of the seminarians had been of zoological nature . . . ; a young student of Asturias told a nightmare about a circle of howling wolves that formed into a blazing ring that melted the snow as it rolled" (105). The ultimate union of sex, religion, and power is the consecration of their marriage in 1473 by Cardinal Borgia, the future Pope Alexander VI, who "anointed his brow" with "a drop of that precious sperm born of the purest and most powerful love" (99).

In keeping with the novel's dialogic characterizations, Isabella's image is not totally negative, particularly alongside Ferdinand's. She supports Columbus's first voyage and then reaffirms her support as a result of the admiral's discovery of the terrestrial Paradise on the Venezuelan mainland. The reader tends to sympathize with her anger over Ferdinand's philandering and with her concern over having given birth to weak children—the Mad Juana and Prince John, her favorite, whose death at the age of twenty devastates her: "She was struck by illness: an insatiable thirst. She turned her back to the world and set her gaze on the realms of the beyond" (294).

In addition to being manifested in the creation of ambivalent characters, the dialogic nature of *Los perros del Paraíso* is evident in the affirmation and subversion of historicity as well. In the tradition of Borges, García Márquez, Vargas Llosa, Fernando del Paso, and Hayden White, Posse distrusts historians. The narrator even accuses them explicitly of suppressing the truth, especially the actual motivations of the entrepreneurs who supported Columbus's expedition: "There are no extant details regarding the meetings of the financiers (very few important facts were written down, hence the essential unreliability of historians)" (124). Historians prefer to write about the grandiose and the pageants, he remarks parenthetically: "History records only the grandiloquent, the visible, acts whose results are cathedrals and processions; that is why history composed for official consumption is so banal" (73).

Nevertheless, the historicity of the novel is apparently affirmed by the chronological outlines that precede each of the four parts, in which each date is followed by a series of very concise sentences or phrases. Like the prologues in some of Brecht's plays, these chronological outlines distance readers from the characters and force us to question rather than to feel what is happening. At the same time, within these chronological sections, history is subverted by the insertion of apocryphal events involving historical characters, or of anachronistic or fictitious events involving historical or fictitious characters, such as the following:

> 1462
> *Cristóbal Colón steals an alphabet from the parish in Genoa. States he is to be a poet. Beatings; threats. "Nothing will save you from your fate as wool carder or tailor."*

> 2-House
> *Failure of Inca-Aztec negotiations in Tlatelolco. Decision against forming a fleet to invade the "cold lands of the Orient." Hot-air balloons of the Incas. Pampa of Nazca-Düsseldorf.*

> 1469
> *Landsknecht Ulrich Nietz, a German mercenary accused of bestiality for kissing a horse, arrives in Genoa from Turin. Land Wo die Zitronen blühen. Angst and the Judeo-Christian swindle. "God is dead."* (2–3).

> 1492
> *. . . The Mayflower. At sea: a rumba by Lecuona.* (142)

The admiral's encounter with the *Mayflower* provides the narrator with an opportunity to criticize still another dogmatic orthodoxy: "the good ship *Mayflower,* laden with terrible Puritans on their way to Vinland" (207). The presence of a twentieth-century rumba by the Cuban composer Ernesto Lecuona during Columbus's first voyage is further developed in the following sentence, in which the mention of the Caribbean princess Siboney, also the name of a twentieth-century song, engenders four other modern song titles (which I've italicized and which are lost in the translation), preceded by the narrator's own reference to the creative process, a touch of metafiction: "Se gesta una nueva forma de imaginación. La *piel canela* de *Siboney,* las *flores negras* en la *vereda tropical.* La supuesta *perfidia* de Anacaona" (216) 'A new form of imagination is in gestation. The cinnamon skin of Siboney, the black flowers along tropical trails. The alleged perfidy of Anacaona' (290). Not only music but painting is intertextualized with references to Nietzsche and to Henri Rousseau's painting *Tropical Storm with a Tiger* (1891), which is reproduced on the cover of the 1987 Plaza y Janés edition of the novel (the English translation has a different cover): "He had the eyes of a caged tiger; glints of yellow and chestnut striation" (19); "Nietz half-opened his yellow eyes, a Rousseau tiger semiconcealed in a jungle clearing" (115).[18]

Within the realm of literary intertextuality, the narrator takes issue with Carpentier's assumption in *El arpa y la sombra* that Columbus and Queen Isabella were lovers: "That is why the great Alejo Carpentier errs when he describes a complete and uninhibited sexual union between the navigator and the sovereign" (136). The narrator ironically attributes Carpentier's error to his "admirable proclivity for the democratic" (136)—an unlikely trait for an author living in socialist Cuba, from Posse's perspective. Cervantes and Descartes, thinly disguised, bid goodbye to Columbus on the eve of his departure for the New World: "That is where a one-armed former soldier, twice rejected in his attempt to be engaged as scribe, is hanging around, and a mad Frenchman who only yesterday was pontificating that intelligence is the most evenly distributed commodity in the world, but that what is lacking is *method.*"[19]

Marx, in the guise of Mordecai, and Nietzsche, in the guise of landsknecht Ulrich Nietz, appear on board the caravels along with some aspects of their ideologies. Mordecai "tells the men they are equal, that they should unite, that private property is a kind of thievery! It is obvious he has misread Saint Thomas, and that humble man from Assisi. He even says religion is the opium of the people" (210). Whatever ambiguity there may be in this quote is eliminated when the narrator establishes a parallelism between the Catholic missionaries of the Spanish Conquest and Marxism: "The plants, the great trees, the jaguars, were the first to discover the imposture of the false gods. The families of monkeys, so nervous and lively in their reactions, realized, too, that the peasants and blacksmiths were using their scythes [the Spanish *hoz* is more properly translated as 'sickle'] and hammers as instruments of destruction" (277).

In the Brechtian chronology preceding Part 3, the narrator's juxtaposition of the hammer and the sickle with the identification of the Inquisition as the gibbet with the cross reaffirms Posse's criticism of all dogmatic, fanatical religions:

1492–1502
A departure that will last ten years. The gibbet-cross (Spanish patent). Virgins at wholesale. Hammer and sickle. . . . (142)

Nonetheless, in true dialogical fashion, the narrator arouses the reader's compassion for Mordecai at the very end of the novel: "the bearded rebel Mordecai, who was paying dearly for his ideas on redemption."[20]

Nietzsche is portrayed more sympathetically and at greater length.[21] The narrator appears to support Nietzsche's contention that human beings should strive to improve themselves rather than being content with the mediocrity represented by the Swiss watchmakers: "In Bern, that odious city of clockmakers, he had dared say that 'man is a thing to be surmounted.' Before the dawn, he was brutally beaten" (19). In Genoa, he consoles the boy Columbus who has just been beaten by his brother-in-law and other port toughs: "'Courage, boy. What does not kill you more strong will make you . . .'" (20). Later, in the terrestrial Paradise, Nietz insists that "God was dead. But men lived on, diminished, like worms upon a mountainous cadaver" (266). When God fails to respond to Nietz's scatological provocations in the Garden of Eden, "Nietz howled with pagan joy. This was the birth of man, finally liberated from the Tyrant's oppression. Of superman" (268).

Nietz's fellow anachronistic landsknecht, (Emanuel) Swedenborg, is also portrayed positively in the novel. Seen by Fray Buil as "a heinous heretic, one of those independent and irresponsible theologians who march alone toward the stake" (246), Swedenborg, "from the eminence of his liberated theology" (248), argues with Fray Buil that the Indians, whatever their "sins," are "creatures from God's garden" (249). Nonetheless, Fray Buil triumphs over both Swedenborg and Bartolomé de las Casas, and the Indians are enslaved and decimated. Nietz's triumph is also short-lived since Columbus and his followers are forced to abandon the terrestrial Paradise by Francisco de Bobadilla, who returns the Admiral of the Ocean Sea to Spain in chains.

The tragic end of Columbus's odyssey is also paralleled by Queen Isabella's death and the advent of a new era of destruction prophesied in the Chilam-Balam text:

We are sure. We have lived the reality.
The era of Sun in Movement has begun,
which follows the ages of Air,
Fire, Water, and Earth. This is

the beginning of the last age; the kernel
of destruction and death has been
sown. The Sun in Movement; the Sun
on earth, that shall pass. (285)

The pre-Columbian text's reference to the four elements, which establishes a link to early Greek philosophy, reinforces the encyclopedic, to-
talizing nature of the novel structured symbolically on the number four.
Like Vargas Llosa's *La guerra del fin del mundo*, *Los perros del Paraíso*
is divided into four parts, and groupings of four are common.[22] However, in *Los perros del Paraíso*, even though the four parts are explicitly
labeled *Air, Fire, Water,* and *Land*,[23] the respective leitmotifs of each
part of the symphonic structure, in keeping with the postmodern, dialogic nature of the whole novel, occasionally cross boundaries.

The air leitmotif of Part 1 may be seen in the metaphorical breath
of fresh air of the Renaissance;[24] the sea breezes that fill the ships' sails
and appeal to the boy Columbus's imagination; the verb "gasping" that
refers to both the death of the medieval world and the sexual awakening
of Ferdinand and Isabella; the wind that carries the Inca balloon to
Düsseldorf; and a great variety of aromas. As a transition to the fire
leitmotif of Part 2, Part 1 ends with two giant Olmecs serving "a dozen
hairless dogs, done to a crisp" on a "white-hot spit" (61), and with the
flames that destroy the Aztec and Mayan scrolls as well as the Library
of Alexandria.

The fire leitmotif of Part 2 is associated with the Inquisition's burning its victims at the stake; the ardent passion of Ferdinand, Isabella,
and Columbus; and the two wars—the four-year civil war against the
supporters of la Beltraneja and the final war against the Moors in Gra-
nada. The air leitmotif from Part 1 reappears toward the beginning of
Part 2: "And Colón, yellow shoes in hand like two Aeolian harps awaiting the fingers of the breeze . . ." (71). In Lisbon, a sudden breeze comes
up from the Tagus and "belled out Felipa's skirts" (83), smiting Columbus. In the final scene of Part 2, the air leitmotif is reintroduced with an
intertextual allusion to Carlos Fuentes's first novel: "It was a splendid
morning. Clear air. Purified air that had arrived with the breeze from
Teotihuacán, the Place-Where-the-Air-Is-Clear" (138). The air leitmotif
is combined with the water leitmotif in an earlier reference to Genesis—"at the time of Genesis there was only water or air (or, if you wish,
mist, which is the combination of the two" (80)—followed by reference
to the terrestrial Paradise and the flatness of the planet Earth. Toward

the end of Part 2, the water leitmotif is foregrounded: "Everyone knew that the cycle of the sea was about to begin, although the fire of the inquisitor's stake was not dimmed" (132). Columbus is taken to the former Mosque of Córdoba, where "the constant murmur of a fountain" (133) provides the musical accompaniment for Isabella's dance, which provokes his "extragenital ejaculation, or intraorgasm" that is compared to "the bubbling wine of Champagne" (135). The water and air leitmotifs are combined in the following sentence: "He was damp from seminal dew, bathed in a milky whey, exuding a slight aroma of crushed tarragon" (136).

Since all of Part 3 is concerned with Columbus's four-in-one voyage across the sea, water is the obvious predominant element. This leitmotif is reinforced by the amphibious Columbus's abnormal "ability to float" even "face downward";[25] by the buckets of "seawater, with lye and disinfectant" (171) that Beatriz de Bobadilla's Galician Guards use to scrub him down; by his escape "through urinary channels" (142); and ultimately by his arrival at the Orinoco delta described in a letter to Queen Isabella: " 'Thence is born a fountain from which issue the four principal rivers of Paradise. At this very moment we are being borne on the waters of the original fountain!' " (224). The air leitmotif is present throughout Part 3, naturally enough, as an indispensable part of ocean navigation, from gentle sea breezes to hurricanes. The search for land is also a very natural part of the discovery voyage, culminating in Rodrigo de Triana's cry on October 12, 1492, of " 'Land ahead!' " (220). What is more unusual are the relatively frequent references to the subdominant fire leitmotif: the "great bonfires" (147) of the Moorish pirates on the beach prior to Columbus's departure from Spain; "the fires of the volcano . . . towers of fire" (164) upon arriving at the Canary Islands; the September 13 "unusual disorder around the firebox and cooking pots" (193) aboard ship; and the September 14 incident of watching "a marvelous branch of fire fall from the sky into the sea. . . . Several arms of fire around the center. It is the unmistakable sweep of the flaming sword, the swastika of fire" (194). After Columbus's September 25 appearance on the poop deck "in expectation of the Saint Elmo's fire" (202), the subdominant fire leitmotif culminates with the October 9–10 crescendo: "The night of tropical calm follows a day of infernal heat. Sun beating down: limp sails drooping like melted candle wax . . . scorching sun and boiling air . . . the horrendous heat is a positive sign. It comes from the fire of the flaming swords guarding the Gates" (211–212). Finally, the sirocco-like *traconchana* (159), cleverly translated as 'menstral' (212; from the French *mistral,* paradoxically, a cold north wind), arouses the crew sexually: "The Iberian crew are as hot as caged dogs in heat" (212).

Part 4 takes place on land, the terrestrial Paradise, and the reappearance of the Catholic monarchs is also identified with the land: "For more than a week the court has been encamped on a picturesque plain not far from Almagro" (231). As one would expect, all four leitmotifs are explicitly mentioned in the passage from the Chilam-Balam quoted earlier. However, to the readers' surprise, they are displayed less prominently than in the novel's first three parts, perhaps so as not to detract from the major theme, which is the denunciation of power: Las Casas "was borne along on the wind of faith" (291); a waterfall generates a rainbow, "a mist with the seven primordial colors of creation" (291); Torquemada "'died in an aroma of sanctity'" (293); and Isabella is stricken by "an insatiable thirst" (dropsy; 294). The fire leitmotif also appears in an intertextual allusion to the cat in what Borges considered his best story, "The South": "The admiral was curled up in time like a cat on a hearth" (286).

The structural importance of the four natural elements, the prevalence of cultural allusions—ranging as far back as Genesis, the pre-Columbian Indian civilizations, and Homer—and the "flagrant rupture with the established spatiotemporal order" (204) create an instantaneous total view of world history that is reminiscent of the final deciphering of Melquíades's parchment at the end of García Márquez's *Cien años de soledad* and, in a more philosophical vein, of Borges's short story "El aleph" (1949). However, in Posse's *Los perros del Paraíso,* no matter "how immense the pleasure of reading" (in the words of Peruvian novelist Alfredo Bryce Echenique), no matter how ludic the chronotopes and the heteroglossia, and no matter how dialogic the characterization of Columbus, the ideological message comes through loud and clear: the denunciation of power, whether it be exercised by God, dogmatic religions, or political systems; by the Aztec, the Inca, or the Spanish empire; or by the twentieth-century Nazis, the U.S. economic and cultural empire, or the Argentine military dictatorship of 1976–1983.

4 The Instant Canonization
of a Bakhtinian Symphony

Fernando del Paso's *Noticias del imperio*

The almost certain canonization of Fernando del Paso's *Noticias del imperio* 'News from the Empire' depends primarily on its artistic complexity.[1] Whereas Roberto González Echevarría attributes the success of Vargas Llosa's *La guerra del fin del mundo* to its "symphony of narrativity" (70), *Noticias del imperio* may be appreciated best as a Bakhtinian symphony: a combination of the dialogic or polyphonic, heteroglossia, the carnivalesque,[2] and intertextuality.

One of the most impressive features of this exhaustively researched, history-dominant New Historical Novel is the expansion of the three-year imperial adventure of Maximilian and Carlota in Mexico (1864–1867) to an all-embracing, encyclopedic mural (characteristic of the modernist Joycean and Boom novels and uncharacteristic of the postmodern novel) that covers over a century of international relations dating from Napoleon Bonaparte's ascent to power at the end of the eighteenth century to the death of Carlota in 1927. Actually, through Carlota's trip to Yucatán and the crisscrossing of Europe by the different royal families, the historical scope is extended back to the days of the Mayan pre-Columbian civilization, to Charlemagne's Empire, and beyond.

Just as Vargas Llosa's condemnation of fanaticism in late nineteenth-century Brazil is obviously applicable to Peru's present-day Shining Path radical guerrillas, Fernando del Paso's description of Juárez's 1861 suspension of debt payments, highlighted on the page after the dedication, is an implicit criticism of today's presidents of Mexico and other Latin American countries for not suspending their debt payments to the United States. Although the novel clearly emphasizes the French imperialism of Napoleon III, it also traces American imperialism from the Monroe Doctrine in the 1820s to the 1925 intervention in Nicaragua. The beginning and the end of the U.S. Civil War (1861–1865) obviously play important roles in influencing Napoleon III's decisions to invade Mexico in 1862 and to withdraw his forces five years later. Even before the invasion takes place, during the masked ball at the Tuileries, Napoleon III (disguised as a Venetian noble) proposes to Austrian Ambassador Richard Metternich (disguised as a Roman senator) the possibility that the future Mexican Empire will recognize the Confederacy in exchange for the emigration of black slaves to Mexico, where they will be granted their freedom: "We'll make Mexico the new Liberia" (51). Toward the end of the novel, the spotlight is turned on the gunboat diplomacy of Theodore Roosevelt and his successors: the blowing up of the "Maine" in Havana harbor as a pretence for U.S. entry into the Cuban War of Independence; the plotting of Panama's independence from Colombia in order to facilitate the construction of the canal; the 1914 invasion of Veracruz; and the eight-year occupation of Nicaragua opposed by Sandino (640–641). Nevertheless, although Fernando del Paso's war against imperialism may be equated with Vargas Llosa's war against fanaticism as the dominant theme in the novel, there are two very significant differences. Vargas Llosa focuses exclusively on the Canudos war, but his ideological message, aimed at his readers of the 1980s, is of prime importance. On the other hand, *Noticias del imperio* has a much broader geographical and historical scope, yet the author's concerns about present-day imperialism are definitely subordinated to his aesthetic concerns about the nature of the novel and his creation of a Bakhtinian symphony.

Noticias del imperio's dualistic symphonic structure reflects not only the prominence of both Maximilian and Carlota but also other double phenomena, such as the French intervention and the Maximilian-Carlota empire; the two-headed Austro-Hungarian Empire led by Maximilian's older brother, Franz Josef; the Belgian Empire, led by Carlota's father and later by her brother, both named Leopold; the French empires of Napoleon Bonaparte and Louis Napoleon; and the two other Mexican empires, led respectively by Agustín Iturbide and by *Su Alteza Serenísima*, Santa Anna. Chapter 2 is entitled "ENTRE NAPO-

LEONES TE VEAS, 1861–62," and in its first section, "Juárez y 'Mosta-chú'," the early lives of Juárez and Louis Napoleon alternate, paragraph by paragraph; comparisons are also made between Napoleon III and both Napoleon I and Santa Anna.

Of the novel's twenty-three chapters, the odd-numbered ones are assigned to Carlota's monologues, all of which bear the exact same title of "Castillo de Bouchout 1927" in order to give the impression that nothing changes for a woman who has been considered insane since Maximilian's execution in 1867, or earlier, and who does not live in the real world. Stylistically, this impression is reinforced by the use of anaphora. In the fourteen pages of Chapter 9, for example, her constant repetition of the following phrases reaffirms Carlota's insanity: "When I tell them that . . ." (233–236); "the world has gone up in flames" (237); "it snowed" (238–239); "ask him/her" (240–241); "I defecated in . . ." (247). At the same time, her rather coherent meandering through history remembering historical figures, themes, and leitmotifs belies that insanity.

In an example of interior metafiction, Carlota characterizes her own discourse: "It's my privilege, the privilege of dreams and of the insane, to invent if I want to a huge castle of words, words as light as the air in which they float" (117) and "I'll write, yes, without stopping, in a stream like a river that never reaches the horizon, like a torrent that rushes towards infinity" (492). She also categorizes her own and the author's approach to history as a jigsaw puzzle, which she can break up and put together again, Borges-style, "converting villains into heroes, heroes into traitors, the victors into the vanquished, and those who were humiliated by defeat into the triumphant" (414). Carlota also equates her jigsaw puzzle with a mirror, where, like Aureliano Babilonia at the end of *Cien años de soledad*, she can see her entire life in one instant (414–415). Although, like many mental patients, Carlota con-stantly challenges the verdict of insanity, the reader is also intrigued by the ability of the mad Empress to recreate such a huge tableau of world history during her sixty years of confinement from 1867 to 1927. Her monologues reveal that she has been able to keep abreast of the news right up to Charles Lindbergh's transatlantic flight in 1927, the year of her death.

In contrast to Carlota's twelve monologues, all bearing the same title, the eleven even-numbered chapters assigned to Maximilian have different titles, and each one is subdivided into three sections, which also have individual titles. In numerological terms, the eleven chapters multiplied by three produce the number thirty-three, the age of Jesus at the time of his crucifixion, thus suggesting the view of Maximilian as a sacrificial lamb. This interpretation is substantiated by Maximilian's need for a traitor—Miguel López—shortly before his execution: "the sacrifice that was requested of the latter, and for which he was being compensated, was to appear that way, like a traitor, in the eyes of history" (555). The comparison of Maximilian to Jesus is made even more explicit in the following sentence: "In that period, as in many others, it was not rare for a martyrdom to be compared to the Calvary" (586).

The novel's dualistic structure, alternating between Carlota and Maximilian, is totally in keeping with its dialogic nature, which is enriched because of the paradox that the abundance of rigorous historical documentation perpetuates rather than clarifies certain doubts. Whereas Abel Posse in *Los perros del Paraíso* plays fast and loose with history by indulging in outrageous anachronisms, Fernando del Paso draws on a large number of historical, literary, and even apocryphal texts in order to present detailed, multifaceted, but nonetheless nondefinitive portraits of his fictionalized historical characters. Nowhere is this method more clearly illustrated than in the final appraisal of Benito Juárez in the novel's penultimate chapter. Although Juárez plays a far less prominent role in the novel than Maximilian and Carlota, and although he is invariably projected in a positive light, in the section *"¿Qué vamos a hacer contigo, Benito?"* 'What are we going to do with you, Benito?' he is alternately cast in the roles of devil and angel, with history alternately condemning and absolving him.[3] His black-cowled accusers are armed with torches associated with the inferno, while his white-cowled defenders are associated with the cool white daisy, the *margarita*—his wife's name. Juárez is proclaimed a hero for establishing and maintaining the separation of church and state and for restoring the republic after defeating the foreign invaders. However, he is condemned by others for his subservience to the United States and Protestantism.[4] Nevertheless, historical judgments are not to be taken too seriously since, in the words of Voltaire recalled by the dying Juárez, "History is a joke . . . that we living play on the dead . . ." (622–623), which subverts Juárez's own earlier invocation of "the tremendous judgment of history" (622) in his 1864 letter to Maximilian.

The dialogic portrait of Juárez is paralleled by the fuller, more complex portraits of Maximilian and Carlota, with all three being punctuated by the true-false leitmotif. In the aforementioned Juárez section, the vague question "Isn't that so, Benito?" (618–619) is posed rhetorically several times in slightly varied forms before it is applied directly to the appeals made by the poor, the peasants, the Liberals, the

Indians, the entire nation, the continent. When the anti-Juárez voices deny that it is true (620), Juárez defends himself: "But no, it wasn't a lie and his Indians knew it, his friends and even his enemies knew it, the fatherland knew it, America, History, isn't that so, Margarita? he said or tried to say" (620).

Carlota and Maximilian are surrounded by lies throughout the novel. Chapter 13 begins with the sentence "Yes, Maximilian, it was the lie, it was the lies that did us in" (349), referring to the lies of their enemies as well as to Max's lies to Carlota. The lie leitmotif continues throughout the chapter and reaches a crescendo in the initial sentence of the final section: "But more than, much more than your lies and mine, and those of the others, Maximilian, what kills me with anguish is the great lie of life, the lie of the world, the one they never tell us, the one that nobody tells us because we're all deceived by it" (360). Although Carlota is obviously referring to a broad philosophical view of the world, she is also referring to her alleged insanity manifested, according to her doctors, by her living in the past. Carlota also makes a convincing case for her sanity with the intertextual aid of Jorge Luis Borges's "El aleph," describing the simultaneous vision in one magic moment of the Earth's totality: geography, history, human beings, aspects of nature, and so on.

> How can I explain to our Spanish teacher, who, furthermore, died many many years ago, that it's useless for him to talk to me about conjugations and verb tenses because I was not the Empress of Mexico, I shall not be Carlota Amalia, I would never be the Queen of América except that I am all the time, an eternal present without beginning or end, the live memory of a century frozen in one instant? (362)

Carlota's next monologue, in Chapter 15, also begins with the lie leitmotif: "Because I am, Maximilian, the Empress of the Lie" (407). Earlier, in Chapter 11, Carlota confesses to Max that she has lied to him about her sexual desires and activities before she met him (306). In the third section of Chapter 16, the lie leitmotif assumes a negative form with a series of sentences that start with variations on the phrases "What Maximilian was unaware of" (458) and "What Maximilian also didn't know" (459). On the other hand, the final section of Chapter 20 asserts categorically, in various forms, the truth of several aspects of Maximilian's final moments: "Regarding the truth of some of these events, there doesn't seem to be any doubt" (584); "it also seems to be free of any doubt" (584); "it's also true that . . ." (585);

"yes, that too was certain" (585). In short, Fernando del Paso is illustrating the postmodern Borgesian contention that it is impossible to ascertain the truth.

Just as Juárez is somewhat demythified by his dialogic portrait in Chapter 22, Maximilian is even more demythified by Carlota's apostrophizing: "you were Maximilian the fearless . . . the noble . . . the just . . . you were also, Maximilian . . . the proud . . . the hypocrite . . . the liar" (601–604). In the second section of the same chapter, Carlota evokes all the different decorations received by Maximilian, only to culminate in the supreme insult: "¿Why didn't you decorate yourself with the great necklace of the Supreme Order of the Big Prick?" (613). With statements such as these, Carlota also demythifies herself. Did she really imagine herself as making passionate love to Maximilian when she "almost died of love for you, of desire, and of tenderness and of lust that night I was alone in my room, in the dark, and my hands crept under the covers" (183)? Was she also so lascivious as a child (307–308) and as a widow (65, 310–312) as she indicates in her monologues? Did she really go crazy as a result of his execution? Did Maximilian really contract a venereal disease during a trip to Brazil? Did he not sleep with Carlota during their entire stay in Mexico?

Despite all the historical documentation in the novel, other doubts persist. Was Maximilian the illegitimate son of his mother, the Archduchess Sophia, and Napoleon II—also known as the King of Rome, the Duke of Reichstadt, *El Aguilucho*, Astiánax, Archduke Franz, and François? Did Maximilian have a son with his Cuernavaca mistress Concepción Sedano, who during World War I became a German spy? Did Carlota have a son named Maxime Weygand with a Belgian, Colonel Van der Smissen (597)?

In addition to the novel's dialogic nature and dualistic structure, my interpretation of it as a Bakhtinian symphony stems primarily from its rich variety of discourses, or heteroglossia, which are often paired. One type of discourse that is common from start to finish is the epistolary, which is derived directly from the first word in the novel's title, *noticias* 'news.' The word also appears prominently in the second paragraph of the novel—"Today the messenger came to bring me news from the Empire" (14)—and in the novel's final sentence—"Today the messenger came to bring me news from the Empire" (668). News is transmitted via word of mouth, via letters, and via telegrams. The style of a war correspondent is used to describe the military events of 1866–1867 in the first part of Chapter 18. However, above all, letters are emphasized. In the very first chapter, the old, mad Carlota expresses the desire to plunge her face into Max's letters, but sometimes she cannot find them and sometimes she even doubts that he ever wrote them (23).

The epistolary discourse between two French brothers presents opposing views on the age-old debate over civilization and barbarism. Whereas the young officer in the invading army complains about the Mexican guerrillas' atrocities—"they are unsurpassed in all of history" (103)—the more educated socialist historian living in France condemns the invasion and maintains that the French have no right to set themselves up in Mexico as the champions of positivism when they and the other Europeans have a long history of violence and barbarism. He also points out that Paris, the so-called City of Light, is really the brothel of Europe, with thirty thousand prostitutes and with four-fifths of its inhabitants living in abject poverty (222). On the international level, he criticizes Napoleon III for having exported "that turbulence in the name of civilization" (595) to Indochina and Algeria as well as Mexico. The Belgians are denounced for their atrocities committed in the Congo (633). Throughout the novel, the royal families of Europe are portrayed as corrupt and immoral and are ridiculed as a "pile of little carnival kings, princes and princesses" (121). In his reply, the army officer confesses that his erudite brother's letter has almost convinced him that the invasion was unjust, but on further reflection, he agrees with Napoleon III that only with a European prince as a monarch can Mexico be saved from chaos and the sharpened claws of the United States (395). Unfortunately, he reports, Maximilian has not been a felicitous choice.

In contrast with the personalized correspondence between the two French brothers, the first three pages of Chapter 8 are saturated with a brief, staccato mention of letters written between 1862 and 1864 by many of the principal political and military leaders of Europe, Mexico, and the United States—some of them in code. The anaphoric use of phrases such as "the Archduke wrote to Louis Napoleon," "Louis Napoleon sent a letter to Bazaine," and "Carlota received a letter from her adored daddy Leopich" (191–192) creates the impression of a veritable deluge of letters influencing Maximilian and Carlota's decision to accept the Mexican crown. The three pages are summed up as follows:

> Letters, easily by the dozens, by the hundreds, from one place or another in Europe and across the Atlantic, from Europe to America, and during the years of 1862 and '63 and the beginning of '64 they came and went, some by ordinary mail, by burro, by stagecoach, on the ships of the Royal Mail Steam Packet Company, others by special

couriers, some innocent, some deceitful, secret or in code, brief, interminably long, optimistic, with private or royal messengers. And as though this were not enough, everybody also traveled from one place to another opining, giving advice, warning. (193)

In addition to the epistolary discourse, the novel is enriched by a variety of other types of discourse with fewer appearances. The doctor's physiological monologue (378–384) as he gives Maximilian a thorough medical examination is spiced with suspense, stemming from the emperor's apparent concern over his possible sterility, and clearly surpasses the much longer physiological passages in the author's previous novel *Palinuro de México*. Physiological discourse appears only one more time, after Maximilian's execution, with a detailed account of the embalming process and the conversion into souvenirs of his blond locks, his heart, and his eyes.

Maximilian's extramarital affairs and Carlota's graphic masturbations are not the only examples of erotic discourse, which has become such an integral part of the Spanish American novel since the Boom masterpieces *La muerte de Artemio Cruz, Rayuela* 'Hopscotch', and *Cien años de soledad*. Two sections of the Maximilian chapters are specifically entitled "*Seducciones*." In the first one, subtitled "*¿Ni con mil avemarías?*" 'Not Even with a Thousand Ave Marias?' a Basque priest stationed in Michoacán relates to his bishop, in a monologue, the confession of a *juarista* spy who was married to a French officer and who performed extraordinary sexual manoeuvres with other French officers in order to obtain secret information for her *juarista* lover. The section culminates with a short story–like climax: the priest confesses his own seduction and offers to accept as penance a thousand avemarías or more. The section is also tied structurally to the civilization/barbarism theme by the equation of the difficult-to-pronounce Tarascan toponyms with the equally or more difficult Basque patronymics. The second seduction section, entitled "*Espérate, Esperanza . . .*" 'Wait, Esperanza . . .', also a monologue, takes place on the eve of Maximilian's trial in Querétaro. The military prosecuting attorney attempts to concentrate on the trial in spite of his mistress's increasingly seductive advances. He ultimately succumbs, but continues to think of the trial in order to hold back his ejaculation. The "*Espérate, Esperanza*" refrain is heard from beginning to end, making this monologue one more example of the author's virtuosity.

In addition to the erotic, physiological, and epistolary discourses, the novel's heteroglossia is further enriched by several others:

1. One of the very few episodes in the entire novel that is narrated dramatically: the gripping torture of an Indian *juarista* by the sadistic French counterinsurgent Colonel Du Pin, entitled appropriately *Con el corazón atravesado por una flecha* 'With His Heart Pierced by an Arrow' (Chap. 10, sec. 2). This episode further subverts the justification of the French intervention on the basis of their being the purveyors of civilization.

2. The multilingual conversation between Maximilian, Carlota, and their Spanish teacher in *El Archiduque en Miramar* (Chap. 4, sec. 2), and its counterpart, eight chapters later (Chap. 12, sec. 3), facetiously entitled *El Emperador en Miravalle*. The latter is a primarily bilingual (Spanish and English) and occasionally trilingual (French) conversation between Maximilian and Commodore Matthew Fontaine Maury on the terraces of Chapultepec Castle, in which the former's comments on the spectacular view of the Valley of Mexico alternate with his racist comments about converting Mexico into a world supplier of cotton with Negro and Asian labor.[5]

3. The delightful first-person narration of a pro-Juárez poet, *evangelista* 'public stenographer', novelist, and typesetter who actually kills a French sniper in the outskirts of Guaymas with his box full of type: "You gentlemen will agree with me that not every day does one kill somebody with the weight of letters, and as my father would say, not so much literarily but literally" (338).

4. The *costumbrismo* of the Mexico City street vendors in *La ciudad y los pregones* 'The City and the Hawkers' (Chap. 6, sec. 3), in which the hawkers' words and observations, written in dialect and printed in italics, alternate with the omniscient narrator's description of General Forey's betrayal by Napoleon III and General Bazaine. Popular speech assumes a greater role in *"Camarón camarón . . ."* (Chap. 8, sec. 2), in which a Mexican spy tells how he enjoys contributing to the defeat of the French . . . and how he also enjoys stealing rings from their corpses.

5. The ceremonial, protocol discourse for the celebration of Maundy Thursday in order to highlight the profligate frivolity of the imperial court in *"Crónicas de la corte"* (Chap. 14, sec. 1). Ironically, the same ceremonial discourse is used to describe Maximilian's execution in *"Ceremonial para el fusilamiento de un Emperador"* (Chap. 22, sec. 3):

Sección Tercera:
"De los procedimientos para la ejecución".

Mientras el Emperador se acerca al lugar de la ejecución, se observará en la plaza un silencio absoluto.

El Gran Maestro de Ceremonias habrá dispuesto la colocación de una alfombra roja en el lugar de la ejecución, a fin de que el cuerpo del Emperador no toque el suelo.

En caso de que el Emperador elija ser ejecutado a caballo, se prescindirá de la alfombra, pero los cuatro ayudantes de campo que acompañan al Emperador permanecerán a una distancia adecuada, a fin de recoger su cuerpo antes de que éste llegue a tocar el suelo.

Section Three:
"On the procedures for the execution".
While the Emperor approaches the place of execution, an absolute silence will be observed in the plaza.

The Chief Master of Ceremonies will have arranged for the placement of a red carpet in the execution spot, in order to prevent the Emperor's body from touching the ground.

In case the Emperor elects to be executed on horseback, the carpet will be dispensed with, but the four aides-de-camp who accompany the Emperor will remain at an adequate distance, in order to catch his body before it touches the ground. (651)

The same execution is earlier described in the section entitled *Corrido del tiro de gracia* (Chap. 20, sec. 2), in which stanzas from the popular *corrido* 'ballad' alternate with the first-person recollections of the coup de grace fired by a repentant *juarista* soldier annoyed at his incredulous listeners.

6. The alternation of discussions or news about affairs of state with the trivial daily activities of family life. In *El Manatí de la Florida* (Chap. 16, sec. 2), Napoleon III plays a game of Educational Exotic Animals Lotto with his wife and his mother-in-law, in which the names of the animals contrast with Napoleon III's concerns over Maximilian, Bismarck, and the United States at the same time as they relate to France's imperialistic interest in the exotic regions of the world. A similar but more complex version of the same technique constitutes the structure of *Escenas de la vida real: La nada mexicana* (Chap. 10, sec. 3), which consists of twenty-five different vignettes ranging in length from one paragraph to two pages each. The scenes change rapidly from palace to palace in Paris, Mexico City, Brussels, England, Vienna, and Rome; all the principal historical figures, including Juárez, participate; and Lincoln's assassination, the celebration of All Souls' Day in Mexico, paintings in the Sistine Chapel, gourmet dishes served

at Carlota's first- and second-class banquets, and the words of *"La paloma"* are all interlaced with the increasing tensions between Napoleon III and Maximilian.

Heteroglossia is combined with intertextuality in the gardener's monologue before a silent judge regarding his wife's infidelity with Maximilian, a technique perfected by Juan Rulfo in short stories such as "El hombre," "Luvina," and "Diles que no me maten" 'Tell Them Not to Kill Me'. The gardener's pathetic situation is intensified by its proximity to Maximilian's first-person account of how he used to dictate frivolous memos to his secretary Blasio in his carriage on the way to Cuernavaca, an account interspersed with observations on the terrain's changing flora and fauna.

In addition to Juan Rulfo, Borges and some of the leading authors of the Boom make intertextual appearances in the novel. Carlota's recreation of Maximilian—*"Te voy a dar a luz"* (118)—is a specific reference to Borges's "Las ruinas circulares" 'The Circular Ruins', and Borges's general views on history are an integral part of the novel's Weltanschauung. *Cien años de soledad* makes its presence felt with the many colored butterflies circling around the corpse of an imperial soldier and the ice machine that Carlota sees in the Paris World's Fair and would like to take to Mexico in order to freeze Lake Chapultepec. Cortázar's story "Axolotl" is evoked by Carlota's "seeing" the axolotl grow in her womb, which is "round and transparent as a fish bowl" (236), while Carlos Fuentes's *La muerte de Artemio Cruz* is parodied in Carlota's final monologue, with the anaphoric use of "I'm going to present you with" culminating in the presentation of Ambrose Bierce and Pancho Villa, a clear reference to *Gringo viejo*. In fact, the inspiration for *Noticias del imperio* may have been the three pages of monologues alternating between Maximilian and Carlota—including the embalming details—in Fuentes's *Terra nostra* (740–742).

Carrying intertextuality one step further, *Noticias del imperio* is a special form of palimpsest in which the allusions to historical and literary sources, present throughout the novel, multiply as the novel progresses. Chapter 4 begins with two pages of questioning reality with the Borgesian use of "or" and "perhaps" before going on to enumerate seven reasons for the French Intervention. The sources are somewhat surreptitiously inserted with phrases like "as Conde Corti tells it" (79); "Hidalgo y Esnaurrízar tells in his Memoirs" (84); "a biographer of Juárez, the Mexican Héctor Pérez Martínez, said" (85–86); and "at least that's what Ralph Roeder says" (91). By the time we reach Chapter 20, devoted to Maximilian's execution, the dialogue between *Noticias del imperio* and its sources has become one of the novel's major themes. The chapter begins with Maximilian's previously unmentioned notebook *"El libro secreto de Maximiliano"* 'Maximilian's Secret Book'. Several accounts of the execution, including the pictorial ones like Manet's famous painting, are specifically mentioned and summarized with the phrase "The bibliography on Maximilian and Carlota's adventure in Mexico and on the French intervention is infinite" (587–588). Paradoxically, it is in this same chapter that the two Mexican literary works on the subject are mentioned for the first time: Juan A. Mateos's novel *El Cerro de las Campanas* 'The Mountain of the Bells' (1868) and Rodolfo Usigli's much more famous play *Corona de sombra* 'Crown of Shadows' (1943).

And here we arrive at the key to understanding and appreciating the quality of *Noticias del imperio*, in the dilemma shared by the author/narrator with his Mexican readers in the metafictional discourse of the penultimate chapter. The challenge faced by Fernando del Paso was how to maintain the interest of his readers throughout 668 pages with a subject that had already been treated by so many international historians and biographers and by the dean of Mexican playwrights. Fernando del Paso addresses the problem squarely by quoting specifically from Usigli, Borges, and Lukács. Whereas Usigli called his play *antihistórico* and regarded history as less exact than literature, whereas Borges stated that he was interested in "More than the historically exact, what is symbolically true" (641), and whereas Lukács wrote in *La novela histórica* (1963) that "it is a modern prejudice to assume that the historical authenticity of an occurrence guarantees its poetic effectiveness" (641), Fernando del Paso poses his own dilemma and defends his fusion of history and literature:

> What happens—what should you do—when you don't want to avoid history and yet at the same time you want to attain poetry? Perhaps the solution lies not in proposing alternatives, like Borges, and not in avoiding history, like Usigli, but rather in trying to reconcile whatever truth history may have with whatever exactness fiction may have. In other words, instead of setting aside history, placing it alongside of fiction, of allegory, and even alongside of unbridled fantasy . . . without concern whether that historical authenticity, or what passes for that authenticity according to our criteria, may not guarantee a poetically effective product, as Lukács warns us: when all is said and done, on the other hand, alongside of history, the poetic re-creation would march, which as we warned the reader—I am warning you—would

not guarantee, likewise, any authenticity beyond the symbolic one (641–642).

It is incumbent on each reader or each literary critic (if we want to make that distinction) to decide to what extent Fernando del Paso has succeeded. In spite of my disappointment with his two previous novels and in spite of, or perhaps because of, my familiarity with the present subject, I am not hesitant about assuming the critic's responsibility and evaluating *Noticias del imperio* as one of the best of the New Historical Novels, deserving instant canonization.

A Comparison: *La lejanía del tesoro*

In addition to its intrinsic qualities, *Noticias del imperio* stands out even more when contrasted with its Liberal counterpart, Paco Ignacio Taibo II's *La lejanía del tesoro* (1992). Obviously a serious attempt to surpass his previous best-selling detective novels, *La lejanía del tesoro* belongs in the New Historical Novel category because of its dialogic approach to history, its historical protagonists, its heteroglossia, and its occasionally carnivalesque tone. Somewhat paralleling the structure of *Noticias del imperio, La lejanía del tesoro* devotes the majority of its chapters to two of Juárez's literary supporters: Guillermo Prieto and Vicente Riva Palacio. Just as Maximilian and Carlota are presented through very different types of discourse, Guillermo Prieto is portrayed through his first-person memoirs, while Riva Palacio's exploits are narrated in the second person. Other famous nineteenth-century literary figures whose names appear frequently are Ignacio Ramírez and Ignacio M. Altamirano. (Although Juárez actually participates in the novel, he has a surprisingly minor role.) Where the structures of the two novels differ is that in *La lejanía del tesoro*, the chapters are not devoted exclusively to Prieto and Riva Palacio. As a reflection of the novel's title, seven of the twenty chapters of Part 1 are devoted to seven different versions of the Juárez government's treasure, which may never have existed. Other groups of interwoven chapters are devoted to the Apache Indians in northern Mexico, the cruel French officer Dupin who is in charge of counter-guerrilla activities (the same officer Du Pin who appears in *Noticias del imperio*), and Mexico's sole balloonist Esteban Padrón, who ultimately carries a message by air from Juárez in San Luis Potosí to General Escobedo in Querétaro and, on Juárez's orders, drops a bucket of horse manure on Maximilian's besieged forces.

Although Taibo II's novel is structurally and historically interesting, it cannot hold a candle to *Noticias del imperio*: the main characters do not come alive, the individual chapters are not based on dramatic events and are lacking in suspense and tension, and the linguistic creativity is mediocre at best. As a well-known Mexican short story writer confided to me in June 1992, "Taibo II is just not in the same league as del Paso."

5 The Bolívar Quartette, or Varieties of Historical Fiction

Gabriel García Márquez's *El general en su laberinto*
Fernando Cruz Kronfly's *La ceniza del Libertador*
Alvaro Mutis's "El último rostro"
Germán Espinosa's *Sinfonía desde el Nuevo Mundo*

In spite of its historical protagonist, Gabriel García Márquez's *El general en su laberinto* 'The General in His Labyrinth' (1989) may not really fit into the category of the New Historical Novel. The portrayal of Bolívar is more or less historically accurate; anachronisms and other ingenious distortions are eschewed; the re-creation of the specific time period is not subordinated to the presentation of timeless philosophical concepts; and metafiction and the Bakhtinian concepts of the dialogic, the carnivalesque, parody, and heteroglossia are for the most part missing. It is, nevertheless, one of the more outstanding historical novels of the past fifteen years and clearly deserves a place of distinction alongside the New Historical Novels of García Márquez's Boom peers Mario Vargas Llosa and Carlos Fuentes. In other words, as we have seen with Taibo II's *La lejanía del tesoro*, not all NHNs are necessarily superior in quality to all other historical novels.

In the broadest sense of the term, almost all of García Márquez's novels may be labeled historical, but only *El general en su laberinto* meets the restriction that all the events of the novel must take place before the author's birth. It is also his only novel that called for a considerable amount of historical research.[1] Within the broad range of historical fiction, *El general en su laberinto* may be categorized as a biographical novel in that it focuses exclusively on Bolívar: the memories of his entire life are interwoven with his final journey down the Magdalena River. Although some Colombian historians and patriots have criticized the novel for demythifying Bolívar, and others have criticized it for portraying Francisco de Paula Santander in a negative light, *El general en su laberinto* is a superior work of art in which certain typically García Márquez elements are skillfully applied to the novel's specific theme.[2]

By designating García Márquez's latest novel as "a superior work of art," I am, of course, expressing a value judgment, which has been frowned upon by many critical theorists in the past twenty-five years. However, before the ruthless invasion of the jargonauts, the universally respected Mexican essayist Alfonso Reyes proclaimed evaluation as the highest form of criticism. In 1942, Reyes wrote that evaluation is "the final step on the scale . . . the ultimate in criticism that situates the work in the balance of human acquisitions" (113). Twenty-five years later, Henri Peyre, the French literary scholar, affirmed that the greatest responsibility of the contemporary critic was to identify those authors who are worthy of being "read and reread, those who are important and who are destined to survive" (37). In the revolutionary year of 1989, Robert Scholes wrote, according to reviewer Robert D. Spector, that "with proper standards and appropriate methods, we should be able to show that 'some readings are better than others and some texts are better than others.'"[3]

In order to establish such "proper standards," all critics, consciously or not, depend on the comparative approach. In fact, what distinguishes the professional critic from the run-of-the-mill reader is not only the theoretical principles for the study of literature but also the tremendous quantity of works read, which permits the critic to place any work at all in a broader and more complex perspective.[4] Just as mid-twentieth-century linguists studied minimal pairs in order to analyze a foreign language's phonemes, morphemes, and tagmemes, the literary critic can better perceive, analyze, interpret, and evaluate the various elements of a literary work by analyzing them in comparison with or in contrast to those of a similar work, and the more similar, the better. For a more complete appreciation of the high quality of *El general en su laberinto,* my intrinsic analysis will be complemented by analyses of three other Bolívar narratives written by Colombians: *La ceniza del Libertador* 'The Ashes of the Liberator' (1987) by Fernando Cruz Kronfly; *Sinfonía desde el Nuevo Mundo* 'New World Symphony' (1990) by Germán Espinosa; and "El último rostro" 'The Last Face'

(1978), a short story by Alvaro Mutis, and the only one of the four works that has some of the traits of the New Historical Novel.

El general en su laberinto and La ceniza del Libertador

Just like García Márquez's novel, La ceniza del Libertador traces Bolívar's final river voyage from his Bogotá departure in May 1830 until his death on an estate near Santa Marta in December of the same year. Most of the action in both novels actually takes place on the river boats. The narration of the trip is interwoven with the evocation of different episodes from the past. Both novels emphasize Bolívar's digestive and pulmonary problems, demythifying him with frequent allusions to his vomiting, his flatulences, and his periodic outbursts of foul language. The Liberator is depressed over being rejected by the Colombian Congress but derives a small degree of solace from the faithful few who accompany him: his oldest servant José Palacios, his young nephew Fernando, and his dogs. In spite of the unusual similarities between these two novels, to my knowledge no comparative study has yet been published. Although it may not be fair to compare the work of a Nobel Prize winner to that of an author whose limited fame has not yet extended beyond the national boundaries of Colombia, the theoretical consequences of the comparison may well justify the venture.

In the final chapter of my 1978 book La novela colombiana: Planetas y satélites 'The Colombian Novel: Planets and Satellites', I present a theoretical guide for distinguishing between "planet-novels" and "satellite-novels." The chapter title "Manual imperfecto del novelista" 'The Novelist's Imperfect Manual' parodies Horacio Quiroga's well-known 1925 decalogue "Manual del perfecto cuentista" 'The Perfect Short Story Writer's Manual'. My nine points for evaluating a novel are (1) organic unity, (2) transcendent theme, (3) interesting plot, (4) skillful characterization, (5) constancy of tone, (6) appropriate structural and stylistic techniques, (7) creative language, (8) originality, and (9) literary impact. Although in no way do I pretend that these nine points are foolproof, nor that they should be weighted equally nor equally applied to all novels, they do provide a functional guide for discerning the relative successes and failures of each work. In the comparison of these two Bolívar novels, the most significant differences occur in points 3, 4, and 7; point 9 is still to be determined.

No matter how impossible it may be to define an "interesting plot," a successful novel must arouse and maintain the reader's interest from the first to the last page. Naturally, tastes and the cultural background of each reader vary greatly. What interests one reader may bore another; what one reader finds intellectually challenging, another may find discouragingly incomprehensible. In the 1960s the search for formal innovation became at times so obsessive that the interesting plot was practically eliminated as a desideratum of serious literature. However, *Cien años de soledad* (1967) reminded readers, critics, and novelists that an interesting plot was not incompatible with the modern experimental novel. What makes the plot of *El general en su laberinto* more interesting than that of *La ceniza del Libertador* is that García Márquez does not feel compelled to devise an artificial plot. He maintains the reader's interest by concentrating on the human qualities of his protagonist within his historical environment. He alternates Bolívar's physiological and psychological ups and downs in 1830 with the evocation of a series of historical and amorous exploits. Particularly important are the assassination of Bolívar's great friend Antonio José de Sucre and Rafael Urdaneta's coup in Bogotá aimed at recalling Bolívar to the presidency. Bolívar rejects the offer because he prefers to try to restore the unity of *La Gran Colombia* by launching a campaign against his compatriot José Antonio Páez. Although the informed reader is well aware of the succession of historical events, he cannot help but feel a certain amount of suspense. Will Bolívar really get personally involved in yet another armed struggle? After finally receiving his passport, will he really fulfill his wish to sail for England? In addition to marveling at the ease with which the principal events in Bolívar's life are recalled, the reader remains interested because at each river port new characters appear who converse with Bolívar, or new characters from the past are evoked.

By contrast, in *La ceniza del Libertador*, Fernando Cruz Kronfly decided to envelop his historical protagonist in a fictitious plot, an artificial attempt to create suspense. Noises from the upper deck arouse Bolívar's suspicions of a conspiracy. His attempts to gain access to the deck are periodically thwarted because the doorway to the staircase is always closed. His requests for an explanation from the captain are unsuccessful because the latter never appears. The mystery is also heightened by the presence of a lawyer seated in the dining room and a rather enigmatic black cook with "one black eye and the other greenish blue" (31), who turns out to be one of Bolívar's former soldiers, "the famous Negro Bernardino" (41). From Chapter 3 to Chapter 47, the noise, the uproar, the sound of music, the sound of dancing, as well as Bolívar's efforts to meet the captain continue but without the mystery's growing in intensity nor varying sufficiently to maintain the reader's interest. Finally, in Chapter 48, Bolívar, his nephew Fernando, and another officer storm the upper deck, only to find dust-laden books and papers and a horde of large rats.[5] In other words, as a result of Bolívar's discovery, the reader realizes that the noise of dancing has symbolized the medieval dance of death, and the trip down the river is thus equated with the trip to the sea of death (325). Upon arriving in Cartagena, Bolívar becomes increasingly aware of his impending death, and indeed, in Chapter 50, he is placed in "a coffin with layers of dried grass" (331).

The idea of a ship with a deck or part of a deck inaccessible to the passengers undoubtedly comes from Julio Cortázar's first novel, *Los premios* 'The Prizewinners' (1960). Cruz Kronfly himself indicates his indebtedness to Cortázar when Bolívar, while traveling through the town of Mompox, shouts gratuitously, "—¿*Qué es la joda, carajo?*" 'What the hell is the conspiracy?' (130), a direct allusion to another of Cortázar's novels, *Libro de Manuel* 'A Manual for Manuel' (1973).[6] However, the symbolic aspect of the sealed-off part of the ship is more appropriate in *Los premios* because it is more intimately linked to the main theme of the novel, which is the panoramic presentation of a variety of human beings, in the "ship of fools" literary tradition.

Characterization has traditionally been an important measure of a novel's success—particularly for European and U.S. readers and critics. In fact, prior to the Boom, European and U.S. critics had difficulty in understanding and appreciating many Latin American novels because their main criteria were the psychological complexity, the verosimilitude, and the constancy of the portrayal of the protagonist and the other characters. In the novels of the so-called developed countries of the capitalist world, social problems are, at least in the novel, subordinate to individual problems, while the search for national unity has not been a major concern for scores of years, if not centuries. On the other hand, Latin American novelists tend to look upon themselves as the consciences of their countries, responsible for denouncing abuses and formulating a new social order. Therefore, in many Latin American novels, the protagonist is not an individual but rather a town (Agustín Yáñez's *Al filo del agua* 'The Edge of the Storm' and Elena Garro's *Recuerdos del porvenir* 'Recollections of Things to Come'), a city (Carlos Fuentes's *La región más transparente* 'Where the Air Is Clear' and *Cristóbal Nonato* 'Christopher Unborn'), or a nation (José Revueltas's *El luto humano* 'The Stone Knife' and Jorge Icaza's *Cholos*). This difference in perspective explains why a splendid novel like Miguel Angel Asturias's *El señor Presidente* has not yet been properly evaluated by most U.S. and European critics in spite of the fact that Asturias received the Nobel Prize in 1967.[7] By the same token, the vast majority of Joseph Conrad scholars have misinterpreted *Nostromo* in their search for a personal protagonist when in reality the protagonist is Costaguana, the geographical and historical synthesis of the typical Latin American nation.

Whereas the Latin American Boom novels as well as the postmodern novels throughout the world have broadened the criteria for evaluating novels among all critics, characterization is still an important consideration in novels like *El general en su laberinto* and *La ceniza del Libertador,* where both authors are primarily concerned with contrasting the dying human being with the mythical continental hero. Here again García Márquez comes out on top. He successfully creates a real live human being who projects his thoughts and his feelings during the last months of his life, which are plagued by declining health. His portrayal is superior in part because Bolívar is constantly the center of attraction: he is present at all times, and the author succeeds in conveying his tragedy to the reader.

By contrast, in *La ceniza del Libertador,* Bolívar's character suffers because of both the artificial plot and the excessive number of poetic, neo-baroque, and at times affected descriptions—plus the occasional insertion of poetry. Furthermore, Cruz Kronfly's portrait of Bolívar is, on the one hand, less sharply focused because of the latter's periodic hallucinations and wild ravings, and on the other, less subtle because of the excessive use of foul language.

In almost all of his fiction García Márquez tends to use a relatively unadorned language, devoid of sensorial adjectives and frequent innovative images. Nonetheless, he is capable of creating unforgettable poetic scenes with a relatively straightforward style. The novel's very first sentence is an excellent example: *"José Palacios, su servidor más antiguo, lo encontró flotando en las aguas depurativas de la bañera, desnudo y con los ojos abiertos y creyó que se había ahogado"* 'José Palacios, his oldest servant, found him floating in the purifying water of the bathtub, naked and with his eyes open, and he thought that he had drowned' (11). The sentence suggests the imminence of Bolívar's death, bestows on him a touch of Magic Realism, and initiates one of the novel's dominant leitmotifs of *flotando* 'floating' in both the literal and the figurative sense.

In view of Cruz Kronfly's more obviously poetic and fantastic portrayal of Bolívar, his more elaborate style, particularly in his descriptions of nature, is justifiable. However, unfortunately, he overdoes it and his repetition of the title word *ceniza* 'ash' and his excessive use of images built on the words *párpado* 'eyelid' and *chorrear* 'to gush forth' create the impression of either a lack of poetic imagination or poor editing. A few examples will suffice to prove the point. When the ghost of his beloved sister warns Bolívar against accepting a floral crown, he replies, "—*Deja, despreocúpate, para qué una corona en medio de todo este mar de cenizas*" '—Don't worry. Why a crown in the midst of this sea of ashes' (82). The narrator refers to Bolívar's reading a letter from Bogotá lamenting his approaching death: *"Toma de nuevo el pliego en sus manos y vuelve a leer aquel misterioso renglón escrito con ceniza de cementerio"* 'He takes the letter in his hands again and reads once more that mysterious line written with cemetery ash' (234). The early morning river scene is cast in a painterly description: *"El vapor vuelve a esponjarse, como un párpado que viene del sueño hondo y adivina el día"* 'The steam fluffs up again like a sponge, like an eyelid that emerges from a deep sleep imagining the break of day' (13). Other descriptions of the sky, which might be effective individually, give the impression that the "painter" is working with a limited palette: *"Las calderas trabajan a toda máquina, el humo se atropella en las chimeneas, el cielo se empaña como un párpado que rueda encima de las cenizas secas"* 'The boilers are working at full blast, the smoke is charging through the stacks; the sky clouds over like an eyelid that rolls over the dry ashes' (132–133); *"Como a través de un cedazo roto de todos lados chorrea el resplandor de una luna diferente"* 'As through a torn screen, the brightness of a new moon gushes forth (125); and, on the very next page, *"Sólo sobrevive en la pupila la niebla luminosa que chorrea de la lámpara"* 'All that remains in his eyes is the luminous mist that gushes forth from the lamp' (126).

However, even disregarding the comparison with *La ceniza del Libertador, El general en su laberinto* is in absolute terms an outstanding work of art. Referring back to the first point in my *"Manual imperfecto del novelista,"* the organic unity of the García Márquez novel is superb. There are eight unnumbered chapters, which correspond to an almost equal number of stops on his final voyage from Bogotá to Santa Marta. The eight chapters contain varying widths of approximately seven different threads or strands each (the woof), which are interwoven in different order and proportions and held together by the warp of time and García Márquez's inimitable style, in order to meet the challenge of writing a novel about such a well-known historical figure. The seven strands will be examined in turn.

1. "SIC TRANSIT GLORIA MUNDI"

The major theme of the novel is the contrast between the deteriorating physical condition of Bolívar the man and the glorious exploits of Bolívar the legendary hero. In each of the eight chapters, Bolívar coughs, vomits blood, runs a high fever, and/or expels gas; he suffers from headaches; he is subject to an "insatiable erosion" (142); and he loses weight and height. In Chapter 5, his friends cannot believe *"que se hubiera desmigajado tanto en tan poco tiempo"* 'that he had crumbled away so much in so short a time' (146). The fact that Bolívar is well aware of his declining health enables the reader to share with the protagonist (and his over-sixty-year-old creator) the emotional as well as the rational impact of the fragility of human life. As Bolívar leaves Bogotá (in Chapter 2), his enemies make fun of his frailty, calling him *"¡Longaniiiizo!"* 'Sausage liiiink!' (49), which is pathetically countered by one woman's compassionate and typically García Márquez phrase: *"Ve con Dios, fantasma"* 'May God be with you, ghost' (49). Soon after, when the mother superior in the mission between Facatativá and Guadua doesn't recognize Bolívar, in another of García Márquez's ingenious succinct phrases Bolívar tells his aide Colonel Wilson, *"Ya no soy yo"* 'I'm no longer me' (52).

Although there is a steady decline in Bolívar's health from chapter to chapter, the reader's interest is maintained by a series of remissions or unexpected miraculous recoveries. For the four previous years he has suffered from fever and delirium, with recovery each time the very next day: *"se le veía resurgir de sus cenizas con la razón intacta"* 'he would resurrect from his ashes with his reason intact' (18). During his three-day stop in Honda, in spite of a severe headache and high fever, he visits a silver mine, swims in the river for a half-hour, and dances for three hours with a variety of partners. Even as he comes closer and closer to death in Chapters 7 and 8, the news of Urdaneta's coup in Bogotá and the prospect of suppressing the rebellion in Riohacha revive his spirits and provide him with the energy to plan a military strategy.

In spite of Bolívar's failing health throughout the novel, doctors—with the exception of Dr. Nicasio del Valle, who makes a brief appearance (118) in Chapter 4—are not consulted until Chapter 7 because, as Bolívar says at the beginning of Chapter 5, "If I had followed my doctors' recommendations, I would have been buried many years ago" (142). The three doctors who are finally consulted enrich the novel with their picturesque traits, including their names. Hércules Gastelbondo is a huge, happy old man who smokes incessantly and justifies his unusual prescriptions by claiming that "the other doctors' patients die as much as his, but his die happier" (218). The American surgeon Dr. Night provokes the reader's snicker by misdiagnosing Bolívar's illness as chronic malaria. The young French doctor, Alexandre Prosper Révérend, comes up with a more accurate diagnosis of a pulmonary lesion (251), but his five abrasive patches applied to the back of Bolívar's neck, along with one on the calf, are probably the immediate cause of death, according to several 1980 doctors: "A century and a half later, many doctors continued to think that the immediate cause of death had been those abrasive patches" (261). Révérend's skill as a doctor is surpassed by his skill as a linguist: he can identify by accent alone the place of origin of every native of France, down to each street corner of Paris.

2. THE GLORIOUS HERO

Chronology is a key element in recounting the entire life of the Liberator. In this strand most of the episodes are pinpointed by variants of the phrase "eleven years earlier" (19)—that is, in 1819. The nonchronological order of the various episodes—an order which, as in Carlos Fuentes's *La muerte de Artemio Cruz,* is more novelistically creative—is complemented by a succinct chronology of Bolívar's life immediately following the final page of the novel. Although almost all of Bolívar's military and political friends and enemies are mentioned, Sucre and Santander are clearly the stars in this thread. Sucre is the man whom Bolívar has counted on to be his successor, and his refusal on June 13 (Chapter 1) causes the Liberator to turn livid (28). Despite his disappointment, however, Bolívar continues to admire and respect Sucre. The latter's name keeps recurring until Chapter 6, when the news of his assassination[8] sends Bolívar into a rage and plunges him into mourning: "He struck himself on the forehead and yanked the tablecloth from under the supper dishes, maddened by one of his biblical fits of anger. . . . After Sucre's assassination, he stopped using all forms of makeup that had concealed his aging" (192–193).

Even more prominent than Sucre throughout the novel is Bolívar's hated enemy, the Colombian highlander Francisco de Paula Santander. Whereas Sucre is featured in Chapter 1, Santander—Bolívar's vicepresident from 1821 to 1828—is featured in Chapter 2. In the 1828 plot to kill Bolívar, Santander was accused of being involved and was condemned to death by General Rafael Urdaneta. He was ultimately pardoned by Bolívar, who sent him in exile to France. According to the Liberator, their main bone of contention was Santander's refusal to accept the idea that this continent would be one big country: "*La unidad de América le quedaba grande"* 'The unity of America was too big a concept for him to grasp' (125). In addition to their ideological differences, Bolívar, from the perspective of the creator of Aureliano Buendía, distrusted the *"truchimán"* 'astute' (224) Santander, prototype of the despised Colombian *"cachaco"* 'stuffy highlander'. Nonetheless, in the novel's final chapter, a more sober Bolívar recognizes that "not having reached an agreement with Santander has ruined us all" (238).

Two other important historical events, that later caused Bolívar difficulties with the people of Riohacha and Santa Marta, were the separate executions of his two heroic mulatto officers, General Manuel Piar and Admiral José Prudencio Padilla. The execution of Piar in Angostura is treated in greater detail in the novel and is further highlighted by its closing out Chapter 7. Bolívar considers that, although the execution constituted "the most ferocious exercising of power in his life, it was also the most opportune because it consolidated his authority, unified his command, and cleared the way for his glory" (234). The chapter ends with the words " . . . I would do it again" (234). Another angle to these executions, although not directly suggested by the author, is the revelation in the previous chapter of Bolívar's own African heritage, via a great-great-grandfather, so evident in his features that "the aristocrats of Lima called him El Zambo" (186). In his typical challenging of official history, García Márquez points out that, as Bolívar's fame grew, his portrait painters "idealized him, washing his blood, mythifying him, until they fixed him in the official memory with the Roman profile of his statues" (186).

Although García Márquez clearly sympathizes with Bolívar, endowing him with the personality of a Colombian *costeño* (from the northern Caribbean coastal area), his characterization of the Liberator is not completely monologic. The conspirators in the failed assassination plot of 1828 justified their actions because of "the extraordinary powers of a clearly dictatorial type that the general had assumed three months earlier" (61). Furthermore, regarding Bolívar's decision to leave Bogotá in 1830, "the truth was that even his most intimate friends didn't believe that he was leaving either the power or the country" (21–22). On the other hand, Bolívar defends himself against the charge of inconsistency by admitting to it (but attributing it to special circumstances) and by saying he never lost sight of his primary goal: *"Porque todo lo he hecho con la sola mira de que este continente sea un país independiente y único, y en eso no he tenido ni una contradicción ni una sola duda"* 'Because everything I've done has been with the only goal of making this continent an independent and united country, and in this respect, I have not had a single contradiction or doubt' (207).

The United States is depicted, on three different occasions, as the enemy of an integrated Spanish America. Bolívar criticizes Santander for inviting the United States to participate in the Congreso de Panamá, which was convoked to proclaim the unity of Spanish America: *"Era como invitar al gato a la fiesta de los ratones"* 'It was like inviting the cat to the mice's party' (194). Bolívar advises Agustín Iturbide against settling in the United States: *". . . que son omnipotentes y terribles, y con el cuento de la libertad terminarán por plagarnos de miserias"* 'which is omnipotent and terrible, and with the tale of freedom, they'll wind up infecting us with a plague of miseries' (227). Although Bolívar doesn't mention the United States in his warning to Santander about debts, he is obviously referring to the economic situation of Latin America in the 1980s: "I abhor debts more than Spaniards . . . because if we accepted debts, we would continue to pay interest for centuries on end" (225).

3. THE 1830 BOLÍVAR

Unlike the historical events before May 8, 1830, the events from May 8 to December 17, 1830, occur in chronological order and constitute an independent thread in the woof of the novel. Whereas the events of the past emphasize in a more or less monologic manner how Bolívar overcame all obstacles to attain glorious victories, the historical events that occur in the present time of the novel, during Bolívar's river journey of 1830, are presented somewhat more dialogically and even with occasional uncertainty on Bolívar's part. Aside from Sucre's assassination, the three most important historical events of Bolívar's final seven months are Joaquín Mosquera's election as president of Colombia in May; Rafael Urdaneta's pro-Bolívar coup in September; and Bolívar's final war, to reintegrate Venezuela into La Gran Colombia. After presiding over the unstable union of three countries (Venezuela, Colombia, and Ecuador) for twelve years (1819–1830), Bolívar is psychologically crushed upon learning that he has failed to garner even one vote against Mosquera. Although Bolívar's bitter departure from Bogotá arouses the reader's sympathies, the inclusion in the novel of his opponents' accusation that he was plotting to be president for life, to be succeeded by a European prince, complicates the picture.

Urdaneta's coup is also presented dialogically. By using the first person plural for the only time in the novel, the narrator unequivocally condemns the coup: *"Era el primer golpe de estado en la república de Colombia, y la primera de los cuarenta y nueve guerras civiles que ha-*

bíamos *de sufrir en lo que faltaba del siglo"* 'It was the first coup d'état in the Republic of Colombia, and the first of the forty-nine civil wars that *we* were to suffer in what remained of the century' (203; emphasis added). Sucre also opposed the plot as it was being hatched. On the other hand, Bolívar's headaches and fevers disappear with the news of the coup. Although he rejects Urdaneta's invitation to reassume the presidency, he does embark on what seems a full-scale campaign to re-unify the nation. With his supporters in control of Colombia and the possibility of enlisting the aid of Juan José Flores in Ecuador and Andrés Santa Cruz in Bolivia, Bolívar decides to mount a military campaign against Páez in Venezuela. However, Bolívar's plans are thwarted when the province of Riohacha sides with Venezuela and is supported by forces sent from Maracaibo under the command of Pedro Carujo,[9] the leader of the failed assassination plot of September 1828. Carujo is victorious, but ten days before his death, Bolívar is still convinced, or fools himself into believing, that if he returned to the Aragua Valley, "all the Venezuelan people would rise up in arms to support him" (257). In a final ironic note, five years later Carujo was to head another "military adventure in favor of Bolívar's idea of integration" (253).

4. BOLÍVAR THE LOVER

Unlike Bolívar's military and political exploits, his amorous adventures, also more or less evenly distributed across the eight chapters, provide greater leeway for the Rabelaisian author of *Cien años de soledad* and *El amor en los tiempos del cólera*. Bolívar is portrayed as a sympathetic Don Juan. Although he balks at confessing the number of his conquests to his friends Mariano Montilla and Daniel Florencio O'Leary, later the same evening, while in his hot bath, Bolívar accepts the apparently unexaggerated accounting offered by his loyal servant José Palacios: "'According to my reckoning, they're 35', he said. 'Without counting the one-night stands, of course'" (162). Although this figure pales in comparison with the operatic prototype's 1,003, Bolívar does resemble Don Juan in that he assures all his women of his undying love: "She asked him heartbroken if he really loved her, and he replied with the same ritualistic phrase that throughout his whole life he had been sprinkling unmercifully in so many hearts: "'More than anyone else in this world'" (217). However, the biggest difference between Don Juan and Bolívar is that while the former dies vigorous and unrepentant, Bolívar's declining health also affects his sexual prowess and is thus intimately tied to the main theme of "sic transit gloria mundi." In Chapter 1, featuring the historically famous Manuela Sáenz, who has been Bolívar's mistress for eight years (1822–1830), the narrator conveys in a low key his sympathy for Bolívar's pathetic plight: "At the siesta hour, they went to bed without closing the door, without undressing, and without sleeping, and more than once they committed the mistake of attempting one last lovemaking, since his body was no longer strong enough to please his soul, and he refused to admit it" (33). Manuela is mentioned throughout the novel, from Chapter 1 through Chapter 8, but it is Chapter 2 where she receives the greatest recognition for having saved Bolívar's life in the September 1828 assassination attempt. Bolívar, however, does not translate his gratitude into fidelity; for example, "in Lima . . . he had to invent excuses to keep her away from him while he frolicked with ladies from the upper classes, and with others somewhat below" (32).

On the other hand, in the final chapter, Manuela upstages Bolívar's young, tragic wife María Teresa Rodríguez del Toro y Alayza, whose memory he has buried so deeply that she is not even mentioned until this chapter: "Never again did he speak of his dead wife; never again did he remember her; never again did he try to replace her" (255). Manuela, upon learning that Bolívar was actually on his deathbed, set out for Santa Marta but did not arrive in time for a final good-bye. The description of her "widowhood" is enhanced by an unexpected historical expansion of the novel up to 1851: she is consoled in her solitude by visits from Bolívar's old teacher Simón Rodríguez, from Giuseppe Garibaldi in 1851, "who was returning from his struggle against the Rosas dictatorship in Argentina, and [from] the novelist Herman Melville in 1841, who was traveling around the oceans of the world gathering documentation for Moby Dick" (263).

In addition to the frequent appearances of Manuela Sáenz, each of the chapters in the novel includes at least one of Bolívar's amatory episodes—almost all of which are apocryphal[10]—with a proper amount of variety and eroticism. Nowhere in the novel is there anything comparable to the detailed accounts of the lovemaking of José Arcadio and Rebeca Buendía or of Amaranta Ursula and Aureliano Babilonia; in fact, Bolívar does not indulge in any actual lovemaking in the novel's present of May–December 1830. The following women are, nonetheless, unforgettable. The beautiful mulatto virgin Reina María Luisa (Chapter 2), told Bolívar that she was a slave, setting him up for the typical García Márquez epigrammatic reply: "'No more', he said, 'Love has made you free'" (58). Miranda Lyndsay, the Jamaican (Chapter 3), saved him in 1815 from an assassin's dagger thrusts into his hammock by previously luring him to an abandoned hermitage and by prolonging the tryst until dawn. The Mompox aristocrat Josefa Sagrario (Chapter 4) made her way through seven guard-posts disguised as a Franciscan monk, with the password *"Tierra de Dios"* 'Land of God' (122). The typical García Márquez anticlerical mockery is complemented by her wearing underneath the habit a thirty-pound gold coat of mail, which she donated to Bolívar for his wars. He later exiled her by mistake in the aftermath of the 1828 assassination plot.

Chapter 5 features Camille from Martinique, "the most beautiful, most elegant, and proudest woman he had ever seen" (163). Although she accompanies the Conde de Raigecourt, who seems madly in love with her, Bolívar is also smitten but he is too weak to accept even her invitation to dance. In Chapter 5, mention is also made, coincidentally (?), of the "five indivisible women of the Garaycoa matriarchy" (the grandmother, daughter, and three granddaughters; 158) with whom Bolívar cavorted at the time of his famous interview with San Martín in Guayaquil.

Bolívar also recalls in this chapter his repeated dream of a woman with illuminated hair who tied a red ribbon around his neck, probably in anticipation of the anonymous firefly-crowned "divine creature" (186) in Chapter 6 who spends the night at his side without his ever even touching her. The next morning, as she leaves, he says, "You're leaving a virgin" (188). Her witty reply and jovial laugh presumably make his spirits rise: "'No one is a virgin after spending a night with Your Excellency'" (188).

Chapter 6 also contains a brief reappearance of Camille; an apparently bitter letter from Josefa Sagrario, who has returned to Colombia on the occasion of Bolívar's fall from power; and the introduction of the languid adolescent harpist who leaves Bolívar in a chaste ecstasy "floating on the waves of the harp" (177). Chapter 7 evokes Bolívar's shaving every last hair off the Bedouin-skinned beauty from Lima and recounts the episode in Angostura with the gorgeous Delfina Guardiola. Bolívar actually crawled through her window after she had slammed the door in his face, furious at his infidelities: "You are an eminent man, general, more than any other, but love is too much for you" (221). Nevertheless, he proceeded to spend three days with her and thereby almost lost a battle and his life.

Bolívar's attitude toward women is also more complex than Don Juan's. In his heyday, he would feel strongly attracted to a certain woman and would be "capable of changing the world" (188) in order to satisfy his desire. However, instead of "loving them and leaving them" à la Don Juan, he would remember them fondly and send them passionate letters and remarkable gifts . . . "but without ever changing a whit of his life for a feeling that more closely resembled vanity than love" (189).

5. BOLÍVAR'S AIDES

A relatively minor thread but one that is also present in each of the eight chapters is that of the servant José Palacios and the seven military aides who accompany Bolívar on the trip down the Magdalena River. Palacios attends to Bolívar's personal needs and in every chapter attempts to provide comfort and relief to his terminally ill master. His total identification with Bolívar constitutes the novel's frame. In the very first paragraph of Chapter 1, Palacios finds Bolívar floating naked in the bathtub (11). The repetition of the aquatic images "floating" (267) and "adrift" (267) in the last chapter gives a sense of finality to the novel and tightens the linkage between the two men. Palacios would have preferred to die together with Bolívar—*"Lo justo es morirnos juntos"* 'What is just is for us to die together' (267)—but instead, he becomes an alcoholic and dies of delirium tremens at the age of 76.

Although the seven military aides are relatively minor characters, each one has some memorable traits. Bolívar's nephew Fernando became his secretary after studying at the University of Virginia. He has a special talent for improvising fictitious episodes, but he would never write any creative literature even though he would live to at least 85 because "destiny had bestowed on him the enormous good fortune of losing his memory" (267).

The son of the short-lived Mexican emperor Agustín de Iturbide joins the entourage in Chapter 3, but he does not break into the spotlight, even briefly, until Chapter 6, when Bolívar has him sing all night long, accompanied by José de la Cruz Paredes on the guitar. In addition to being a singer, Iturbide is characterized as being lonely and taciturn, capable of spending the whole night staring at the dying embers of a campfire. His father's military and political careers reflect the novel's major theme of "sic transit gloria mundi," as well as exemplifying the treachery and coups that were to characterize nineteenth-century Colombia, Venezuela, and most of the other Latin American republics. After Bolívar's death, Iturbide would be appointed secretary of the Mexican legation in Washington and would disappear from view. However, in a strange turn of events, his two sons would be adopted by Mexico's second emperor, Maximilian, and would be named successors to the almost equally short-lived throne.

Irish Colonel Belford Hinton Wilson was Bolívar's aide-de-camp at the battle of Junín but suspects that Bolívar does not like him. He longs to return to England and is upset at Bolívar's wavering. He plays a prominent role in the card-game scene at the end of Chapter 2, first defeating the enraged Bolívar and then, on the orders of General José María Carreño, allowing Bolívar to win, but in such an obvious way that the latter calls an end to the game.

General Carreño, who is convinced that he has counted 7,882 stars in the river at the end of Chapter 4, is also capable of standing up to Bolívar by alluding to the latter's never having been wounded while he, Carreño, lost his right arm and has suffered from many other wounds. Although Bolívar has heard this criticism before, he accepts it coming from Carreño. Nonetheless, Carreño's resentment festers, and at the end of Chapter 5, he is determined to escape to Venezuela in order to head an armed movement in order to carry out Bolívar's wish to restore *La Gran Colombia*.

Captain Andrés Ibarra's right arm was also incapacitated by a sabre wound, but he stands out as the youngest and happiest of the group. Just before the card game in Chapter 5—the first one that has been played since the unpleasant experience between Bolívar and Wilson—Bolívar grabs Ibarra's shoulders from behind and asks him if he, too, thinks that the Liberator looks like he's dying. When Ibarra replies in the negative, Bolívar says, "Well, you're either blind or you're lying" (168). Ibarra's clever rejoinder—"Or I've got my back to you" (168)—eases the tension immediately.

Whereas most of Bolívar's aides come from upper-class Venezuelan families, José Laurencio Silva is a mulatto, the son of a river fisherman and of a small-town midwife. In preparation for going blind from cataracts, he sleeps during the day and works at night, creating beautiful pieces of furniture in the darkness (134). Bolívar raised his social status by marrying him to one of his nieces. However, one episode stands out in the reader's memory: when one of the local aristocratic women refused to dance a waltz with him, Bolívar had the orchestra repeat the waltz and danced with Silva himself.

6. THE VISITORS

In contrast to Bolívar's aides, who remain with him throughout the trip down the Magdalena River, a sixth thread in the novel's unobtrusively rich texture is constituted by a series of visitors who appear at each port, beginning in Chapter 3. Although this thread is perhaps the least important, it too makes a significant contribution to maintaining the reader's level of interest. Most of the visitors are foreigners, and no matter how briefly they appear, they leave an indelible mark on the reader. Even the fraudulent German astronomer and botanist in Chapter 3, in spite of his anonymity, becomes important because of his insulting jokes about Baron Alexander von Humboldt's homosexuality, which disgust Bolívar and provide him with the opportunity to express his admiration for Von Humboldt's beauty—". . . y tanto como su inteligencia y su sabiduría lo sorprendió el esplendor de su belleza, como no había visto otra igual en una mujer" '. . . and just as he was surprised by his intelligence and his knowledge, he was surprised by the splendor of his beauty, which he had never seen equaled even in a woman' (104)—as well as his gratitude to Von Humboldt for his early conviction that the Spanish colonies were ripe for independence—"Humboldt me abrió los ojos" 'Humboldt opened my eyes' (104). The anonymous German is further degraded by the importance given to a filthy, lame, mangy dog who comes aboard on the same page. While the German is unceremoniously dropped off the afternoon of the same day without his name's ever being revealed, the dog's importance is magnified in the last line of the chapter by the Liberator's bestowal on him of his own name: Bolívar (107).

Although the Frenchman Diocles Atlantique, who lives in the river port of Zambrano (Chapter 4), is more genuinely intellectual than the anonymous German, he is equally repugnant to Bolívar. His pontificating about the contributions of "Western civilization," the "cultural defects of criollo cooking" (129), and the most appropriate form of government for the new republics increasingly enrages Bolívar, prompting him to question Europe's high degree of civilization: ". . . Well, if any area's history is drowned in blood, indignities, and injustices, it's Europe's" (131). The four-page conversation comes to an end with the Bolívar/García Márquez exclamation, often cited by the critics, "¡Por favor, carajos, déjennos hacer tranquilos nuestra Edad Media!" 'God damn it to hell, stop bugging us and let us live our own Middle Ages!' (132).

During the twenty-nine-day stay in Turbaco (Chapter 5), Bolívar is visited by his friend General Mariano Montilla, who arrives from Cartagena with three of Bolívar's political supporters, referred to as "los tres juanes del partido bolivarista" 'the three Juans of Bolívar's party': Juan García del Río, Juan de Francisco Martín, and Juan de Dios Amador. The narrator reports that Montilla is "célebre por sus chispazos de ingenio aun en las situaciones menos oportunas" 'famous for his sparkling wit even in the most inopportune moments' (146), but García Márquez gives still one more indication of his own writerly talent by providing an actual example of Montilla's wit. Montilla and the three Juans are hard put to conceal their dismay at the reduced size of Bolívar's body. Montilla relieves the tension by saying, "What is important for us is that Your Excellency not shrink in your inner fortitude," and then he laughs loudly at his own joke: *"Como de costumbre, subrayó su propia ocurrencia con una carcajada de perdigones"* 'As usual, he underlined his own joke with a buckshot burst of laughter' (146–147). In the same chapter Bolívar is visited by another Frenchman, the Count of Raigecourt, who invites him to travel to Europe on an English packet boat. Although the trip to Europe is an important theme in the novel, Raigecourt's only claim to fame in the novel is that he is accompanied by Camille from Martinique.

Chapter 6, which transpires in Cartagena, is noteworthy for the visits of two other Europeans: the Italian painter Antonio Meucci, which allows the narrator to comment on how Bolívar was transformed in his portraits, and the Polish Count Napierski, a military hero in the Napoleonic Wars who arrives in Cartagena with a recommendation from General Poniatowski to enter the Colombian army. Napierski does not make a real impact in the novel except that he takes notes in his diary "which a great Colombian poet was to rescue for history one hundred and eighty years later" (196)—a clear reference to Alvaro Mutis's "El último rostro"—the deliberate (?) mathematical mistake (one hundred eighty years later would be the year 2010) notwithstanding.

In the final two chapters of the novel, Bolívar enjoys the visits of two doctors, the picturesque Hércules Gastelbondo and the third Frenchman in the novel, Alexandre Prosper Révérend. Gastelbondo's company is so delightful that Bolívar tolerates the awful smell of his cigar even though he has never been able to put up with tobacco smoke, except for the even more foul-smelling cigars of Manuela Sáenz. Dr. Révérend gains Bolívar's confidence with his bedside manner and his skill as a conversationalist. He issues thirty-three medical bulletins and hears Bolívar's final words, which allude to Borges's favorite metaphor: "'Carajos', suspiró. '¡Cómo voy a salir de este laberinto!'" 'God damn it', he sighed. 'How am I going to get out of this labyrinth!' (269).

7. METEOROLOGICAL AND OTHER SPACE

Although García Márquez does not usually indulge in long, realistic descriptions of the physical settings of his novels and short stories, allusions to the tropical heat of the Caribbean coast do appear from time to time. In *El general en su laberinto*, the seventh and final strand that is interwoven into each of the eight chapters is the narrative space, with emphasis on the weather. This focus on space is not too surprising, considering the inclusion in the volume of the schematic map of Bolívar's final voyage from Santa Fe de Bogotá down the Magdalena River to Cartagena and on to Santa Marta.

The references to Bogotá's inhospitable climate in the early chapters reflect Bolívar's distrust of Santander and the polite, proper, dark-clad *cachacos* 'stuffy highlanders'. When José Palacios announces that "'on Saturday, May 8, 1830, the day that the English wounded Joan of Arc with their arrows . . . it has been raining since three o'clock in the morning'," Bolívar, who has not been able to fall asleep, replies angrily, "Since three o'clock in the morning in the seventeenth century" (12). The narrator reinforces the hyperbolic image with the phrase "the millennial drizzle" (39) and the explanation of Bolívar's hostess's attempt to keep him from leaving Bogotá: "Doña Amalia tried to retain him until it cleared up, although she knew as well as he did that it wouldn't clear up until the end of the century" (43). And yet, in a touch of magic realism, the rain does clear up as Bolívar leaves a Mexicanized (the two volcanoes) Bogotá in Chapter 2: "The sky turned a radiant blue and two snow-capped volcanoes remained immobile the rest of the day" (49). García Márquez further enhances the miracle of the sunshine by elaborating on it at the beginning of Chapter 3, when Bolívar is already suffering from the heat of the river port of Honda—"the air was boiling with bubbles" (78). In a letter, newly elected President Domingo Caycedo describes the picnics celebrated by numerous Bogotá families. They actually ate sitting on the grass, "under a radiant sun that had not been seen in the city since the times of the Big Bang" (80). Bolívar's ironic explanation of the miracle tinges the humor with personal bitterness: "'My departure was all that was needed for the sun to shine again'" (80). However, in keeping with the novel's simultaneous re-creation of the epic hero and the dying man, the interior spaces where Bolívar is lodged are often described in more realistic terms: "Well, they were in Santa Fe de Bogotá, at 2600 meters above the level of the remote sea, and the enormous bedroom with its arid walls exposed to the chill winds that filtered through the loosely sealed windows was not the most appropriate for anyone's health" (13).

After the descent from Bogotá, García Márquez resorts to all his talent in order to maintain interest in the meteorological strand. How does one distinguish between the humid heat and thunderstorms in Honda (Chapters 2 and 3) and those in the other river ports and in the Caribbean ports of Cartagena, Soledad, and Santa Marta? Metaphors, hyperbole, humor, and specific local details constitute the author's approach. Honda's boiling air (75, 78) is also *"un aire de vidrio líquido"* 'an air of liquid glass' (74), and the narrator pokes fun at the very common saying in the tropics, *"la tontería eterna: 'Aquí hace tanto calor que las gallinas ponen los huevos fritos'"* 'the age-old stupid joke: "It's so hot here that the hens lay fried eggs" ' (77). The cloudburst is described vividly with the neologism *desventrarse: "Una nube negra . . . se desventraba en un diluvio instantáneo"* 'A black cloud . . . emptied its bowels in an instant flood' (77). The decadence of Honda, reflecting that of Bolívar, is achieved by the contrast between the phrases "the very famous city of Honda with its Spanish stone bridge" and "its walls in ruins and the tower of the church destroyed by an earthquake" (76).

In the middle of Chapter 3, the scene shifts to the river, with an unusually straightforward, realistic description of the fleet of eight relatively large sampans. However, the García Márquez touch reappears in the description of the captain of the fleet, a man "with a thunderous voice and a pirate's patch over his left eye, and a rather intrepid notion of his command" (94). The following episode knocks the captain off his pedestal and enhances Bolívar's image as the mythical hero. During a thunderstorm Bolívar countermands the captain's orders to the oarsmen, and the captain steps aside because he realizes that "once again he had confused port and starboard" (96).

In the description of the river, García Márquez combines humor with his ecological concerns by observing the immobile crocodiles "with their jaws open to hunt butterflies" (100) and the large number of tree trunks tied into rafts to be sold in Cartagena. Bolívar exclaims: "The fish will have to learn how to walk on land because there won't be any more water" (100).

Chapter 4 begins in Mompox, which like Honda has seen better times. It is described in some detail as being located where the river widens and as having been the prosperous commercial port between the Caribbean coast and the interior of the country in the colonial period. However, it has been "ruined by war, perverted by the disorder of the republic and decimated by smallpox" (110). The stone dikes which the stubborn Spaniards built to control the periodic flooding are in ruins. Although Bolívar spends twenty-nine days in Turbaco (Chapter 5), the town is not described in any detail, but it does differ from the other locales in that its climate is cooler and healthier.

Nowhere is the spatial illustration of the "sic transit gloria mundi" theme better exemplified than in Cartagena (Chapter 6), former capital of the viceroyalty, hub of the slave trade for all of Spanish America, and often extolled in verse as one of the most beautiful cities in the world

(175). Cartagena had been sacked by various foreign pirates during the colonial period, but "nothing had ruined it like the struggle for independence and the subsequent wars among the different factions" (176). Although García Márquez mentions specifically the old convent on Popa Hill, the market, the slaughterhouse, and the inner walled city, he does not indulge in any lengthy *costumbrista* description which would have upset the novel's geographical balance. Bolívar's imminent death is reflected in the city's hovering vultures; a rabid dog; and the huge rats, "as big as cats" (176), emanating from the dilapidated colonial mansions that have been taken over by the poor. Even in the midst of this depressing decadence, García Márquez manages to maintain his hyperbolic sense of humor: "The belt of invincible bulwarks that Philip II had wanted to see with his long-distance telescopes from the Escorial lookouts, was hardly imaginable because of the overgrown weeds" (176). Cartagena's decadence is further heralded by García Márquez in the following chapter (7) when Bolívar moves to the tiny—"four streets of poor houses, hot and desolate" (215)—town of Soledad, "which in a few years was to become the most prosperous and hospitable city in the country" (215): the author's tribute to Barranquilla.

Bolívar's final trip (Chapter 8) is by ship, through the estuary of the Magdalena River, with a view of the salt beds and the distant snow-capped sierra, to Santa Marta; and then by carriage to Señor de Mier's sugar plantation, where he dies on December 17, 1830.

VERTICAL STRANDS

The seven strands that García Márquez weaves in and out of the novel's eight chapters could possibly be rearranged or reduced to five or six. On the other hand, an eighth strand to mirror the eight chapters would be inappropriate because it would make the structure too mathematically perfect, something that García Márquez would hardly tolerate. What does tighten the various strands—the woof on the loom—is the warp, the vertical strands comprised of the inexorable passage of time in the last seven months of 1830, the author's all-pervasive typical style, and a sprinkling of self-intertextuality.

Closely linked to the deteriorating-physical-condition thread is the inexorable march of time. Unlike all of García Márquez's previous novels, *El general en su laberinto* is punctuated with precise dates. The novel opens on May 8, 1830, and ends on December 17, 1830, with Bolívar's death. In fact, it ends at 1:07 P.M., a time magically predicted by the octagonal clock with Roman numerals in the Mompox parochial school where Bolívar is lodged in Chapter 4. The clock has stopped at

1:07 P.M. prompting Bolívar's pathetic remark, *"¡Por fin, algo que sigue igual!"* 'Finally, something that stays the same!' (116). The significance of time is also underlined by the leitmotif of José Palacios's twin watches with their respective crossed chains on his vest and Agustín Iturbide's gold watch sent to him by his father before going out to face the firing squad (98).

Unlike most of the NHNs, and ironically unlike *Cien años de soledad*, *El general en su laberinto* is devoid of intertextuality—except for references to García Márquez's own works,[11] and particularly *Cien años de soledad*. Bolívar's mistresses are marked forever with *"una cruz de ceniza"* 'an ash-colored cross' (219), reminiscent of that borne by Colonel Aureliano Buendía's seventeen illegitimate sons. The "widowed" Manuela Sáenz, like Ursula Buendía, manufactures and sells little candy animals; and, like Pilar Ternera, at the ripe old age of 59 (!) confined to a hammock because of a fractured hip, she "told fortunes with decks of cards and gave advice to people in love" (263). Bolívar discourages his aide Carreño from embarking on another war to restore the unity of *La Gran Colombia* with a remark at the end of Chapter 5 very reminiscent of the one made by Colonel Aureliano Buendía to Gerineldo Márquez in *Cien años de soledad:* " 'No delires más, Carreño', le dijo. 'Esto se lo llevó el carajo' " " 'Stop raving, Carreño," he said to him. "This has gone down the drain forever" ' (172).

"El último rostro"
(fragmento)

Gabriel García Márquez has more than acknowledged his debt and gratitude to Alvaro Mutis for having inspired him to write *El general en su laberinto*. The novel is dedicated to Mutis; García Márquez explicitly recounts having ascertained with Mutis that the latter no longer planned to proceed with his novel-length project on the last months of Bolívar's life (271); and in Chapter 6 of the novel, Colonel Miecieslaw Napierski, the focalizer of Alvaro Mutis's short story "El último rostro" 'The Last Face' (1978), makes a brief appearance.

Despite the word "Fragment" that in parentheses accompanies the title of Mutis's work, "El último rostro" is far from being either an incomplete short story or a chapter of an incomplete novel. It is a complete and superb historical short story,[12] probably the best of its kind in all of Latin America.[13] Although Juan Gustavo Cobo Borda assigns the date of 1978 to the story, which seems to coincide with García Márquez's assertion that he waited for ten years for the Mutis novel to be completed (271), it does not seem to have been published in an accessible book until 1985, when it appeared in volume 2 of Mutis's *Obra literaria*. Even so, to my knowledge, it did not receive widespread recognition before the publication of *El general en su laberinto* (1989), and it has not yet been sufficiently analyzed and evaluated.

"El último rostro" would be an excellent historical short story even if García Márquez had not written *El general en su laberinto*. Nevertheless, given the tremendous popular and critical success of the latter, a comparison of the two works is inevitable. Actually, the minimal pair is the Mutis story and Chapter 6 of the novel. What is most striking about the comparison is the discovery that "El último rostro," like Chapter 6 and the entire García Márquez novel, is structured on the interweaving of seven horizontal threads reinforced by the vertical inexorable march of time. Of the seven identifiable threads in *El general en su laberinto*, five coincide closely with those of the short story: Bolívar's deteriorating physical condition, his heroic past, his few loyal aides, his women, and the narrative space. The two additional threads in the story that are less emphasized in the novel are the frigate anchored in Cartagena harbor and the allusions to world geography and history. However, in spite of the presence of these threads in the Mutis story, it would be a mistake to overemphasize them.

As is befitting a short story, "El último rostro" is much more tightly knit than the novel. From the title and the epigraph to Napierski's final comment on Bolívar's dream, the unifying theme is, in the words of the epigraph—taken from an anonymous eleventh-century manuscript in the library of the Mount Athos Monastery—*"El último rostro es el rostro con el que te recibe la muerte"* 'The last face is the face with which death receives you.' For that reason, Colonel Napierski describes in detail Bolívar's face when he first meets him on June 29, 1830, and during his second and third visits on June 30 and July 1. In the fourth and final visit on July 10, there is no description of the face, but the word *rostro* does appear after Bolívar completes the two-page account of his ominous dream: *"Calló por unos minutos y alzó el rostro interrogándome no sin cierta ansiedad"* 'He remained silent for a few minutes and raised his face questioning me with a certain look of anxiety' (117). In fact, the word *rostro*, aside from the title and the epigraph, appears seven times; not once does the author use the more common, less literary word *cara*. Although Bolívar's physical deterioration is signaled by his coughing up blood, vomiting, and perspiring with fever, these physical symptoms are not emphasized nearly as much as in the novel. On the other hand, what is emphasized is the archetypal death mask, which is justified artistically as an elaboration of the epigraph, and justified in realistic terms by focalizer Napierski's European culture, as evidenced in his observations: *"Me recordó el rostro de César en el busto del museo Vaticano"* 'He reminded me of Caesar's face in the Vatican museum bust' (103–104); *"Dos noches de fiebre marcaban su paso por un rostro que tenía algo de máscara frigia"* 'Two nights of fever left their toll on a face that looked somewhat like a Phrygian mask' (107); *"Su rostro tenía de nuevo esa desencajada expresión de máscara funeraria helénica"* 'His face once again had that frightful expression of the Hellenic funeral masks' (112). These allusions to ancient Greek masks and the Roman bust are reinforced by Bolívar in contrasting his fate to that of the blind Oedipus, who was allowed to leave the land that hated him (105), and in referring to the news of Sucre's assassination as Death testing the sharpness of her scythe's blade (113). The allusions to classical culture are further reinforced by Bolívar's detailed and vivid account of the death dream, replete with the wooded labyrinth; the folding of the hands on his pocket watch which have been turned into a fragile, paper-like substance; and the personalized, sexy, simultaneously realistic and grotesque figure of Death—preceded by an allusion to the importance that the Romans attached to dreams (115–117).

In addition to Sucre's death and Bolívar's impending death, the death theme in the Mutis story is strengthened by two deaths that occur before the real action of the story commences. First, it was the death of Napierski's wife which prompted the Polish colonel to travel to America in order to continue his struggle for liberty over fifteen years after Napoleon's defeat (somewhat reminiscent of Bolívar's oath in Rome to dedicate his life to the struggle for independence against Spain after the death of his young bride). Second, Napierski's commanding officer, Field Marshal Poniatowski, whom Bolívar had met in Paris, died the kind of heroic death at the battle of Leipzig that Bolívar would have preferred (105). Moreover, after equating the walls of Cartagena with the medieval walls of what is now Syria and Lebanon, as seen during the Crusades, Napierski himself feels a Jungian sensation of having previously experienced "this lonely struggle of an admirable warrior with death which besieges him in a circle of bitterness and disillusionment. Where and when did I live all this?" (106).

Unlike *El general en su laberinto,* "El último rostro" does not amaze the reader with a series of unexpected "recoveries" by Bolívar. Whereas García Márquez individualizes the three or four doctors and presents them in a picturesque manner in spite of—or because of—their ineptness, Mutis reduces them to one anonymous doctor and sees nothing funny in the lack of skill of this doctor, "about whose training I have greater doubts every day" (110). Bolívar's spirits remain low throughout the story, except after reading the letter from Manuela Sáenz: "he was very changed; one might almost say rejuvenated" (109). Only upon receiving the news of Sucre's assassination does he react energetically, in the most dramatic moment of the story, which is all the more dramatic because of the almost constant dirge-like tone leading up to it: "*Un gemido de bestia herida partió del catre de campaña sobrecogiéndonos a todos. Bolívar saltó del lecho como un felino y tomando por las solapas al oficial le gritó con voz terrible . . .*" 'a moan of a wounded beast came from the army cot startling all of us. Bolívar leaped up like a tiger and grabbing the officer's lapels, shouted at him with a dreadful voice . . .' (111).

Just as Bolívar's face is described in greater detail in the short story than in the novel, so is the narrative space. The tropical heat and cloudbursts are conspicuous by their absence, but the description of the large, underfurnished house where Bolívar is lodged emphasizes deterioration: the geraniums are somewhat *"mustios"* 'withered' (103); the living room has unmatched and dilapidated pieces of furniture; the walls are bare and spotted with humidity; Bolívar's bedroom is larger but is sparsely furnished and the walls are equally spotted; the one high-backed chair is faded and has no seat. In contrast, the room looks out on an interior patio with flowering orange trees. Napierski's second visit transpires in the patio, where Bolívar has been sleeping in a hammock because of his high fever.

The exterior space of the city of Cartagena seems to interest Napierski and Mutis somewhat less than the interior space. The former mentions by name the Cerro de la Popa, the San Felipe fortress, and the city walls, but the longest description of the city is in the four lines that compare the center of the city (today's old, walled city) to Cádiz, Tunisia, and Algeciras: "white streets in the shade, with houses full of balconies and large patios whose splendid fresh moist vegetation was most inviting" (109). This unusually positive description is appropriately placed between Bolívar's rejuvenation upon receiving Manuelita's letter and his aide Ibarra's description to Napierski of Bolívar's love for Manuelita. By contrast, in the García Márquez novel, the rabid dogs in the street, the vultures, and the run-down condition of the city contribute to the foreshadowing of the Liberator's death. The space strand in the Mutis story is further enriched by the frigate *Shanon* to which Napierski returns after visiting Bolívar.

Whereas the "Bolívar the Lover" strand provided García Márquez with the opportunity to display his Rabelaisian imagination, Mutis reduces this strand to Manuela Sáenz and the comment that Bolívar "was a man extremely fortunate with the women" (107). Manuela does not actually appear in the story—nor do any of Bolívar's women—but Mutis skillfully inserts her in the story on four different occasions. Bolívar receives her letter without identifying her (109); his aide Ibarra tells Napierski about Bolívar's love affair with the still unnamed "Ecuadoran lady who had saved his life . . . standing up to the conspirators who were going to assassinate the hero in his quarters in the Palace of San Carlos in Bogotá" (109–110); Bolívar recalls how well Manuelita was able to imitate Sucre's manner of speaking (113); and Napierski and Santander's ex-aide Captain Arrázola speak about Bolívar's *"capricho"* 'infatuation' (115) with Manuelita Sáenz.

As in the novel, three of Bolívar's aides (Ibarra, Carreño, and Silva) and his friend Montilla are mentioned by name and play minor roles in the story. What are somewhat surprising are the absences of his servant José Palacios, his nephew Fernando, and Agustín Iturbide.

In the comparison of the various strands, the greatest difference in the two works is that within the confines of the short story Mutis does not attempt to reconstruct the Liberator's entire life or even his most heroic moments. The focus is constantly on his despair over his rejection by those whom he has liberated and his resentment over "the empty rhetoric and the bloody violence that wipes out everything" (108). Mutis skillfully evokes some key moments in the struggle for independence when Bolívar complains about how many of his own companions opposed his decision to free the slaves. Particularly noteworthy is the balance between the glorious and the disastrous moments, and the alliteration of the latter: *"Las voces clandestinas que conspiraron contra el proyecto e impidieron su cumplimiento fueron las de mis compañeros de lucha, los mismos que se jugaron la vida cruzando a mi lado los Andes para vencer en el Pantano de Vargas, en Boyacá y en Ayacucho; los mismos que habían padecido prisión y miserias sin cuento en las cárceles de Cartagena, el Callao y Cádiz de manos de los españoles"* 'The clandestine voices that conspired against the project and prevented it from being carried out were those of my fighting companions, the same ones who risked their lives crossing the Andes at my side in order to triumph in the Vargas Swamp, in Boyacá and in Ayacucho; the same ones who had suffered imprisonment and constant misery in the jails of Cartagena, Callao and Cádiz at the hands of the Spaniards' (108). Bolívar attributes his companions' mean-spiritedness to their not knowing who they are, or where they come from, or why they are on earth—phrases that smack of the search for national identity in the writers of the 1930s like Rómulo Gallegos and Eduardo Mallea.

The figures of Santander and Sucre are present, as in the García Márquez novel, but in different proportions. In the novel, Bolívar's dislike for Santander is coupled with García Márquez's fondness for poking fun at the Bogotá *cachacos,* but in the short story, there is no room for any humor at all. (Moreover, Mutis is from Tolima and not from the Caribbean coast.) Bolívar indicates his dislike for Santander only briefly, upon the arrival of the latter's ex-aide Captain Arrázola. Actually it is Arrázola who describes Santander to Napierski as being *"sabio en artimañas de leguleyo y dedicado a hacerle el juego al grupo de familias que comienzan a cosechar con avidez los frutos de la independencia"* 'wise in the ways of the cunning shyster lawyers and committed to playing ball with the group of families that are beginning to harvest greedily the fruits of independence' (115). Arrázola, on the other hand, admires Bolívar, although he considers him too idealistic. As in Chapter 6 of the novel, in the short story Bolívar is devastated by the news of Sucre's assassination. The dramatic scene occupies one and one-half pages, and Sucre reappears in Bolívar's final death dream when a blind beggar asks the Liberator for a contribution for the monument to the Field Marshal from Berruecos—the place where Sucre was assassinated.

Within the strands of the Liberator's glorious past and of the foreign visitors there are distinct differences between the novel and the short story, which undoubtedly reflect the contrasting ideologies of the two authors. Whereas pro-Marxist García Márquez introduces the repugnant Frenchman Diocles Atlantique in order to allow his Bolívar to criticize the barbaric history of Europe and to request permission for Latin America to live its own Middle Ages, the anti-Marxist Mutis gives a much more prominent role to the Polish Count Napierski. When Bolívar complains about the barbaric nature of Latin American geography and of his mean-spirited companions, Napierski tries to console him by alluding to the confusion of those who still long for the glories of the Napoleonic Empire (108), the silliness of those restored absolute monarchs who are trying to stop the irreversible process of history (109), and the tyranny of Russian rule in Poland. Bolívar's reply not only reveals his great despair for the future of Latin America but also confirms the traditional civilization/barbarism dichotomy which the García Márquez Bolívar denounces in the novel: "—You will come out of those crises, Napierski, you have always been able to overcome those periods of darkness, soon new periods of prosperity and greatness for everyone will come to Europe. In the meantime, we here in America will continue sinking into a chaos of sterile civil wars, of sordid conspiracies, and in them all of our energy will be lost, all our faith, all our reasoning necessary to take advantage of and to give meaning to the effort that made us free. There is no hope for us, Colonel, that's the way we are, that's the way we were born . . ." (109). In the light of the contrasting attitudes of the two authors to the civilization/barbarism theme, it is not surprising that the Mutis story contains no allusions to U.S. imperialism.

As befits a finely wrought short story, the final death dream in "El último rostro" closes the frame that is initiated by the Borgesian introduction, which establishes a connection between "El último rostro" and the New Historical Novels. The labyrinthine quality of the dream is anticipated by the labyrinthine beginning, which is similar to that of Borges's "Tema del traidor y del héroe." In this introduction, Count Napierski's diary is found by the narrator among a group of manuscripts sold at auction by a London book dealer shortly after the end of World War II. The Nimbourg-Napierski family had arrived in England a few months before the fall of France. The narrator came upon the diary by chance while looking for details about the battle of Bailén. However, the folios are not in order, and the narrator has to look through eight volumes of legal documents in order to piece together the Napierski diary by checking the color of the ink and certain names and dates.

Napierski wrote the diary in Spanish, which he learned while serving in Spain as part of Napoleon's army, but the narrator informs us that the tone of his language was influenced by some Polish poets living in exile in Paris, especially Adam Nickiewiez—a typically Borgesian gratuitous bit of information calculated to mislead the reader into thinking that it's important.

What *is* important in the introduction is the mention of World War II and the fact that Colonel Napierski's last male descendant died in battle, fighting for the Free French at Mers-el Kebir, in North Africa—just as Colonel Napierski's commanding officer, Field Marshal Poniatowski, died in the battle of Leipzig during the Napoleonic Wars: history repeats itself. If history repeats itself, great historical figures, famous and unique as they may be, also tend to repeat each other, so that Bolívar is also Napoleon and Julius Caesar. Therefore, in the introduction, it is only logical that Bolívar's name is withheld. The narrator has transcribed only "the pages of the Diary that refer to certain events related to *a man* and the circumstances of his death" (102; emphasis added). At the same time, Napierski is specifically tied to Bolívar in the introduction through his participation in Napoleon's 1808 invasion of Spain which gave the Spanish American colonies the opportunity to initiate the wars of independence between 1808 and 1810. Furthermore, the fact that Napierski is a *"coronel de lanceros"* 'a lancer colonel' (101) is a minute but structurally significant detail, since Bolívar's great victory at the Vargas Swamp, mentioned in the body of the text, was accomplished by his lancers, and the victory has been immortalized by the famous monument sculpted by Rodrigo Arias Betancourt.

Although "El último rostro" may not qualify as a New Historical short story, despite its Borgesian introduction and its relatively archetypal presentation of Bolívar, it is, like *El general en su laberinto,* a beautifully crafted work of art, destined to be canonized as soon as it has been read by a sufficient number of astute critics, which it will be in preparation for the June 1993 Eighth Conference of the Asociación de Colombianistas Norteamericanos to be held at the University of California, Irvine, and at which Alvaro Mutis will be the guest of honor.

Sinfonía desde el Nuevo Mundo

Although Germán Espinosa's *Sinfonía desde el Nuevo Mundo* is another very recent historical novel involving Bolívar,[14] it can hardly be analyzed and evaluated with the same criteria as were used for the three previously discussed works. Despite the musical title and the novel's symphonic division in four parts, entitled *"Allegro ma non troppo," "Andante con brío," "Scherzo assai vivace,"* and *"Finales senza conclusione,"* this is not a serious work of literature, not a *novela culta* or a *novela elitista* or a potentially canonical novel. It is, rather, a popular, best-seller type of novel, like Margaret Mitchell's *Gone with the Wind,* which may appeal to large numbers of readers who do not belong to the cultural elite, but which, prior to the current interest in popular culture, would never have found its way into a university syllabus.[15] Because of its intended readers, *Sinfonía desde el Nuevo Mundo* is an action-packed, melodramatic historical novel with a fictitious romantic, swashbuckling French hero who, after Napoleon's 1815 defeat at Waterloo, joins Bolívar in Jamaica and Haiti and participates in the invasion of Venezuela. The chapters are short (one or two pages!); the sentences are short; the emphasis is on plot; and dialogue predominates. The action skips from Paris to Jamaica to Haiti and then to Venezuela. The French hero, Victorien Fontenier, is captured by the Spaniards during their siege of Cartagena and is imprisoned in the underground vaults of the city walls. He is rescued by a French pirate disguised as a monk.

In Haiti, while Fontenier defends himself in the street against the same French pirate, the carriage drawn by mules in which Fontenier and his beautiful mulatto mistress Marie Antoinette have been riding plunges off a cliff, killing the latter. In Part 4, Fontenier saves Bolívar's life twice: first by preventing him from committing suicide (135) and then by jumping into the path of a bullet intended for Bolívar (137). In the romantic tradition of José Mármol's *Amalia* (1845), our wounded hero is nursed back to health by María Antonia (cf. Marie Antoinette), who turns out to be General Páez's goddaughter. Unlike the characters in *Amalia,* however, Fontenier and María Antonia swim nude in a river channel and *"con ademanes lúbricos, ella atrae al francés hacia sí, lo tumba sobre su cuerpo y, en la vasta soledad de esas barrancas salitrosas, se anuda con él en el juego ansioso del amor"* 'with lascivious movements, she draws the Frenchman to herself, pulls him down onto her body and, in the vast solitude of the salty sand dunes, becomes entwined with him in the feverish game of love' (147). Also unlike the characters in *Amalia,* they get married, with Páez's blessing. This novel's lack of artistic pretensions[16] confirms the existence of a boundary between popular and elite literature despite the current postmodern fad to eliminate it.[17] What is particularly strange is the novel's epilogue, in which Espinosa extols his own creativity by calling his *Sinfonía desde el Nuevo Mundo* a "novel," like those of Stefan Zweig, in contrast to a "novelized historiography" like *El general en su laberinto* by Gabriel García Márquez: *"En ella sí es exigible una fidelidad minuciosa a los hechos reales, fidelidad que algún novelista comercial se impuso a sí mismo en cierto libro hoy muy en boga, cuyo protagonista es Simón Bolívar, y que hace de él no una* novela, *sino una* historiografía novelada" 'In it, there is a requirement to adhere faithfully to the real facts, a requirement that a certain commercial novelist imposed on himself in a certain book, very much in vogue today, whose protagonist is Simón Bolívar, and which makes of it not a *novel* but a *novelized historiography'* (154). What is even more paradoxical about this gratuitous criticism is that Germán Espinosa is the author of the relatively complex New Historical Novel *La tejedora de coronas* 'The Weaver of Crowns' (1982), which I have elsewhere contrasted with the best-seller *Los pecados de Inés de Hinojosa* 'The Sins of Inés de Hinojosa' (1986) by Próspero Morales Pradilla in order to prove that the distinction between the *novela culta* and the *novela popular* continues to be valid today—in spite of the pronouncements by some critics who enjoy theorizing about the postmodern and the post-Boom novel.[18]

6 Bending the Rules, or The Art of Subversion

Ricardo Piglia's *Respiración artificial*

In keeping with the dialogic and parodic aspects of some of the New Historical Novels, it is only fitting and proper that I should subvert my own definition of the historical novel in order to discuss one of the most unusual of the NHNs: *Respiración artificial* 'Artificial respiration' (1980) by Ricardo Piglia (1940), a widely exalted novelist of the Left who was a "Marxist political activist in the 1960s" (75) according to Kathleen Newman. Contrary to my definition of the historical novel, most of the dialogues and correspondence in *Respiración artificial* are actually set in the present of the late 1970s. One of the principal narrators is Emilio Renzi.[1] Born, like the author, in 1940, he is a would-be writer who travels to Concordia, in the province of Entrerríos, in 1979 in search of his uncle (his mother's brother), history professor Marcelo Maggi. Nevertheless, the 1979 present is apparently "disappeared," along with Renzi's father who is never even mentioned, in order to reflect Maggi's disappearance and to make way for a complex reconstruction of nineteenth- and twentieth-century Argentine history and literature, culminating in the revelation of a Hitler–Kafka connection, which in turn is linked to the Argentine military junta of 1976–1979. The labyrinthine structure, which moves back and forth between past and future, and the *matrioshka*-like succession of narrators[2] are presumably aimed at deceiving the censors. On the other hand, if Piglia had really wanted to deceive the censors, why did he spell out the significance of the novel's title on the back cover: *"tiempos sombríos en que los hombres parecen necesitar un aire artificial para poder sobrevivir"* 'depressing times in which men seem to need an artificial breeze in order to be able to survive'?

Whereas Posse in *Los perros del Paraíso* disguises his criticism of the Argentine dictatorship with a most un-Argentine, carnivalesque treatment of Columbus's discovery of the Caribbean, Piglia's novel is very much in the Argentine tradition and might even be thought of as the Borgesian novel that Borges never wrote. Like Manuel Gálvez's *El mal metafísico* 'The Metaphysical Disease' (1916), Eduardo Mallea's *La bahía de silencio* 'The Bay of Silence' (1940), Leopoldo Marechal's *Adán Buenosayres* (1948), Ernesto Sábato's *Sobre héroes y tumbas* 'About Heroes and Tombs' (1962), and Julio Cortázar's *Rayuela* 'Hopscotch' (1963), *Respiración artificial* is an essayistic novel in which action is reduced to a minimum and intellectual monologues, dialogues, and letters predominate. Renzi criticizes most Argentine writers from Sarmiento to Borges (a real paradox given Borges's constant presence in the novel). He despises Lugones and goes so far as to claim that Argentine literature "no longer exists" (160) since the death of Roberto Arlt in 1942.[3] Borges is dismissed as a nineteenth-century writer, while Cortázar is mentioned only once (170)—probably in order to keep the novel's apparent focus on the past.

The eternal search for Argentine identity, usually represented as the schizophrenic conflict between the Europeanized "civilization" of Buenos Aires and the *criollo* traditions of the "barbaric" hinterland, is reflected in the novel's dualistic structure. Part 1, narrated by the aspiring writer Emilio Renzi, is a convoluted family saga featuring dictator Juan Manuel Rosas's private secretary Enrique Ossorio, but actually originating with Enrique's grandfather, who prospered by buying sick slaves, curing them, and reselling them at a higher price. The actual writing of the saga is spelled out metafictionally as a collaborative effort involving Renzi and his uncle, Maggi: "Shall we construct the great family saga working as a duo?" (22). The duo, in true dialogic fashion, must be made up of two people with opposing views; Maggi the history professor is obsessed with history, while Renzi claims that he is not interested in either history or politics: *"Después del descubrimiento de América no ha pasado nada en estos lares que merezca la más mínima atención"* 'Since the discovery of America, nothing has happened in our homeland worthy of the slightest attention' (21).

Part 2, narrated by Marcelo Maggi's Polish friend Tardewski, is a

Joycean peripatetic conversation between the latter and Renzi that lasts from 10 A.M. to the following dawn, as they wait in vain for Maggi's reappearance in Concordia. In spite of the novel's indebtedness to Joyce, Tardewski expresses his preference for Kafka over Joyce because he considers the latter too much of a virtuoso (270). Although Piglia himself does not indulge for the most part in the neo-baroque stylistic adornment and puns of Joyce, Carpentier, Lezama Lima, Carlos Fuentes, Abel Posse, or Fernando del Paso, *Respiración artificial*, because of its complex manipulation of time and narrative point of view, is not readily accessible to the masses and hardly deserves to be included in what Marta Morello-Frosch designates as the new fictional biography, which "overthrows the carnivalesque fiction of the preceding Latin American novel."[4]

If Part 1 represents Argentina's more traditional historical roots, then its title, *"Si yo mismo fuera el invierno sombrío"* 'If I myself were the gloomy winter', can be interpreted as a negative as well as an enigmatic view of the national image. At the same time, the selection of Italian names—Renzi, Maggi, and Ossorio (with the double s)—for the protagonists of the "Argentine" half of the novel reveals a greater degree of complexity in Piglia's view of Argentina than is found in the clear-cut conflict between Argentine *criollos* and Italian immigrants in Florencio Sánchez's early twentieth-century play *La gringa,* for example. The T. S. Eliot epigraph for Part 1—"We had the experience but missed the meaning, and approach to the meaning restores the experience"— reinforces the negative image of Argentine history and reaffirms the Argentine intellectuals' obsession with European culture. Part 2, on the other hand, is entitled "Descartes," a reflection of French and possibly European rationality—a concept that is totally subverted by the importance given to the probably apocryphal encounter between Hitler and Franz Kafka in Prague in 1909–1910. As one of the many examples of metafiction in the novel, historian Maggi writes to his nephew Renzi that "everything is apocryphal" (18).

Perhaps the principal justification for labeling *Respiración artificial* a New Historical Novel is the almost total absence of the re-creation of historical space and time. Although the characters are all situated in specific chronological periods and geographic places, and although many historical figures from Rosas to Yrigoyen are mentioned by name, no attempt is made to re-create the flavor of those periods. The novel is much more concerned with projecting Borges's philosophical views on history in general. As in "Tema del traidor y del héroe" and "Historia del guerrero y de la cautiva," history repeats itself. Maggi's abandoning his wife Esperanza six months after the wedding to live with an older cabaret dancer named Coca follows the pattern of Enrique Ossorio's living in New York City with Lisette, the black prostitute from Martinique, and of Enrique's grandfather's abandoning his family at the age of seventy to live with a fourteen-year old black Jamaican whom he called *La Emperatriz*. All three cases constitute protests against bourgeois marriage, like those that appear in the works of Cortázar. Maggi, who was jailed in the late 1930s and early 1940s—either for being affiliated with the Amadeo Sabattini wing of the Radical Party or for having absconded with his wife Esperanza's money—specifically criticizes his oligarchic wife in terms that are reminiscent of Fernanda del Carpio in *Cien años de soledad*: *"No ves que es loca, siempre cagó de parada, me consta, porque alguien le dijo que era más elegante"* 'Don't you see that she's crazy. She would always shit standing up, believe me, I know, because someone told her it was more elegant' (19).

Four of the family members are authors. Emilio Renzi published his first novel in 1976, which he characterizes as a kind of parody of Onetti in the style of Faulkner's *Wild Palms* as translated by Borges (16). Renzi later tells Tardewski that he is convinced that "experiences and adventures no longer exist; There are no more adventures, he said to me, only parodies. He thought, he said, that adventures today are only parodies" and that parodies have become "the very center of modern life" (137). Shortly after the publication of his novel, Renzi receives the first of a series of letters from his uncle Marcelo Maggi. The latter is writing a book about Enrique Ossorio, the law-school companion of Juan Bautista Alberdi, and later dictator Rosas's private secretary. Ossorio himself is writing his autobiography and is planning a novel set in 1837–1838 and an encyclopedia of American ideas. His father, who participated in the wars of independence, jotted down a series of antiwar maxims which he called *Máximas sobre el arte de la guerra* (89).

There are two other examples of history repeating itself. Enrique Ossorio commits suicide; Emilio Renzi enjoys thinking of himself as *"un suicida que camina"* 'a walking suicide' (45), and Maggi himself *may* also have committed suicide. (Maggi is presumably dead because he does not appear for his rendezvous with Tardewski and Renzi; he has therefore either committed suicide or been "disappeared.") Enrique Ossorio's son as well as Luciano Ossorio are posthumous children in that one's father abandoned the family and the other's father was killed in a duel before the children were born.

Continuing in the Borgesian—and, to a great extent, Jungian—vein, if history repeats itself, then all human beings are one, united by the collective unconscious. In 1850, Enrique Ossorio writes that he is "all the names in history. They are all in me, in this drawer where I keep my writings" (83). If all human beings are one, then there are no differences between heroes and villains. In Borges's "Tres versiones de Judas," Judas may be the true (?) Christ; the traitor Kilpatrick is an Irish hero and martyr to everyone who does not read Borges's story "Tema del traidor y del héroe"; and Moon, the treacherous Communist in "La forma de la espada," narrates the story from the perspective of his heroic victim. Similarly, Piglia's Enrique Ossorio proclaims that "he struggled indefatigably for freedom" (83), but that he has also been "a traitor and a spy and a disloyal friend and will be so judged by history" (91).

If history repeats itself and all human beings are one, then everything is predictable, a concept at odds with two other Borgesian concepts: the importance of chance and the impossibility of ascertaining the truth. Maggi writes to Renzi, "I'm convinced that nothing ever happens to us which we have not foreseen, nothing for which we are not prepared" (29). More specifically, in 1850, Enrique Ossorio envisions the future of Argentina *"tal cual va a ser dentro de 130 años"* 'just as it's going to be within 130 years' (97): full of "murders, massacres, civil wars" (84). The predictability of the future is symbolized by the Borgesian leitmotif of the chess game, where patterns of moves are predetermined. However, Tardewski proposes a change in the rules to allow for random moves by each of the pieces so as to make the outcome more unpredictable (26–27). Chance is actually the key factor in Tardewski's great discovery of the 1909–1910 Prague meetings of Kafka and Hitler. If he had received the writings of the Greek sophist Hippias in the British Museum as he had requested, he would never have discovered the Hitler-Kafka connection, but by mistake, instead of the Hippias volume, he received a copy of Hitler's *Mein Kampf*.

The impossibility of arriving at the incontrovertible truth, be it of history or of contemporary reality, is announced by Piglia as the theme of his novel in the ironic dedication to Elías and Rubén, "who helped me get to know the truth of history." Maggi expresses the same idea nonironically in his remarks on the anachronistic epistolary genre of the eighteenth century, when "the people who lived in that period still trusted the straight truth of the written word" (38). If there is no ascertainable reality, then, according to Tardewski, "everything that surrounds us is artificial" (38), a clear reference to the novel's title.

Borges's concept of the interaction between literature and reality expressed in "Tema del traidor y del héroe" (in the interactions between

Shakespeare's *Julius Caesar* and the assassinations of Kilpatrick and Abraham Lincoln) also appears in Piglia's novel. The dying words of Maggi's wife Esperancita are "Buenos Aires, Buenos Aires" (22), an affected imitation of José Hernández, the author of *Martín Fierro*. Renzi states that he is more interested in style than in politics and registers surprise that no one has discovered that President Yrigoyen's speeches are the source of Macedonio Fernández's writings.

Not only is *Respiración artificial* informed by Borges's philosophi-cal views of history, but at least five of his short stories are intertextually present. One of Maggi's ancestors was Pophan, an "Irish gentleman in the service of the queen . . . who admired Parnell" (20); the Irish-English oxymoronic connection is a favorite Borges leitmotif that appears in "El jardín de senderos que se bifurcan," "Tema del traidor y del héroe," and "La forma de la espada." Maggi's father-in-law, Luciano Ossorio, who was one of the founders of the Unión Conservadora and a senator from 1912 to 1916, was shot in 1931 by a drunkard or a Radical and has been paralyzed ever since. His looking out the window (57) recalls the paralyzed Recabarren in Borges's "El fin." However, Luciano is more than an observer; in one of the many metaphors of the novel, he is Argentina: *"Estoy paralítico, igual que este país, decía. Yo soy la Argentina, carajo"* 'I'm paralyzed, just like this country, he said. I am Argentina, damn it'(24). When Luciano's anonymous father (also En-rique Ossorio's son), who has never fired a pistol in his life (61), dies in the 1879 duel, he is prefiguring the death of Juan Dahlmann, the pro-tagonist of Borges's "El sur." This man, Enrique Ossorio's son, had used the money his father accumulated in the California gold rush to become one of Argentina's most powerful ranch-owners in the 1860s. Since he is a supporter of President Bartolomé Mitre, his fatal duel marks a turning point in Argentine history because the survivor is brought to trial, symbolizing the end of internecine struggles among the members of the oligarchy and the recognition that they have to unite against their common enemies, "the immigrants, the gauchos, and the Indians" (63)—thus paving the way for General Roca's ascension to the presidency in 1880.

Dahlmann's death in "El sur"—preceded by his train trip south, a trip to the past—is evoked ironically by Renzi's train trip north to Con-cordia: "Some guys who were playing cards on a cardboard valise in-vited me to have a drink of gin with them. For me, it was like moving into the past and at the end of that trip I realized to what extent Maggi had foreseen everything" (21). In the second half of the novel, Renzi comments on Borges's predilection for "El sur," attributing it to the crisscrossing and integration of the two Argentine literary currents of the nineteenth century: European erudition and the populist *gauchesco* nationalism (163–164).

Although Part 2 of *Respiración artificial* actually transpires in Concordia in 1979 in less than twenty-four hours, its present is also "disappeared" because Renzi, Tardewski, and the latter's local friends— Antón Tokray, son of a Russian nobleman, the ex-Nazi Rudholf Von Maier, and the *lunfardo*-speaking Bartolomé Marconi (heteroglossia)— converse about the totality of Argentine literature and about specific periods of European history. In a kind of counterpart to the family saga in Part 1 of the novel, Tardewski narrates in Part 2 Professor Marcelo Maggi's "family saga" of literary duos made up of European intellectuals settled in Argentina who have served as models for their Argentine friends. The progenitor, he says, was Pedro de Angelis, an expert on Vico and Hegel, cultural attaché in St. Petersburg, and collaborator on the *Revue Enciclopédique,* who became Argentine dictator Juan Manuel Rosas's right-hand man. According to Maggi, "Echeverría, Alberdi, Sarmiento, seemed like desperate copiers, dilettantes corroded by second-hand knowledge" (138–139). The "family tree" continued in the 1880s with Paul Groussac and Miguel Cané; in the 1900s, with Charles de Soussens, a kind of Verlaine, and Leopoldo Lugones; in the 1920s, with William Henry Hudson and Ricardo Güiraldes; in the 1940s, with Witold Gombrowicz and Borges; and in the 1970s, with the fictitious protagonists Tardewski and Marcelo Maggi, backed up by the fictitious secondary characters, the ex-Nazi phrenologist Rudholf Von Maier and his Argentine friend and admirer Pedro Arregui. To make the labyrinth more complex, the European models for their Argentine admirers were usually patterned after other European models. Thus, Charles de Soussens was a model of Verlaine, and Tardewski was deeply influenced by the dialogic Wittgenstein, "the only man in history to produce two totally different philosophical systems in the course of his life, each one of which prevailed over at least one generation and generated two currents of thought with their absolutely antagonistic protagonists, commentators, and disciples" (207).

The subservience of Argentine intellectuals to their European counterparts is highlighted in the 1970s portion of the novel by the Argentine fascination with the latest European trends in critical theory.[5] Marconi asks Renzi if they're still *"jodiendo con la lingüística"* 'bugging everyone with linguistics' (177). Renzi seems happy to report that linguistics has been replaced by psychoanalysis. However, around Concordia, according to Marconi, a report on the regional folklore might be entitled

"*Hjelmslev entre los gauderios entrerrianos o un ejemplo de gauchesca semiológica*" 'Hjelmslev among the gauchos from Entrerríos or an example of gaucho semiology' (178), and in the rural *pulpería,* several of the gauchos converse about themes related to writing and phonetics.

On another, more serious plane, Adolf Hitler is posited as the antecedent for the Argentine military regime of 1976–1979. Although the Hitler-Kafka connection may seem somewhat far-fetched, it is crucially important in the novel. After almost one hundred pages of labyrinthine intellectual meandering in Part 2, narrator Tardewski links Kafka's name to the Nazis for the first time on page 227. For the next thirty pages, the author builds up suspense by not revealing the nature of the connection. When he finally does, the reader realizes how thoroughly this episode is integrated into the novel's main theme, the denunciation of the Argentine military dictatorship of 1976–1979. Tardewski's discovery is that in 1909–1910, Hitler, in order to avoid being drafted, disappeared from Vienna and took refuge in Prague and frequented the Café Arcos. In two letters to friends, Kafka refers to an Austrian exile, a "strange little man who says he's a painter . . . he calls himself Adolf" (259). Kafka (Tardewski discovers) actually transcribed a conversation between himself and Hitler about the latter's plans for the future, which informed Kafka's novels, which in turn prefigured the reality of the Third Reich, thus paralleling somewhat the responsibility of Enrique Ossorio's 1850 vision for the 1980 Argentina:

> . . . Immediately, on the following line, Kafka transcribes this: Discussion A. I didn't mean that, he tells me, reads Tardewski. You know me well Doctor. I am a completely inoffensive man. I had to get it off my chest. What I said are only words. I interrupt him. This is precisely what is dangerous. Words prepare the road, they are the precursors of future acts, the sparks of the future fires. I had no intention to say that, A answers me. That's what you say, I answer him trying to smile. But do you know what aspect things really have? It may be that we are seated on top of a powder keg that will convert your desire into reality. . . . Adolf Hitler knew how to plan so marvelously well what he planned to do with the future of the world, he knew how to explain his plans and his projects in such a fascinating way, read Tardewski in his notebook, that one could have listened to him indefinitely, such was the enchantment and the seduction of his words and the exaggerated and at the same time meticulously detailed character of his descriptions of what the world was going to receive from him in the future. . . . The atrocious utopia of a world converted into

an immense penal colony, that's what Adolf, the insignificant and grotesque deserter, talks about to Franz Kafka, who knows how to listen to him, at the tables in the Café Arcos in Prague in late 1909. And Kafka believes him. . . . Kafka's genius consists of having understood that if those words could be said, then they could be realized. (260–261, 264)

Kafka foresees the transformation of the frustrated Austrian painter into the Führer. Since the word *transformación* 'transformation' in the following lines certainly suggests the title of Kafka's novel *Metamorphosis,* and since the multiple use of the somewhat ambiguous possessive pronoun *su* 'his' fuses the identity of the two men, in true Borgesian fashion Kafka *is* Hitler:

> Con su estilo, que ahora nosotros conocemos bien, el insignificante y pulguiento pequeño burgués austríaco que vive semi clandestino en Praga porque es un desertor, ese artista fracasado que se gana la vida pintando tarjetas postales, desarrolla, frente a quien todavía no es pero ya comienza a ser Franz Kafka, sus sueños gangosos, desmesurados, en los que entreví su transformación en el Führer, el Jefe el Amo absoluto de millones de hombres, sirvientes, esclavos, insectos sometidos a su dominio, dice Tardewski.
>
> With his style, well known to us now, the insignificant and flea-infested Austrian petit bourgeois who lives somewhat in hiding in Prague because he's a deserter, that failure of an artist who earns his living painting post cards, develops, in front of the man who is still not but who is already beginning to be Franz Kafka, his nasal, distorted dreams in which he perceives his transformation into the Führer, the Chief, the absolute Master of millions of men, servants, slaves, insects subjected to his power, says Tardewski. (263)

The Nazis used the word *Ungeziefer* 'vermin' (264) to refer to those detained in concentration camps—the same word used by Kafka to refer to the transformation of Gregor Samsa upon awakening one morning in *Metamorphosis.*

Tardewski discovers that Hitler's plans for the future, which Kafka believed could be carried out, served as the basis for *The Trial.*

> You read *The Trial,* Tardewski says to me. Kafka knew how to see, even in the most precise detail, how horror accumulated. That novel presents in an hallucinating manner the classic model of the State converted into the instrument of terror. He describes the anonymous machinery of a world where everyone can be accused and be

found guilty, the sinister insecurity that totalitarianism injects into the lives of men and women, the faceless boredom of the assassins, the furtive sadism. Since Kafka wrote that book, the nocturnal knock on the door has arrived at innumerable doors and the number of those who were dragged to their deaths *like dogs,* just like Joseph K., is legion. (265)

In the thirty-page suspenseful build-up prior to the above revelation, Piglia intertwines the Hitler-Kafka connection with the texture of the whole novel. The five-year period of 1905–1910 in Hitler's life, described as "incredible and pathetic" (251), is of particular interest to Tardewski during his own similar five-year period of 1940–1945 in Buenos Aires. Upon arriving in the Argentine capital, Tardewski stays at the appropriately named, but real, Hotel Tres Sargentos, where he writes his essay on the relationship between Kafka and the Nazis. One day, however, he returns to his room to find that a thief or thieves have broken in and stolen all his belongings, including Kafka's works. As an excellent example of the use of metaphor, which is praised metafictionally in different parts of the novel,[6] Tardewski compares his own situation to that of Europe in the summer of 1940: ". . . I entered my room and confronted a reproduction in miniature but real, of Europe demolished by war" (229). Tardewski finds employment as a clerk in the Banco Polaco of Buenos Aires. The fact that shortly after being transferred to the Concordia branch in 1945 he resigns without a reason and spends his time giving private lessons in foreign languages and playing chess suggests a desire to break out of the Gregor Samsa world. His friendship with history professor Maggi is explained in terms of "the unity of opposites" (237). Tardewski considers himself a skeptic who lives outside of history, while Maggi is a man of principles who thinks only in terms of historical perspective. The "unity of opposites" theory is also exemplified by Tardewski's realization that *Mein Kampf* "was a kind of perfect opposite or apocryphal continuation of *Discurso del método*" (241), which Valéry called the first modern novel "because it's a monologue where instead of the history of a passion's being narrated, it's the history of an idea" (244)—an allusion to Eduardo Mallea's well-known *Historia de una pasión argentina.*

In another example of metafiction, Tardewski recalls that Prof. Maggi used to tell him frequently that he suffered from the same eagerness for digression as did General Lucio Mansilla (250). This remark is generated by Tardewski's telling two mini-anecdotes in support of attaching great importance to chance. First, if Tardewski had not received *Mein Kampf* by mistake that day in the British Museum, he would not have realized that he no longer wanted to continue studying philosophy, and he would not have been able to escape to Buenos Aires. By the same token, if Hitler had been admitted into the Vienna Academy of Fine Arts, a science fiction writer could make up a great plot about how the world might have been different. In keeping with the theory in the novel that Argentine writers were influenced by Europeans in Buenos Aires and these, in turn, by other Europeans, Hitler derived his racist theories from his namesake, the ex-monk Adolfo Lenz von Liebenfels (253), who published in the journal *Ostara,* also known to Kafka. Since the Spanish translation of Kafka's *The Trial* is '*El proceso*', there is an obvious connection here to the Argentine military junta of 1976–1979, and its Proceso de Reorganización Nacional.

If the past two pages of this chapter seem overly long and drawn out, they are calculated to reflect Piglia's method of hiding his true goal—the denunciation of the abuses committed by the Argentine military dictatorship, particularly in the 1976–1979 period—in a Borgesian labyrinthine manner, à la "El jardín de senderos que se bifurcan," designed to confuse the censors.

The censorship theme is actually represented in the novel by the intercepting and decoding of letters written by people under suspicion. In the second chapter of Part 1 (56), ex-Senator Luciano Ossorio informs his grandson Renzi that he has received threatening letters from a man named Francisco José Arocena, who also intercepts and tries to decipher—as Luciano himself does—other letters sent to him. Arocena's examination of all correspondence is described briefly but sufficiently to create the impression that his responsibilities go beyond the Renzi–Maggi–Luciano Ossorio correspondence: "He revised the envelopes and rapidly established an initial system of classification. Caracas. New York. Bogotá; a letter to Ohio, another one to London; Buenos Aires; Concordia; Buenos Aires. He numbered the letters: there were eight of them. He put aside the letter from Marcelo Maggi to Ossorio that he had just read" (92). Subsequently the narrator pokes fun at Arocena's clumsy attempts (118) to decipher an incestuous letter signed *Juana, la loca* to her putative brother, a post-doctoral physics student in Oxford. The significance of this letter and of Arocena's role as a government censor is foregrounded by his reappearing hard at work at the very end of Part 1 decoding a brief message with the use of numerical techniques in order to uncover the sentence *"Raquel llega a Ezeiza el 10, vuelo 2203"* (125)—probably a reference to Juan Perón's long-awaited return to Buenos Aires (the Ezeiza airport) from Madrid to assume the presidency on June 20, 1973.[7]

Arocena's official role as part of the government plan to create an atmosphere of terror in all of Argentina is complemented by his receiving a letter from Echevarne Angélica Inés (whose three names seem to be in reverse order in order to suggest the art of deciphering) addressed to the señor Intendente. She explains how a TV transmitter has been surgically implanted near her heart while she slept, enabling her to see the killing of Jews in Poland with baling wire and the crematory ovens in northern Argentina[8]—prefiguring the appearance of Hitler in Part 2. She has become the *"Cantatriz oficial"* 'Official Singer' (99), a possible euphemism for "spy" as well as an allusion to Perón's two professional entertainer wives, Evita and Isabelita. Echevarne has become a singer in order to avoid going crazy from seeing all the misery and suffering in this world (99–100). Perón himself, like Renzi's father, does not appear in the novel, in order to reinforce the image of the ten-to-thirty thousand *desaparecidos*.

Nevertheless, the novel ends on a positive note, or at least, on a dialogic note. Tardewski admits to Renzi that Maggi will not appear, but he implies that, in spite of everything, we should not be cynical. He quotes from Immanuel Kant, who on his deathbed affirmed, *"The meaning of Humanity has not yet abandoned me"* (273). Tardewski goes on to comment at some length on the meaning of the German word *Humanität* and applies it to Maggi. On the other hand, Tardewski then proceeds to give Renzi three of Maggi's file folders full of documents and notes. Renzi opens one of them, and *Respiración artificial* ends with a half-page suicide note from Enrique Ossorio, implying that Maggi also may have committed suicide, an ending hardly in keeping with Kant's *Humanität*.

Am I justified in including *Respiración artificial* in a book on the New Historical Novel? By my own definition the action of any historical novel must take place before the author was born, and in this case, the characters exchange letters and converse between 1976 and 1979. Furthermore, the major theme of the novel is the denunciation of the Argentine military dictatorship, particularly in those same three years. On the other hand, the author was too young to have actually experienced the period of Hitler and World War II or the pre-1942 Argentine political and literary world (Perón came to power in 1943, and Roberto Arlt died in 1942). Moreover, like *El reino de este mundo* and many of the other New Historical Novels, *Respiración artificial* definitely subordinates the re-creation of a given historical period to the presentation of philosophical ideas about history in general, derived to a great extent from Borges. Also like many of the NHNs, Piglia's novel is dialogic, abounds in intertextuality and metafiction, and may even be a parody of the novel that Borges never wrote—and, given the general perception of Borges's political views, *might* never have written.

7 Over Two Thousand Years of Exile and Marginality — The Jewish Latin American Historical Novel

Pedro Orgambide's *Aventuras de Edmund Ziller en tierras del nuevo mundo*

Moacyr Scliar's *A estranha nação de Rafael Mendes*

Homero Aridjis's *1492: Vida y tiempos de Juan Cabezón de Castilla*

Angelina Muñiz's *Tierra adentro*

You see your people as slaves; my race is the most hounded in history.—Ludwig Wittgenstein to Irish revolutionary James Connolly in Terry Eagleton's historical novel *Saints and Scholars*

In 721 B.C. the Northern Kingdom of Israel and its capital Samaria were destroyed by the Assyrians, and what became known as the ten lost tribes were deported. In 586 B.C. the city of Jerusalem was destroyed by Babylonian King Nebuchadnezzar, and the people of the Southern Kingdom of Judah were deported to Babylon. Although their descendants returned fifty years later and rebuilt the temple, the majority continued to live in the Diaspora: Babylon and the cities bordering the Mediterranean. Subsequent conquests of the area by Alexander the Great in 333 B.C., by the Romans in 70 A.D., by the Arabs in the seventh century; by the Seljuk Turks in 1071, by the Crusaders in the subsequent two centuries, and by the Ottoman Turks in 1453 perpetuated the Diaspora. Wherever Jews have lived in the past 2,713 years, with the exception of the state of Israel since 1948, they have been, in the words of Alan Dershowitz's *Chutzpah* (1991), "expelled, pogromed, crusaded, inquisitioned, jihaded, and holocausted out of countries that we helped to make great" (8). Even in the United States, according to Dershowitz, "despite our apparent success, deep down we see ourselves as second-class citizens—as guests in another people's land" (3).

Although some Sephardic Jews undoubtedly arrived in the New World during the three hundred years of Spanish and Portuguese colonial rule, most Latin American Jews today, concentrated particularly in Argentina and Brazil, are descended from the Eastern European Jews who arrived between 1881 and 1930.[1] Given the Jews' tragic history and miraculous survival over the centuries, it is not surprising that they are fascinated and obsessed with history. Nor is it surprising that, in the 1979–1992 period in which the New Historical Novel and the historical novel in general have been dominant, Jewish Latin American writers should be attracted to this genre. The four novels to be discussed fall into two very different but nonetheless related themes, of the "Wandering Jew"[2] and the Spanish Inquisition.

Two Versions of the "Wandering Jew": Edmund Ziller and Rafael Mendes

Argentine Pedro Orgambide's *Aventuras de Edmund Ziller en tierras del nuevo mundo* 'Adventures of Edmund Ziller in the Lands of the New World' (1977) and Brazilian Moacyr Scliar's *A estranha nação de Rafael Mendes* 'The Strange Nation of Rafael Mendes' (1983) both attempt to capture in an experimental fashion the total history of the Jews[3] in Latin America, but in very different ways. The protagonists represent two types of "Wandering Jews": the immortal, ubiquitous Edmund Ziller, who assumes many different guises, from that of the Old Testament prophet Jonah to that of an Argentine philologist and Hebraist who identifies with revolutionary causes up to the end of the novel in 1976; and Rafael Mendes, who is the Brazilian descendant of the same Jonah, Habacuc ben Tov, and Maimonides, and all of whose descendants in Portugal and Brazil up to 1975 bear the same name, Rafael Mendes. Strictly speaking, neither novel conforms to my definition of the historical novel since in each instance roughly 30–40 percent of the action transpires during the author's lifetime. However, as was the case with *Respiración artificial,* the novels have a very strong historical component, and the Orgambide novel in particular contains many of the characteristics of the New Historical Novel.

AVENTURAS DE EDMUND ZILLER

Pedro Orgambide's thrice-problematic *Aventuras de Edmund Ziller* (1977) deserves greater recognition as one of the relatively early

NHNs.[4] To borrow from the opening words of the Passover ceremony, how is this novel different from all the other novels studied in this book? Stated very simply, it is not what could be called a traditional novel. There is no continuous plot; there are no psychologically developed characters; 67 of its 317 pages are devoted to the often interrupted reading of a 1791 play in verse; and 31 pages are devoted to an alphabetically ordered, anti-imperialist encyclopedia. In true metafictional fashion, Edmund Ziller rails against the novel as a bourgeois genre (182, 228) and proclaims the impossibility of a "linear narrative discourse" (217). The Argentine narrator/author, who participates in the text as a character referred to as Pedro, P.O., or Piotrer, is receptive to his Mexican friend Santiago Santillán's suggestion that he write "a fragmentary novel" (254) about Ziller, and in Madrid his friend Professor Jesús de la Fuente y Mira ironically consecrates his enterprise with "a theory of the fragmentary novel" (313).

Another way of identifying Orgambide's work in terms of genre is by picking up on its intertextual clue, *"cantaba boleros"* 'he sang boleros' (254, 255, 260). The source is Guillermo Cabrera Infante's well-known Boom novel *Tres tristes tigres* 'Three Trapped Tigers' (1965), which has many sections entitled "Ella cantaba boleros," referring to the enormous mulatto nightclub singer *La Estrella*. The two novels resemble each other in their lack of a "linear narrative discourse" as well as in their carnivalesque tone and the preeminence of parody. In *Tres tristes tigres*, Cabrera Infante recounts the murder of Trotsky seven times, in the respective styles of José Martí, José Lezama Lima, Virgilio Piñera, Lydia Cabrera, Lino Novás Calvo, Alejo Carpentier, and Nicolás Guillén. In the very first chapter of Orgambide's novel, Edmund Ziller's letter to Emperor Charles V is an extravagant parody of Hernán Cortés's letters. In an archaic style suggestive of the sixteenth century, Ziller describes the Río de la Plata, without naming it. He then proceeds to re-create in great detail an imaginary sumptuous banquet, only to transform it brusquely into the reality of desperate cannibalism. In order to lay the groundwork for the interplay in the novel between Argentina and Mexico, the letter is signed "Don Edmundo de Ziller y Sigüenza," with the name Sigüenza constituting an evocation of Carlos Sigüenza y Góngora, the Mexican contemporary and friend of Sor Juana Inés de la Cruz. Only two chapters later, Orgambide parodies Borges's "Historia del guerrero y de la cautiva" by telling the "incredible story" (21) of the seventeenth-century Sephardic pirate who went to live among the Chilean Indians and became their chief. Borges is present, of course, in many of the Argentine novels of the past two decades and, as has been pointed out in Chapter 1, shares with Carpentier the distinction of having engendered the New Historical Novel. In Chapter 2, Ziller tells his German friend Albert Dürer that "he is repeating the words of an Aztec poet, of that man who, like you, like me, is everyman" (18), alluding to the Jungian-Borgesian concept that is most appropriate for the "Wandering Jew's" multiple reincarnations.

Aventuras de Edmund Ziller may also be compared to Orgambide's own previous novel, Los inquisidores (1967). Ideologically similar, Los inquisidores alternates several novelistic threads in which the "inquisitors" are the colonial Inquisition in Peru; Argentina's rural police of the nineteenth century and its fascist Tacuaras of the 1960s; the Ku Klux Klan and white supremacists in Selma (Alabama), New York City, and Watts (Los Angeles); the anti-Communist senator Joseph McCarthy; the Nazis; and the Stalinists. The victims for the most part are Jews and Blacks, who are linked amorously and sexually in both novels: Ziller and Yembá; Francisco Maldonado de Silva and María Martínez; and Efraín Azevedo and Zenobia. Where the two novels differ is that Los inquisidores is written in a straightforward, realistic manner without any of the parody or other carnivalesque devices of the New Historical Novel.

Now that the question of genre has been resolved, we may proceed with the second and more difficult Passover question: how is this dialogic novel different from all the other dialogic novels studied in this book? The more specific question is, to what extent is this a revolutionary Marxist novel and to what extent is it subversive to the Marxist cause? Francisco Hinojosa's very negative review calls it Manichaean, monolithic, proselytizing, and rhetorically militant: "an unnecessary summary of the dogmatic literature that the Latin American novel has begun to forget" (25). From a different ideological perspective, Saúl Sosnowski's very favorable analysis of the novel praises Orgambide for including Brazil in the Latin American liberation movement (9), for using humor to combat alienation, and for effectively integrating "the literary praxis and the militancy that embraces it" (11). In other words, both critics, from opposite ideological positions, affirm the novel's monologic revolutionary posture.

A close reading of the novel, however, raises doubts about its single-mindedness and Aventuras de Edmund Ziller may be as dialogic as the other New Historical Novels. On the one hand, there is no question that Latin American history is presented from a Marxist revolutionary, anti-imperialist point of view. Ziller, in the guise of the Jewish pirate Subatol Deul, denounces the proud Spanish conquistadors for having decimated the Mayans, the Aztecs, and the Incas, and for having destroyed their temples, their codices—their culture (26). At the end of the eighteenth century, Ziller lives with his black girlfriend Yembá among the Indians of Mato Grosso and identifies with the sick Brazilian sculptor "O Aleijadinho" and the revolutionary dentist Tiradentes. Later he directs the struggle of the Argentineans against the English invaders in the early years of the nineteenth century. In accordance with Marxist revisionist historians, Ziller is critical of the "civilized" Bernardino Rivadavia (71) and the Unitarian *"cajetillas"* 'dandies' (102) and seems to support the "barbarous" Rosas and his gauchos. Ziller then proceeds to southern Brazil where he becomes the leader of a ragtag army engaged in guerrilla warfare; the historical referent is the Guerra das Farroupilhas (1835–1845) waged by the Rio Grande do Sul republicans and federalists against the imperialist central government of the Regency. Placing that war within the anti-imperialist world view, Ziller tells his troops that they are fighting against pride and all the imperialist powers: "the adolescent Alexander the Greek, the Roman legions, the ships of the Invincible Spanish Armada, the proud British on the island of Java, and all those fearful princes, thieves, cardinals, popes, *encomenderos*,[5] Dutch merchants . . ." (79–80).

Two decades later, Ziller finds himself on the side of the Paraguayans fighting against the imperialist forces of Brazil, Argentina, and Uruguay. At the very end of the nineteenth and the beginning of the twentieth centuries, the imperialistic power to be feared has become the United States: "The storm is coming from the North" (103). Although Ziller and the narrator seem genuinely anti-imperialist, there are indications that Orgambide may be parodying anti-imperialist literature. A U.S. confidential report indicates that one of Ziller's advisers is Manuel Ugarte, who is about to publish a twenty-two-volume *"Anti-imperialist Encyclopedia"* under the supervision of *"un tipógrafo enfermo de anarquismo"* 'a typesetter suffering from anarchism' (107).

Santiago Santillán, the narrator's friend from the Mexico City slum of Tepito, says that he has been interested in the racial problems in the United States for many years. However, his friendships with people there—"professors, liberal people . . ." (194)—and his memory of being threatened by a gang in Harlem are inconsistent with the anti-imperialist attitude of a single-minded revolutionary radical. In the 1960s liberals were despised by radicals, and it doesn't help the radical cause to evoke gang violence in Harlem. Furthermore, if the novel is so critical of United States imperialism, why does the author have Santillán later go to Houston for a serious operation which saves his life? Perhaps the thirty-one-page digest of the *Encyclopedia* should be taken as a parody, a criticism of dogmatic anti-imperialism.

Around 1910 Ziller shows up in Mexico as a photographer to take pictures of Zapata, Villa, and "another foreigner, a guy by the name of Reed,[6] who, like him, loved justice and adventure" (146). After World War I, Ziller takes part in labor conflicts, as described in the discourse of the rabid anti-Communists: ". . . The Jewish-Marxist conspiracy allied with the Sinarquist movement, has as its forerunner: Edmund Ziller. This miserable renegade, traitor, and mercenary whom the Inquisition condemned to be burned, today has won new supporters: homosexuals, ideological delinquents and drug addicts" (159). Other twentieth-century revolutionary names and events that appear are the Peruvian Marxists José Carlos Mariátegui and César Vallejo and the Chilean Luis Emilio Recabarren; the long march of the Prestes Column in Brazil; the 1960s revolutionary politician Francisco Julião from northeastern Brazil; the Tlatelolco Massacre of 1968; the Ezeiza Airport massacre of June 1973 perpetrated by the López Rega Peronists against the revolutionary *montoneros* as they waited for Perón to return from Madrid; the military coup that overthrew President Allende in Chile in September 1973; and the 1976 violent intervention of the Mexican government against the independent newspaper *Excelsior*.

If I have described Ziller's revolutionary exploits in excessive detail, it is because I do not want my comments on the aberrations in his militancy to be construed as denying his revolutionary image. However, I would like to demonstrate that the novel is more heterodox than appears at first sight. After participating in the War of the Triple Alliance (1865–1870), Ziller marries a wealthy Argentine rancher and enjoys the good life of the oligarchy, which is described twice in the novel. In Chapter 12 of Part 1, entitled *"De los placeres de la música"* 'About the Pleasures of Music', Ziller becomes so enthralled with the classical music performances at the famous Teatro Colón in Buenos Aires that all thoughts of social injustice and unrest are forgotten. However, his wife and her cousins bring him back to his revolutionary senses with their strong condemnation of the "Red plague" (189), the anarchists. The classical music becomes trivial in Ziller's mind in contrast to his vision of a firing squad, led by his wife and her cousins, that is preparing to shoot workers and their families and students who are taking Mozart's corpse to be buried (90). Instead of hearing the elite music being played in the Teatro Colón, Ziller "hears" the "leprous musician from India, the minstrels from Provence, a blind violinist from a London suburb, another one from Cuernavaca, the zitherists, African drummers . . ."

(90). Can this opposition between elite and popular culture be taken seriously in a novel in which a parodic, carnivalesque tone predominates from the very first chapter? Could it be that Orgambide is parodying orthodox Marxist literature? "On the other hand," to quote Tevye from *Fiddler on the Roof,* this same phase of Ziller's life crops up again toward the end of the novel with a letter to the author from a former Argentine oligarchic government minister. The letter describes Ziller as a "bon vivant" who frequented the Jockey Club, hobnobbed with the wealthy landowners, and practiced fencing, gambling, extramarital lovemaking, and betting at the race tracks. Ziller's sudden disappearance from Argentina in 1910, recounted in the letter, might confirm the monologic revolutionary view of the novel if one interprets these activities as Ziller's infiltration into the Argentine oligarchy in order to undermine it, and his leaving in 1910 as a move to participate in the Mexican Revolution.

More clearly dialogic are the Marxist roles of Ziller and the narrator. Ziller is reputed to be the author of *Manual de Revoluciones,* published in Ecuador around 1920 (46). In 1943, during the military takeover in Argentina that initiates the first Peronist period, Ziller explains to himself why he joined the Communist Party: "They have their place in the world, they know what they want" (230). Nevertheless, he feels uncomfortable as he listens to the Party's official reaction to the inability of a Polish comrade to resist police torture. He compares the questions and answers to those of the catechism in the Catholic parochial school (232). This third part of the novel is pointedly entitled *"Las leyes del juego"* 'The Rules of the Game' (225). When cell leader Julio González quotes Lenin's remark that "extremism is the childhood disease of communism," Ziller's idealistic friend Nino announces that he is leaving the cell in favor of the Shock Brigade (232–233). That night both Nino and González are shot by the police, and Ziller casually reports that he has replaced González as the cell leader (234). Later, the narrator's Brazilian artist friend Plinio Bandeira criticizes Ziller as "that strange man who preferred the cabala to Marxism" (248), but the section ends with positive references to Ziller's Party allegiance: "hiding comrades, providing them with passports, with faith in their immediate needs (a house, a weapon, a plate of food, a plane, a friendly country)" (249–250).

The novel's position with regard to Marxism is further clarified in a later chapter entitled *"Vindicación de la escuela de la sabiduría"* 'Vindication of the School of Wisdom'. The tone of the chapter is definitely ironic and pokes fun at dogmatic Marxism through the character Tito's advocacy of "Pavlov's theory (conditioned reflexes)" (287) and Urrutia's obsession: *"se calentaba con la tesis y la antítesis y la síntesis y la negación de la negación"* 'he got all excited about the thesis and the antithesis and the synthesis and the negation of the negation' (288). Given the many examples of intertextuality in the novel, the name "Urrutia" may be an allusion to the director of Guatemala's Communist Party in Mario Monteforte Toledo's *Una manera de morir* 'A Way to Die' (1957), a bitter denunciation of the Communist Party whose dogmatism is equated with that of the Catholic Church (one of Latin America's most "disappeared" novels).[7]

The narrator states in a nonironic tone that he, Ziller, and the historical poet Raúl González Tuñón formed the dissident wing of the Escuela de la Sabiduría and proposed *"una Poesía Total, una poética que abarcara diferentes disciplinas del pensamiento y la acción"* 'a Total Poetry, a Poetics that would embrace different disciplines of thought and action' (290). Raúl was affiliated with Peronism, Ziller was a member of the Communist Party who had fought in the International Brigades in Spain during the Civil War, and the narrator had joined the Communist Youth at the age of fourteen after reading González Tuñón's poetry.

The chapter entitled *"Edmund Ziller cartógrafo de la isla de utopía"* 'Edmund Ziller Cartographer of the Island of Utopia' reinforces the novel's heterodox or dialogic position by questioning the Left's equation of the Cuban Revolution with utopia: "the illustrious Mexican intellectual Jesús Silva Herzog and the no less illustrious Argentine writer Ezequiel Martínez Estrada agree that the Island of Utopia and the Island of Cuba are one and the same thing" (269). Ziller's collection of poems, with its ambiguous title *Poemas lunares* 'Lunar Poems' or 'Blemished Poems', refers to revolutionary Cuba disguised as a late fifteenth-century map. As Santiago Santillán leaves for Cuba, the narrator tells him, "—I hope that the images of the Revolution don't keep you from finding that map" (271).

To summarize the answer to the second question posed earlier, *Aventuras de Edmund Ziller* is a revolutionary novel but not at all an orthodox Marxist revolutionary novel—which may account for its not being more widely disseminated. The narrator himself, in true metafictional style, describes his own approach to the revolutionary novel. Ziller's several amorous escapades—including one with his first wife in New Spain, the grotesquely obese Genoveva (possibly inspired by Colombian artist Fernando Botero)—are not considered by the narrator to be detrimental to Ziller's revolutionary activities. The verses dedicated to Yembá "allude to both erotic pleasure and the warm and dangerous love for liberty and justice" (47). Inspired by the Mexican lithographer José Guadalupe Posada, Ziller gives a Bakhtinian lecture entitled "Theory of the Popular and the Comic" in which he argues that

> ...las verdades absolutas, las leyes, las estatuas, la pompa, la represión, caen destruidas ante el embate de lo Cómico. La Muerte Cómica de Posada, la muerte de carnaval y fiesta, se burla de las jerarquías, aparece como un exabrupto entre las buenas costumbres. Y, sin duda, quien maneja así la comicidad es un rebelde. Como Aristófanes, Rabelais, Defoe o Sade. Y nada importa que Posada desconociera a esos parientes de la Subversión. El era uno de ellos. ¡Viva Posada, carajo!

> ...the absolute truths, the laws, the statues, the pomp, the repression are destroyed in the face of attack from the Comic. Posada's Comic Figure of Death, the death figures of Carnival and fiestas, poke fun at the hierarchies, appear as a sudden attack on good manners. And, without a doubt, whoever handles the Comic in that way is a rebel. Like Aristophanes, Rabelais, Defoe, or Sade. And it doesn't matter at all if Posada was not acquainted with his subversive relatives. He was one of them. Long live Posada, damn it to hell! (281)

Later Ziller adopts a similar attitude in the Escuela de la Sabiduría:

> ...Ziller defended, so to speak, a humanistic position, not at all belligerent; he was proposing an opening to diverse approaches to knowledge, he was vindicating François Villon and Enrique Santos Discépolo, Agustín Lara and hermetic poetry. This heterodoxy, which Raúl and I considered the spice of life, was combated by Tito in the most energetic way. Each week he would ask for our immediate expulsion. ... (290)

Toward the very end of the novel, Ziller comes up with a Borgesian "*Teoría de la Contradicción*" 'Theory of Contradiction', perhaps with a touch of irony, in which "the assassin of gauchos (Sarmiento) is also the Poet of the Future, where Guido y Spano could be Homer, Matraca could be Hernández, Hernández could be Martín Fierro, and all in some way could be Ziller" (314).

As a follow-up to the novel's heterodox revolutionary attitude, the third question, couched in ritualistic terms, is as follows: how is this Jewish historical novel different from all the other Jewish historical novels considered in this book? The answer is relatively simple: Edmund Ziller, like his creator Orgambide, is only half-Jewish. Whereas a name like Ziller in Latin America sounds Jewish, a name like Edmund is more typically Anglo-Saxon, like that of the eighteenth-century English statesman Edmund Burke. Ziller's Jewishness derives from his association with the legendary "Wandering Jew" (142); from his identification with all the downtrodden and persecuted people of the world regardless of religion or race; and from his being a heterodox intellectual. On the other hand, his Jewishness is not highlighted at all, and there is hardly any mention of Jewish customs or traditions. In fact the absence of Jewish *costumbrismo* becomes obvious during the descriptions of how Mexicans celebrate the *Día de los Muertos* 'All Souls Day' (261, 279) and of how Ziller spends the day at the touristy Xochimilco (161).

The novel opens with an illustrated "Wanted" poster in which Edmund Ziller is accused of being everything from a highwayman and pirate to a surgeon, poet, and merchant. His Jewishness appears only in the word *converso* 'converted Jew', which hardly stands out, appearing as it does between "magician, Voodoo and Macumba witch doctor" and "heretic, Huichol shaman, scribe for the Insurgents" (9).

Although Ziller is the author of "The Trial of Francisco Maldonado de Silva," an account of the trial of a Chilean surgeon accused by the Inquisition in 1626 of being Jewish,[8] and although the narrator believes that Maldonado de Silva and Ziller are almost the same, Ziller, the author of the 1791 text, is called a Jesuit by the narrator (159) and an "old Christian" (173) by Santillán. Later the narrator asks, "Doesn't it seem curious that Ziller should choose as a character a Jew who is not completely Jewish, a Christian who is not completely Christian? He's a mestizo. . . . Neither Jew nor Christian, neither white man nor Indian" (191).

On a more autobiographical note, Ziller recalls his childhood in a Jewish colony in Entrerríos (256), and the narrator closes the novel by recognizing the great resemblance between Ziller and his crazy grandfather who marched in the labor demonstrations as Secretary of the Socorro Rojo Internacional (International Red Cross), who escaped unharmed from the sabre thrusts of the mounted police during the Tragic Week (1919), and who grew up in Odessa (the home town of my own maternal grandmother, Esther Abramowitz).

To close out the discussion of Orgambide's novel, I obviously need a fourth question. How is this New Historical Novel different from all the other NHNs discussed in this book? The answer is that it isn't. In addition to its Bakhtinian characteristics of the dialogic, the carnivalesque, intertextuality, parody, and metafiction, *Aventuras de Edmund Ziller* obviously attaches greater importance to the Borgesian philo-

sophical concepts of history than it does to the realistic re-creation of
any particular period. Besides, although it does not have a historical
protagonist, it does have some historical characters with minor roles
whose lives are playfully altered, as in many of the other New Historical
Novels. Even before the publication of Carpentier's *El arpa y la sombra*
(1979) and Abel Posse's *Los perros del Paraíso* (1983), Orgambide included in *Aventuras de Edmund Ziller* (1977) a comic opera entitled
Don Cristóbal staged by Ziller in the theater of Manaus before an au-
dience of rubber barons and their wives. In it, Columbus is portrayed
as the son of Américo Vespucci and any one of several mothers from
Italy, Spain, England, Portugal, and Holland. A love affair between Columbus and Queen Isabel is insinuated in the royal court of Spain. The
historical distortions, however, are far surpassed by the musical distortions. Along with the traditional nineteenth-century arias, Ziller's production includes the *"Danza de los ratoncitos"*—a possible reference
to "Three Blind Mice"—and a cancan. The most ingenious part of this
four-page chapter is that it is narrated as an act-by-act summary in the
discourse of a professional music critic and thus constitutes still another
example of the novel's heteroglossia.

Ziller is also both Jonah and Jesus. The narrator relates how he
saw Ziller on the cross as an actor representing *The Passion* in a street
theater production during Holy Week—a reference to the annual pro-
ductions in Ixtapalapa, a precinct of Mexico City. Ziller, however,
comes to life as the real Jesus, escapes from the cross, goes to India
where one of the saints teaches him humility, and dies at the age of 76
in Rome (257). Earlier in the novel Ziller assumes another reincarnation
of Jesus, as the gaucho Buenaventura (a possible reference to the Colombian revolutionary dramatist Enrique Buenaventura), called *El Nazareno,* who relies on his army of downtrodden Indians, Blacks, mestizos, and mulattoes (50) to avoid being captured or killed by the Capitán
General of Río de la Plata Province. *El Nazareno*'s exploits are sung by
his folkloric *Cantor* 'cantor' or 'singer', while the Capitán General is
accompanied by Jiménez Toledo, a young playwright who claims to
have seen portentous signs in the sky and proceeds to dream a play
about the Capitán General's pursuit of *El Nazareno*.[9]

Regardless of its lack of a coherent plot and of clearly defined and
developed characters, regardless of its including such recent historical
developments as the Chilean military coup of 1973 and the Mexican
Excelsior scandal of 1976, and regardless of the protagonist's ambiguous Jewish identity, *Aventuras de Edmund Ziller* merits greater atten-

tion from the critics. Although I am not suggesting that it deserves to be placed in the same masterpiece category as the New Historical Novels by Vargas Llosa, del Paso, Posse, Piglia, and Fuentes, it does share with them many of the NHN characteristics and is among the earliest of the New Historical Novels, even preceding Carpentier's *El arpa y la sombra*.

A ESTRANHA NAÇÃO DE RAFAEL MENDES

A estranha nação de Rafael Mendes might well have been entitled *Aventuras de Rafael Mendes no Brasil*, but the differences between Orgambide's New Historical Novel and Moacyr Scliar's magic realist historical novel far outweigh the similarities. Both novels share the concept of the "Wandering Jew"; both cover over twenty-five hundred years from the prophet Jonah up to 1975–1976; and both include among their list of characters Jonah, Jesus, Christopher Columbus, and Tiradentes. Nevertheless, *A estranha nação de Rafael Mendes* comes much closer to being a novel than to being a collage or "fragmentary novel" like Orgambide's work; it is more realistic than carnivalesque; and it's much more a Jewish novel than *Aventuras de Edmund Ziller*. Scliar's novel, for all its strangeness, more closely resembles the traditional form of the novel. In fact, the first 67 pages—roughly 25 percent of the novel—and the final 37 pages are set in Porto Alegre, Brazil, in 1975, with a dramatic plot and realistic characters. The protagonist, Rafael Mendes, a nominal Catholic, is a naive partner in a corrupt investment firm headed by the appropriately named Boris Goldbaum (meaning 'gold tree'), who, in addition to being an unscrupulous businessman, is a notorious womanizer. Mendes is primarily concerned about his rebellious Bohemian daughter. However, what starts out as a realistic psychological novel with some social protest takes a strange magic realist twist from the very beginning with the protagonist's nightmares of the mailed fists of the Crusaders, the bonfires of the Inquisition, and the decapitated head of Tiradentes. No matter how assimilated Rafael Mendes may be, his Jewish heritage is lurking in his subconscious.

The bridge between present and past is supplied by the unexpected appearance at Mendes's door of a mysterious box containing historical books, a notebook, and a 1938 photo of him as a baby with his parents. It turns out that the box has been left by Professor Samar-Kand, a genealogist who knew Rafael's father and traced the latter's genealogy back to Jonah. Most of the novel—roughly 60 percent—is devoted to narratives, in chronological order, about Rafael Mendes's ancestors from Jonah to his father, who abandoned his family in 1938 to fight in the Spanish Civil War on the side of the Loyalists, against Francisco Franco. Ironically, the present Rafael Mendes is obsessed with Franco's comatose state in 1975.

The novel ends with an accelerated tempo, suggestive of a movie thriller. Mendes realizes that his daughter is running off with his crooked partner Boris. He makes a mad dash to the airport and arrives in time to prevent them from leaving. Boris and Rafael are arrested on charges of embezzlement. Boris escapes from jail with the aid of a doctor. Franco finally dies. Rafael faces up to his being Jewish and reviews all his ancestors.

In the 164 pages devoted to tracing Rafael Mendes's genealogy, the stories of each of the ten generations of his ancestors (with some chronological gaps), all of whom were named Rafael Mendes, are narrated in a concise, unadorned discourse with a sprinkling of magic realism. Each generation is covered in roughly 7 to 14 pages except for the present Rafael's father, whose story is told in much greater detail—over 55 pages. Prior to the individual stories of the ten Rafael Mendeses, the "First Notebook of the New Christian" narrates the stories of three of their important predecessors: the prophet Jonah, he of the whale; the Essene Habacuc ben Tov[10] at the time of Jesus; and the twelfth-century doctor and philosopher Moses Maimonides.

The wandering of the Jews as well as the dichotomy between the perplexed good Jews and the self-confident, greedy, bad Jews are presented as beginning with Jonah. In fact, the section on Jonah begins with the word *perplexo: "Perplexo, recebeu Jonas do Senhor a missão de profetizar contra a corrupta cidade de Nínive"* 'Perplexed, Jonah received from the Lord the mission to prophesy against the corrupt city of Nineveh' (77). On the one hand, Jonah rejects his father's insinuation that he intervene with God to locate the gold tree and rejects both the hustler and the seductive priestess of Astarté inside the whale's belly. On the other hand, he does not understand why his threatening prophecies to the sinners of Nineveh are not executed by Jehovah. In very simple, everyday language, typical of the novel in general, he explains his decision to abandon his mission: *"Não podemos trabalhar juntos: eu, perplexo e Tu enigmático, isto não vai dar certo. Chega"* 'We can't work together: I, perplexed, and You, enigmatic; this just won't succeed. I've had enough of it' (84). Jonah leaves Nineveh and wanders feverishly in the desert until he angers God by mistakenly identifying a shade tree, put there by God, as the gold tree.

Habacuc ben Tov also starts out as a good Jew. He rejects the quarrels between the Saducees and the Pharisees; he abandons his unfaithful wife in Jerusalem; he does not accept Jesus as the Messiah in spite of seeing him walk on the water; and he goes to live with the Essenes. However, while fleeing with Naomi after killing his rival for her love, he commits the error of asking her if she has brought along the seeds of the gold tree. That puts an end to their idyllic love: "Greed poisoned their lives. Like Adam and Eve after the fruit from the Tree of Knowledge of Good and Evil, they will no longer have any rest" (92). God condemns Habacuc's descendants to wander throughout the world "until the word of the Children of Light is heard" (93)—a different version of the origin of the "Wandering Jew" legend.

Nevertheless, Habacuc and Naomi arrive in Spain and prosper. Their descendants live in Toledo under the Romans, the Visigoths, and the Moors. In the twelfth century, the "Wandering Jew" syndrome reappears with the expulsion of Maimonides and his family by the fanatic Amoadas Arabs. They go to Cairo, where, in the first of many examples of the dualistic pair of Jews (the present-day Rafael Mendes and his partner Boris Goldbaum), Maimonides becomes an altruistic doctor and philosopher while his brother David is obsessed with the jewelry business and the search for the gold tree. Maimonides becomes the court doctor to the Sultan Saladin and satisfies his conscience by treating other imaginary patients. The simple matter-of-fact way in which this strange undertaking is introduced is clearly in the magic realist vein and recalls Fernanda del Carpio's letters to the imaginary doctors in *Cien años de soledad: "Maimonides dedica-se a tratar doentes fictícios"* 'Maimonides devotes himself to treating imaginary patients' (100). Not only does he write his masterpiece *The Guide of the Perplexed* (1190), but also he himself is perplexed over the dilemma of whether to cure Saladin of cholera or let him die because Saladin is planning to sign a treaty with the Crusader Richard, which would be bad for both Muslims and Jews. Ultimately, Maimonides does not have to make a choice because Saladin dies quickly, and Maimonides' descendants return to Spain.

Once the dualistic pattern is established, the scene shifts to Portugal and Brazil. The first Rafael Mendes is so named in honor of Maimonides: Rafael in Hebrew means "doctor of God" (108), while Mendes is a telescoping of Maimonides. The sons are named after the fathers in order to fool the Inquisition authorities in northern Portugal into thinking that they are not Jewish.[11] Before proceeding with the story of the Rafael Mendes family, the narrator summarizes, in a scant half-page, the medieval origins of anti-Semitism:

The Jews aroused envy and fear. They were doctors and poets, as-
tronomers and philosophers; but they were, above all, merchants and
financiers. During the entire Middle Ages, the Jews were the only
commercial intermediaries between the West and the East. . . . In order to purchase this precious merchandise—and more importantly, in
order to wage their frequent wars—the feudal lords needed money.
Since Christians were prohibited from practicing usury, this activity
was reserved for the Jews, who, moreover, were admirably suited for
it; so, if the barons could not pay their debts, all they had to do was
unleash a massacre. (108–109)

Because of the picaresque nature of *Aventuras de Edmund Ziller*
and because of its emphasis on the historical conflicts between the hegemonic forces and an array of marginalized, exploited people—Blacks,
mulattoes, Indians, anarchists, communists, and others—the protagonist's Jewishness is relatively minimized. By contrast, in *A estranha nação de Rafael Mendes,* the main theme of the novel is not the denunciation of the enemies of democracy or socialism; rather, the principal
themes are the strange survival of the Jews, with emphasis on their almost 500-year history in Brazil, and the dual nature of the archetypal
Jew: the money-oriented, unscrupulous businessman, symbolized by the
tree of gold, and the moral, perplexed philosopher who disdains material wealth and sides with the underdog. Scliar, a practicing Jew whose
grandparents migrated to Brazil from Russia, has described his relationship with Judaism as dialectical. In the *Los Angeles Times* review of the
English translation of the novel, he is quoted as saying, "Judaism itself
is dialectical. . . . Within it there is a Marx and a Rothschild, the philosopher Martin Buber and the gangster Meyer Lanski" (2, 9). Although Goldbaum and his materialistic ancestors are portrayed negatively, fortunately for the novel, the two archetypes are not always
presented as neat opposites.

The first Rafael Mendes is a Portuguese cartographer who fails to
participate in Christopher Columbus's first voyage to the New World
because of his father's opposition and because he loses a chess game[12]
with Columbus at La Rábida Monastery. At the time, one fifth of Portugal's population is of Jewish origin and subject to persecution by the
Inquisition. Although the cartographer's son and his friend Afonso
Sanches are imprisoned and tortured, and although succeeding generations of Rafael Mendeses continue to be persecuted by the Inquisition
until 1773, when the Marquês do Pombal abolishes the distinction between New and Old Christians, Scliar's novel dwells less on the Jews'

suffering and more on their strange, miraculous survival. Although the cartographer's grandson is baptized in 1591, he observes the religious practices of Judaism secretly, as do his descendants for the next two centuries and more.[13]

One exception to the persecution is the strange occupation of Pernambuco between 1630 and 1654 by the more tolerant Dutch and the conversion of Recife into "the Jerusalem of the New World, the city where the glories of the Mosaic faith could be proclaimed in a most beautiful synagogue, all decorated in jacaranda and gold" (132). With the Portuguese reconquest of Pernambuco, persecution of the Jews by the Inquisition is resumed. With the advent of the eighteenth-century Enlightenment, a friend of another Rafael Mendes proposes an ingenious solution. He plans to found a *Nova Sião* 'New Zion' on a gigantic airborne wooden platform supported by 120 balloons, to be called *Passarolas* (159)—an intertextual allusion to the highly successful Portuguese novel set in early eighteenth-century Portugal, José Saramago's *Memorial do convento* (1982), translated into English as *Baltasar and Blimunda* (1987).

The New Christians continue to practice their Judaism secretly until the late 1840s, when the ex-companion of Garibaldi in the Farroupilha War marries, has a child, and does not tell him that he is Jewish—but does sing him to sleep with a Ladino lullaby, first mentioned in connection with Maimonides's Spanish descendants: *"Duerme, duerme, mi angelico / Hijico chico de tu nación . . . / Creatura de Sión, / no conoces la dolor"* 'Sleep, sleep, my little angel / Little son of your nation . . . / Creature of Zion, / you do not know pain' (106). The lullaby is passed on from generation to generation, but by the time it reaches the present-day Rafael Mendes's father, he sings it to his son without realizing its significance or its origins. Nevertheless, this man is the doctor who in 1936, like Maimonides, prefers to help the poor Indians in rural Rio Grande do Sul suffering from an epidemic caused by polluted water rather than collaborate with the government of Getúlio Vargas and the wealthy landowners. This is also the man who, thanks to the genealogist, discovers his Jewish roots and abandons his family to fight in the Spanish Civil War although he never gets there because he dies on board the ship, probably from the epidemic.

The strangeness of the Jews' survival in Brazil is further reinforced by their contact with the Brazilian Indians and Blacks. When the cartographer's son and his friend Afonso Sanches first arrive in Brazil in the early sixteenth century, they are captured by Indians who take them to their village, where the chief, in true magic realist style, welcomes them in Hebrew: *"Bruchim habaim,"* literally 'Blessed be those who come' (124). The chief explains that he is descended from one of King Solomon's sons who, in punishment for having rebelled against his father, was set adrift in a rudderless ship with his fellow rebels and their families. They have maintained their Jewishness over 2500 years thanks to the Torah brought from Jerusalem, which has been entrusted to one man in each generation. Four generations later, Rafael Mendes and his friend Alvaro are taken prisoners in the hinterlands of Bahia by a group of Blacks. They are taken to the village, where the chief saves them because he recalls meeting a black Jew in Africa who claimed to be descended from King Solomon and the Queen of Sheba, a reference to the stranger-than-fiction survival of the present-day Ethiopian Jews, the Falashim.

Although the word *nação* in the novel always refers to the Jews, it could also be interpreted as referring to Brazil. The various generations of Rafael Mendeses provide a geographical and historical summary of the country (particularly of its economic history). The cartographer's son and his friend live among the Indians in northern Brazil and plant sugar cane. Rafael Mendes then moves south to Olinda, starts a business, and in 1593 becomes friends with Brazil's first poet, Bentos Teixeira. During the Dutch occupation, a Rafael Mendes becomes a prosperous optician in Recife. The next Rafael Mendes goes to Maranhão, becomes a teacher, and, along with Padre Antonio Vieira, defends the Indians against the abuses of the tobacco and sugar-cane plantation owners. From there it's on to Bahia, Rio, and Minas Gerais for succeeding generations. In the late eighteenth century, a Rafael Mendes almost dies when his dentist friend Tiradentes extracts a molar. After recovering in time to witness Tiradentes's execution, Mendes proceeds to São Paulo, where the Jews have always enjoyed prestige as doctors, pharmacists, and merchants who finance the expeditions to capture and enslave the Indians and search for gold and other precious metals. While looking for the gold tree, Rafael Mendes and his perplexed companion Bentos Seixas come upon what they decry as a useless coffee plantation, "tropical poison" (174). Mendes proceeds south to Rio Grande do Sul where he and his descendants remain, participating in the Guerra das Farroupilhas, working as a railroad engineer for the French Rothschilds in the mid-nineteenth century, and working as a public health official during the Getúlio Vargas government in the 1930s.

The image of the Jewish nation within the Brazilian nation that is projected in the novel may be dualistic, but overall the image is positive for two reasons. First, the good, perplexed Jews are usually the Rafael Mendeses with whom the reader identifies, while the bad gold-tree seekers are the others, even if they are friends of the Mendeses. Second, the magic realist tone of the whole novel reflects an optimistic world view: in spite of the persecutions and the assimilation, the strange nation of Rafael Mendes will continue to survive, if only thanks to a centuries-old Ladino lullaby.

How Different Can You Get? The Inquisition Novels of Homero Aridjis and Angelina Muñiz

Although the Inquisition plays an important role in Orgambide's and Scliar's "Wandering Jew" novels, the importance of its implacable persecution of the Jews is somewhat undermined in both cases by the muralistic focus and carnivalesque tone. In contrast, Homero Aridjis's *1492: Vida y tiempos de Juan Cabezón de Castilla* '1492: The Life and Times of Juan Cabezón of Castile' (1985) and Angelina Muñiz's *Tierra adentro* 'Homeward Bound' (1977) are respectively narrated by a *converso* and a Jew whose entire lives are tightly intertwined with the Inquisition. Aridjis's protagonist recounts, "My grandfather was born in Seville on the sixth day of June in the Year of Our Lord 1391, the same day in which the Archdeacon of Ecija, at the head of the Christian mob, burned the gates of the Jewish quarter, leaving in its wake fire and blood, looting and death" (11); and Muñiz's protagonist begins, "My name is Rafael. I was born in Toledo, one autumn day in 1547. From childhood on my grandfather would seat me at his side and would carefully and with respect take out a Hebrew Bible and would teach me how to read. . . . Years ago the Inquisition had prosecuted him, he had been tortured, and his mind was left unhinged" (10). However, despite their similar beginnings, it would be difficult to find another pair of novels on the same theme that are as different as these two.

1492: VIDA Y TIEMPOS DE JUAN CABEZÓN DE CASTILLA

As the title of the Aridjis novel suggests, the re-creation of the times of Juan Cabezón is of at least equal importance to the narration of his life. Actually, the characterization of Juan Cabezón is subordinated to the interweaving of a broad panoramic tapestry of Spain covering a period of 101 years, from 1391 to 1492, but with greater emphasis on the final 11, between the establishment of the Inquisition in Spain in 1481 and Columbus's departure for the New World, which coincides with the expulsion of the Jews.

Although Juan Cabezón is the only narrator throughout the novel, he serves a double function. He is both alternately and simultaneously the Bildungsroman protagonist and the well-documented, omniscient narrator. His childhood is mediated through *Lazarillo de Tormes,* and his association with the blind *converso* Pero Meñique continues throughout most of the novel, until the latter is killed in Avila for attacking an Inquisition scribe, having mistaken him for the notorious Chief Inquisitor, Torquemada. The most personalized part of Juan Cabezón's life is his love affair, and sexual initiation, with Isabel de la Vega, a *conversa* refugee who, along with her brother, have been burned in effigy in Ciudad Real. Unlike the romances in most of the New Historical Novels, the love affair is not described with exaggerated carnivalesque eroticism. Instead, like the protagonist of André Schwarz-Bart's *Le dernier des justes* 'The Last of the Just' (1959), Ernie Levy, and his girlfriend Golda, Juan Cabezón and Isabel perform their own wedding ceremony in the privacy of their bed as the pursuers' net tightens. Soon thereafter, the pregnant Isabel flees. The entire love episode occupies only 50 pages of the 410-page novel, but as Juan searches for Isabel, it provides the author the opportunity to enlarge his muralistic vision of Spain with detailed descriptions of Zaragoza, Calatayud, Teruel, Toledo, Avila, and Cádiz, where Juan finally catches up with his beloved, but only in time to bid her a final farewell. With their son, she boards the ship of expelled Jews after telling Juan to look for her in Flanders. He indicates that he will, but after seeking his fortune in the New World.

The relative weakness both of the plot and of the characterization of the protagonist is offset by the author's re-creation of fifteenth-century Spain: the reigns of Juan II, Enrique IV, and Ferdinand and Isabella; the geography; the power of the Inquisition; the gallery of prostitutes, beggars, and other lower-class characters lifted from *Lazarillo de Tormes* and other picaresque novels; and above all, the variety of discourses (heteroglossia), including the official announcements of the town criers, the salacious slang of the prostitutes and their friends, the archaic dialect of the Jews and *conversos,* and the legal documents of the Inquisition.

Although *1492* does not qualify as a New Historical Novel, it has been, despite its flaws, one of the more successful of the recent historical novels—not only because of its intrinsic qualities, but also because it has benefited from a series of circumstances which are clearly different from those surrounding the publication of *Tierra adentro.* Whereas the latter was published in 1977, before the historical novel had become the dominant tendency that it is now, *1492* was published in 1985, when some of the key New Historical Novels had already been published and when the critics were beginning to recognize the signifi- cance of the tendency. The title of the Aridjis novel clearly points to the celebration of the Columbus Quincentennial, while the title of Muñiz's novel gives no clue to its time or space. Although both novels were originally printed in the usual limited edition of three thousand copies, *1492* has also benefited from the notoriety given to the follow-up volume, *Memorias del Nuevo Mundo* 'Memoirs of the New World', which traces the adventures of Juan Cabezón on Columbus's voyage of discovery and subsequently as an active participant in the Con- quest of Mexico. *Memorias del Nuevo Mundo* was awarded the Novedades-Diana International Novel Prize for 1988, and Editorial Diana published a second edition of *1492* and distributed it in an attractively illustrated cardboard box together with *Memorias del Nuevo Mundo*. Even before the publication of *1492*, Homero Aridjis (1940) was a well-known poet who was described in the 1967 *Diccion- ario de Escritores Mexicanos* as "one of the young Mexican poets with the most clearly defined personality" (22). In addition to his literary fame, Aridjis achieved national and international political fame by founding the Group of the One Hundred, an ecological organization made up of some of the most important creative artists and intellectuals in the world, including Carlos Fuentes. *1492* was translated into English by Betty Ferber and was published in 1991 by Summit Books. In the July 28, 1991, issue, the *New York Times Book Review* printed a half-page advertisement featuring promotional quotations from news- papers in Paris, Brussels, Madrid, Boston, and New York and, in larger type, a quotation from Carlos Fuentes consecrating Aridjis's work as an epic novel that comes to life with both historical and poetic resonance" (13). The previous month, the same newspaper printed a rave review by Allen Josephs. Josephs does recognize, however, the excessive evocation of late fifteenth-century street names (and family names, I might add) and the failure of Juan Cabezón to become emotionally involved in the sufferings of his beloved Isabel and of the other persecuted Jews and *conversos:*

> If this richly textured novel has any defect, it is the author's relentless desire to re-create late fifteenth-century Spain in all its myriad, hor- rific detail, down to every sight, scent and street name. Yet Mr. Arid- jis's meticulous research and painstaking reconstruction have a deep and resonating appeal for devotees of revisionist history. True to his

epoch, Cabezón usually limits himself to witnessing events, however complex, withholding judgment. (June 16, 1991, p. 11).

Narrator Cabezón's relative detachment from the world he describes may be attributed to Homero Aridjis's own non-Jewish background. Although his father was a Greek who sympathized with his Sephardic friends, Homero's mother was Mexican, and the poet was born and raised in the town of Contepec, Michoacán, where he was unlikely to have been exposed to Jewish culture.

TIERRA ADENTRO

Angelina Muñiz and her novel *Tierra adentro*, in contrast to Aridjis and *1492*, have, until recently, been relatively marginalized. In fact, it would be tempting to say that, as a Spanish Jew who traces her genealogy back to the times of the Inquisition and earlier, Angelina Muñiz has been thrice marginalized: as a Spaniard, as a Jew, and as a woman. Obviously she was not in the mainstream of the Mexican literary world of the 1970s. And yet, a 1984 interview reveals that she was really not that marginalized. Because she arrived in Mexico at the age of five, her schooling was completely Mexican, and she was encouraged to write by her professors in the Escuela Preparatoria and in the Facultad de Filosofía y Letras of the U.N.A.M. She was welcomed into a group of young Spanish exiles that included short story writer José de la Colina, and her own first stories were published in literary journals directed by Mexican critics and writers Huberto Batis, Beatriz Espejo, and Margarita Peña. A more plausible explanation why her novel is not better known is that the subject of the Spanish Inquisition was unlikely to appeal to Mexican readers in 1977, during the post-Tlatelolco decade. Furthermore, President Luis Echeverría, toward the end of his six-year term (1970–1976), in his ill-fated campaign to become United Nations Secretary-General, had cultivated the friendship of other Third World countries to the extent that he even voted with them on the 1975 General Assembly's resolution equating Zionism with racism. This act led to a tourist boycott of Mexico by many American Jews, and a corresponding Mexican reaction of anti-Semitism.

Whatever the reasons, *Tierra adentro* 'Homeward Bound', one of three lyrical historical novels by Angelina Muñiz, may be the least known of all the historical novels analyzed in this book.[14] It also has little in common with the New Historical Novel. The protagonist is not a well-known historical figure, nor do any historical figures appear, even in the background.[15] The only date mentioned in the entire novel is the protagonist's year of birth, 1547, which coincides with that of Cervantes. Although the focus is more on the re-creation of sixteenth-century Spain than on the projection of Borges's philosophical views on history, the absence of specific historical references and the eschewing of the language of the period do allow for an allegorical interpretation to a certain extent. On the other hand, unlike many of the New Historical Novels, *Tierra adentro* does not consciously distort history through outrageous anachronisms; its tone is certainly not carnivalesque; and the usual NHN heteroglossia is replaced by a single narrative voice.

The uniqueness of *Tierra adentro* lies in its apparent simplicity. Unlike the complex, muralistic New Historical Novels and their Boom antecedents, *Tierra adentro* does not require several readings in order to identify and evaluate its structural and stylistic techniques and its archetypal underpinnings. The challenge for the critic, rather, is to identify and evaluate the different aspects of its minimalist approach.

As a lyrical novel, *Tierra adentro* features the narrator/protagonist's thoughts and sentiments in reaction to the events of the outside world. There are no elaborate descriptions of autos-da-fé, and yet Rafael's poignant and at the same time delicate comments on the burning of his own parents at the stake leave a deep impression on the reader:

> Mañana habrá una quema de herejes, y mis padres estarán entre ellos. Ya no importarán el dolor, ni la tortura, ni la sangre. El fuego subiendo al cielo, purificado con las almas de mis padres. Y yo solo. Para siempre solo. Sin que le importe a nadie y nadie me importe a mí. La columna de humo, recta, hacia arriba. Nada vale para mí: tengo el derecho de burlarme de todo, a no creer en nada. Ni Dios, ni rey, ni pueblo. La columna de fuego no camina delante de mí, como lo hizo para Moisés, la columna de fuego se eleva al cielo. (54)

> Tomorrow there will be a burning of heretics, and my parents will be among them. Neither pain, nor torture, nor blood will matter any longer. Fire going up to the sky, purified with my parents' souls. And I alone. Alone forever. Without anyone's caring about me or my caring about anyone. The column of smoke, straight, upward. Nothing has any value for me: I have the right to mock everything, to not believe in anything. Neither God, nor king, nor a people. The column of fire does not proceed in front of me, as it did for Moses, the column of fire goes straight up to the sky.

As in the above quote, the lyric quality of the novel is maintained throughout by the use of the present tense (except in the first six and a half pages); the relatively simple contemporary prose devoid of archaic forms; the brevity of the sentences, which at times even omit verbs; and a gentle rhythm established by a discreet use of repetition and of parallel phrases usually based on two or three component parts. The poetic quality of the prose is enhanced by the unobtrusive insertion of a small number of italicized words in Hebrew taken from prayers, such as *Shemá Israel* 'Hear, oh Israel' (54), *Adonai ejad* 'God is one' (103), and *Lejá dodí* 'Come, my friend' (176). Although Rafael travels throughout Spain, the only identified cities are Toledo and Madrid. The small city with its white-walled houses (probably in Andalusia) where Rafael finds the alchemist is described poetically with the anaphoric repetition of the word *ciudad* 'city' (61–62).

The novel's unique lyric quality culminates in the unusually harmonious ending. The protagonist and his bride Miriam survive the long and dangerous trek to "Eretz Israel" (170); they see *"la ciudad de oro"* 'the city of gold' (i.e., Jerusalem; 172), and they rapidly integrate themselves into the Safed settlement of Spanish Jews. The final words of the novel capture the long-sought tranquility and pay a final tribute to the protagonist's guardian angel, the mysterious muleteer:

> Cada día y cada noche. El ciclo que empieza y el ciclo que acaba. El recuerdo y el olvido. Las palabras que suenan y los sueños del silencio. Las ráfagas y la calma. La lluvia, cuando cae. El viento, cuando sopla.
>
> A lo lejos, contra el horizonte, pasa el arriero con su carreta. Tierra adentro. (177)

> Every day and every night. The cycle that begins and the cycle that ends. Remembering and forgetting. The words that are heard and the silent dreams. Gusts and calm. The rain, when it falls. The wind, when it blows.
>
> In the distance, against the horizon, the muleteer passes with his cart. Homeward bound.

The frequent and somewhat magical appearances and disappearances of the muleteer throughout the novel establish his role as the wise mentor in the archetypal voyage of the hero. The novel starts with Rafael's crossing the threshold, running away from home as he nears his thirteenth birthday because his father, for fear of the Inquisition, refuses to arrange for his bar mitzvah. His maturing experiences include his first sexual experiences with the Muslim Almudena and the Greek Helena, and his intellectual encounters with Rabbi Josef el Cohen and the alchemist. His descent into the underworld is represented by his loss of faith: "What good did it do me to study the Bible with the Rabbi? And alchemy. One madness after another. . . . It's better to sink into the mud. . . . The abyss attracts me and to the abyss I shall go" (84–85). The underworld consists of the society of beggars and thieves, where Rafael is befriended by one old beggar who warns him against the *Santo,* the archetypal false guide who introduces him to the "absolute happiness" (94) of the brothel: sex, drugs, and weird rites. Rafael escapes from the underworld and then, at the point of his rebirth, the muleteer gives him Miriam's letter which convinces him to set out on the long voyage to the Promised Land: "I was holding on to Miriam's letter as a secret cure, I knew that you would be reborn" (105).

Perhaps the most unusual aspect of *Tierra adentro* is the fine blend of three elements: the Jewish fear of persecution, the determination to remain true to both faith and nation—*"un judío español que ama a España y que ama a Sión"* 'a Spanish Jew who loves Spain and who loves Zion' (49–50)—and the possibility of harmonious coexistence with Christians and Muslims. Rafael and Miriam set out for the Holy Land in the company of a procession of nuns and friars without revealing to the latter their Jewish identity. Nonetheless, the sharing of dangerous experiences establishes a bond between them, and the leader of the pilgrimage, Don Alvaro, turns out to be a Spanish nobleman of Jewish descent whose Jewish wife was burned at the stake. Their route takes them across the Pyrenees, through France, and into war-torn Germany. The death, destruction, and pestilence caused by the religious wars between Catholics and Protestants are vividly described, but the absence of specific historical references converts them into a graphic archetypal representation of the horrors of war *"como si fueran un grabado de la muerte"* 'as though they were an engraving of death' (153). The passage through Italy is totally free of danger, full of light and beauty: *"Post tenebras lux"* 'After the darkness, light' (153). The pilgrims cross the Mediterranean without incident, land in North Africa, and proceed eastward, crossing over mountains, through deserts, and past inhospitable towns. Their ranks are decimated by cutlass-wielding Moors. The few who survive take refuge in a monastery on a cliff overlooking the sea. When a ship finally arrives to pick up Don Alvaro, his page, and Rafael and Miriam, a monk waves goodbye and Rafael realizes that he is the muleteer, who earlier in the novel has been characterized as *"de cara cambiante"* 'with a changing face' (58). Once they arrive in Turkey, they narrowly escape being sold as slaves. They continue their journey with a caravan on the road to Damascus—an allusion to Saul's conversion to Christianity—but they never lose sight of their final goal.

Unlike the other three novels discussed in this chapter, or any of the several other historical and partially historical Latin American novels about the experiences of European Jewish immigrants in the late nineteenth century and the first third of the twentieth century,[16] *Tierra adentro* ends happily, and in the Promised Land. The ideological message is that the only way for Jews to achieve happiness is to be true to their religion *and* to their respective nations, without harboring resentment against their enemies. However, what makes this novel worthy of being more widely disseminated is not its message but—as is the case with all works of art—the way the message is expressed.

8 La campaña *by Carlos Fuentes*

Crónica de una guerra denunciada, or Chronicle
of a War Retold

The double subtitle of this chapter is a take-off on García Márquez's
novel *Crónica de una muerte anunciada* 'Chronicle of a Death Foretold'
and reflects the intertextual and carnivalesque nature of Carlos Fuentes's
latest novel, as well as its serious message. Indeed, the complexity of *La
campaña* (1990) belies the simplicity of its title. Its 240 easily read
pages, with widely spaced print, may be analyzed according to at least
six different codes:

1. The *neo-criollista* 'neo-regionalist' novel
2. The archetypal novel
3. The Bakhtinian dialogic and carnivalesque novel
4. The intertextual novel
5. The parody of the popular historical novel
6. The New Historical Novel

Although I could have reduced or expanded the number of codes
necessary to analyze *La campaña*, I have preferred to stay with six in
order to focus on the mathematical product of two times three.[1] Strange
as it may seem, the novel is built on both a binary and a trinary base in
order to reflect its highly flexible and pluralistic ideology. Regardless of
all its farcical ingredients, the novel constitutes a plea to put an end to

the Manichaean struggles that have plagued the Spanish American republics throughout their history: the violent encounters between Spaniards and patriots during the wars of independence; the endless civil
wars between Liberals and Conservatives, mainly in the nineteenth century; and the more recent struggles, from the 1960s on, between revolutionary guerrillas and government troops. Coincidentally, in Fuentes's
collection of lectures given at Harvard, *Valiente mundo nuevo* 'Brave
New World', published almost simultaneously with *La campaña*, he
argues for "the Erasmist tradition,[2] in order to prevent the moderniza-
tion project from becoming a new absolute, a totalitarianism of the Left
or the Right, a religious fanaticism on behalf of the State or private
enterprise, a servile model of one or the other 'great powers', but rather
a relativist fountain, sensitive to the presence of multiple cultures in a
new multipolar world."[3]

As far as the novel itself is concerned, the title refers to the two
campaigns of the fictitious Argentine protagonist Baltasar Bustos: the
1810–1821 campaign for Spanish American independence and the
campaign to win the love of his Dulcinea, the beautiful Ofelia, the Chilean wife of the president of the Río de la Plata Audiencia (High Court).
The binary rhythm is reinforced by his two beloved Chileans, Ofelia
and Gabriela, and by the particularly picturesque *double* execution in
Veracruz of the Virgin of Guadalupe, the patron saint of the Mexican
insurgents—an execution ordered twice by royalist Captain Carlos
Saura[4] of the Fifth Regiment of Grenadiers of the Virgin of Covadonga
(197), which means that the War of Independence, at least in Mexico,
is portrayed as a war between the two national virgins.

> El comandante del fuerte de San Juan de Ulúa volvió a repetir la or-
> den, apunten, fuego, como si un solo fusilamiento de la imagen de la
> virgen independentista no bastase y apenas dos ejecuciones diarias
> mereciese la efigie venerada por los pobres y los alborotadores que la
> portaban en sus escapularios en las banderas de su insurgencia.

> The commander of Fort San Juan de Ulúa repeated the order again,
> aim, fire, as if a single execution of the image of the pro-independence
> virgin were not enough, and as if she deserved at least two executions
> every day for being venerated by the poor and the rabble-rousers
> who bore her image on their scapularies, and on the flags of their
> insurgency.[5]

At the same time, Baltasar belongs to a trio of Argentine friends
who are devoted to the three principles of the French Revolution—
liberty, equality, and fraternity—but who differ from each other accord-

ing to their respective adherence to the principles of the impassioned romantic Rousseau, the cynical rationalist Voltaire, and the flexible Diderot. This trinary structure is reinforced by another trio of friends (Baltasar, Father Francisco Arias, and Lieutenant Juan de Echagüe), who cross the Andes to join San Martín in Mendoza, and by Mexico's three rebel priests: Miguel Hidalgo in Guanajuato, José María Morelos in Michoacán, and the apocryphal Anselmo Quintana in Veracruz— a gambler, womanizer, and cockfight enthusiast whose advisers are lawyers straight out of García Márquez's *Cien años de soledad*. Even in the midst of battle they never remove "their black top hats and funereal frock coats" (211). They urge him to beat Iturbide to the punch by proclaiming himself *"Alteza Serenísima"* 'Most Serene Highness' (210), an obvious allusion to Santa Anna.[6] The binary and trinary rhythms are clearly marked throughout the novel with series of two or three parallel nouns, adjectives, or verbs. In Chapter 1, as a reflection of the three revolutionary principles and the three friends, the trinary rhythm predominates:

> Quiere ser abogado en un régimen que los detesta, acusándolos de fomentar continuos pleitos, odios y rencores. . . . ¡La seducción! ¿Qué es, dónde empieza, dónde acaba? (12) . . . nuestra máxima atracción son los relojes, admirarlos, coleccionarlos y sentirnos por ello dueños del tiempo . . . (13). Ardía la hiedra, ardían las gasas, ardía la recámara (29) . . . van a tener que decidirse entre abrir las puertas al comercio o cerrarlas. . . . Si las cierran, protegerán a todos esos vinicultores, azucareros y textileros de las provincias remotas (30).

> He wants to be a lawyer in a regime that detests them, accusing them of fomenting continuous arguments, hatred, and resentment. . . . The seduction! What is it, where does it start, where does it end? (12) . . . our greatest attraction is clocks, admiring them, collecting them, and therefore considering ourselves masters of time (13). The ivy was burning, the sheets were burning, the bedroom was burning (29) . . . they're going to have to decide between opening the doors to trade or closing them. . . . If they close them, they'll be protecting all those owners of vineyards, sugar plantations, and textile factories in the remote provinces (30).

However, in Chapter 2, as a reflection of the father-son relationship, the rhythm is binary. After the narrator mentions the double founding of Buenos Aires by the two Pedros—by Pedro de Mendoza in 1535 and by Pedro de Garay forty years later—the prose assumes the binary rhythm:

> Estaba una ciudad soñada para el oro y ganada para el comercio. Una ciudad sitiada entre el silencio del vasto océano y el silencio de este mar interior, igualmente vasto, por donde Baltasar Bustos corría al tranco, arrullado por el paso largo y firme de los caballos, soñando, soñándose en medio de este retrato del horizonte que era La Pampa, con la impresión de no avanzar. (38)

> It was a city dreamed up for its gold and conquered for its trade. A city under siege between the silence of the vast ocean and the silence of this interior sea, equally vast, through which Baltasar Bustos was loping along, lulled by the horses' long, firm strides, dreaming, dreaming of himself in the midst of this picture of the horizon that was the pampas, with the impression of standing still. (38)

In Chapter 6, as a possible reflection of the number six, the binary and trinary rhythms are fused in the description of San Martín's campaign to cross the Andes:

> ... una empresa que en Buenos Aires era comparada a las de Aníbal, César o Napoleón: ahí van, desde la capital porteña, los despachos de los oficiales, los vestuarios y las camisas. Van dos mil sables de repuesto y doscientas tiendas de campaña. Van, en un cajoncito, los dos únicos clarines que se han encontrado. Y basta ya, escribió Pueyrredón: "Va el Mundo. Va el Demonio. Va la Carne." (155)

> .... a feat that in Buenos Aires was being compared to those of Hannibal, Caesar, or Napoleon: there they go, from the port capital, the officers' dispatches, the uniforms, and the shirts. Two thousand replacement sabres and two hundred military tents. In a small box, the only two bugles that could be found. And that's it, wrote Pueyrredón: "There goes the World. There goes the Devil. There goes the Flesh."

Furthermore, the majority of the nine chapters are subdivided into two, three, or six numbered sections, in order to make the reading easier; Baltasar has a total of six archetypal mentors; and the number of independent rebel leaders in Alto Perú is six.[7] After this numerological introduction, we are ready for the analysis of the novel according to our six codes.

1. The *Neo-criollista* Novel

In 1969, in *La nueva novela hispanoamericana,* Carlos Fuentes euphorically proclaimed the superiority of the novels of Alejo Carpentier, Julio Cortázar, Gabriel García Márquez, and Mario Vargas Llosa—and implicitly his own—over the "geographical" novels, not only of the

1915–1945 *criollistas*,[8] but of all the previous Spanish American novelists. In this respect, he was echoing Vargas Llosa's 1967 declaration in Caracas that the decade of the 1960s was the dividing line between the primitive novel and the creative novel:

> "The jungle swallowed them up!" says the final sentence of *La vorágine* by José Eustasio Rivera. The exclamation is something more than the tombstone of Arturo Cova and his companions; it could be the commentary on a long century of Latin American novels: the mountains swallowed them up, the pampas swallowed them up, the mines swallowed them up, the rivers swallowed them up. Closer to geography than to literature, the Spanish American novel had been written by men who seemed to assume the tradition of the great explorers of the sixteenth century. (9)

In 1990, a repentant Carlos Fuentes modified his previous excessive contempt for the *criollista* novel by reevaluating Rómulo Gallegos's *Canaima* in *Valiente mundo nuevo* and by incorporating elements of the *criollista* novel in *La campaña*. Like so many *criollista* novels, *La campaña* is replete with geographical, historical, ethnic, and regional linguistic elements. Divided into nine titled chapters, the novel moves over a large portion of Spanish America from Buenos Aires to Orizaba, Mexico, with stops on the Argentine pampa, the high plateaus of colonial Alto Perú (today's Bolivia), Lima (Peru), Santiago (Chile), Mendoza (Argentina), and Maracaibo and Mérida (Venezuela). Perhaps parodying the *criollista* novels,[9] Fuentes includes some of the more picturesque names from the different regions of Spanish America: from Argentina's *Jujuy* and Alto Perú's *Cochabamba* and the *Sipe-Sipe* River to Mexico's *Xoxotitlán,* the *Chachalacas* River and the Peak of *Citlaltépetl.* The tragicomic aspect of Spanish American history is exemplified by Bolívar's defeat at the battle of *Semen* and José Antonio Páez's defeat at the battle of *Cojedes* (*coger* is the most common equivalent in Spanish for 'to fuck'): "these funny words" (174), as the narrator observes. These geographical names are complemented by a moderate use of regional vocabulary: the Argentine *pago* 'region', *pingo* 'horse', and *pibe* 'kid'; the Chilean *damasco* 'peach'; the Venezuelan *lechosa* 'papaya'; and the Mexican *tejocote* 'a cherry-like fruit'. Unlike the *criollistas,* however, Fuentes does not include phonetic transcriptions of the local dialect.

Fuentes's approach to history in *La campaña* is more complex. On the one hand, he follows the chronicler's technique of recording the political events in Buenos Aires year by year from May 1810 to 1821— that is, from the government of Mariano Moreno to that of Bernadino

Rivadavia. This chronological approach is symbolized by the leitmotif of the clocks, as quoted earlier: "The clocks in the squares are striking on these eventful days in May and we three friends confess that our greatest attraction are clocks: admiring them, collecting them, and therefore considering ourselves masters of time."[10] In contrast with this precise, linear, Newtonian chronology, the novel probes more vaguely into the past and the future,[11] with only general references to the Conquest of Mexico by Cortés; the two distinct foundings of the city of Buenos Aires; the reforms introduced by King Carlos III in the mid-eighteenth century; and the predictions of anarchy in the postindependence era, which may be extended in the novel to include the present of the 1990s.

Like a typical *criollista* novel, *La campaña* also captures Spanish America's ethnic panorama: the whites and blacks of Buenos Aires, the Indians of Alto Perú, the blacks of Maracaibo, and a variety of mestizos. However, Fuentes not only represents and describes the different groups, but also foregrounds the struggle for racial equality as one of the constant goals of the wars of independence: " . . . The creole military officers promised to protect the interests of the upper classes and to prevent the accursed races, Indians, Negroes, *zambos,* mulattoes, *cambujos,* quadroons, and *tentenelaires*[12] from taking over the government" (196), whereas the Veracruz priest Anselmo Quintana is proud of the law that he sponsors in the Congress of Córdoba "which says that from now on there will no longer be Negroes or Indians or Spaniards, but only Mexicans" (208).

The *neo-criollista* code of *La campaña* goes beyond the geographical, historical, ethnic, and linguistic continental mural; Fuentes also deals dialogically with the most frequent theme of the *criollista* novels, the civilization/barbarism dichotomy. The encounter between Baltasar Bustos, the enlightened citizen of Buenos Aires, and his rancher father refers intertextually to Benito Lynch's *Los caranchos de la Florida* 'The Buzzards of La Florida' (1916). However, in contrast to the rancher in the Lynch novel, the rancher in Fuentes' novel, in spite of living among the gauchos, does not represent barbarism. His pleasant, even-tempered, Solomonic personality with his patriarchal flexibility (44) and his "extraordinary sixth sense"[13] stand in sharp contrast to the revolutionary fervor of his urban son. In addition to raising cattle, he has absorbed some of the progressive ideas of the eighteenth century, and several years earlier initiated "a small textile and metal industry" (46). He may even be more flexible than his son: "If his son had to be implacable in the city, the father perhaps[14] had to be flexible in the country" (44).

The father's predilection for evolution rather than revolution makes him, in Fuentes's eyes, less barbaric than his impassioned son. With a dramatic symbolism reminiscent of Rómulo Gallegos, Fuentes has the father tell Baltasar that, if he finds him dead "holding a candle in his hand" (37), it will mean that he has died accepting Baltasar's revolutionary ideas. On the other hand, if Baltasar finds him "with his hands crossed on his chest and intertwined with a scapulary" (37), it will indicate that he died clinging to his own evolutionary ideal, of "a confederation of Spain and its colonies, sovereign but united" (61). In keeping with the dialogic ideology of *La campaña*—it's impossible to maintain the six codes totally separate from each other—Baltasar, after fighting on the side of the original *montoneros* 'guerrillas', returns to find his father's corpse "with his hands folded, his fingers entwined in a scapulary, and a candle erect like a black phallus" (110).

Since *La campaña* is Carlos Fuentes's first novel with an all-encompassing Spanish American vision, the obvious question that arises is what prompted it. The probable answer lies in the author's reservations about the Free Trade Treaty between Mexico, the United States, and Canada which is currently being strongly promoted by Presidents Carlos Salinas de Gortari and George Bush. Writing in the Winter 1991 issue of *New Perspectives Quarterly*, Fuentes argues in favor of a Spanish American federalism—based on a cultural continuity of five hundred years (16)—that would start with Mexico and extend southward to Chile and Argentina (17), excluding the United States. In other words, while he was writing *La campaña*, Fuentes was also re-creating Bolívar's dream of a united Spanish America. At the same time, Fuentes was writing the script and narrating a series of five television documentaries under the title "The Buried Mirror" that interweave pre-Columbian, Spanish, and Spanish American culture.[15]

2. The Archetypal Novel

A second way of analyzing *La campaña* is through the archetypal codes of the adventure of the hero and the negative image of the Great Mother, both of which Fuentes subverts somewhat in keeping with the ideological posture of the novel.[16] Although Baltasar and his father disagree ideologically, they—unlike the characters in the *criollista* novels—do not allow their political differences to affect their personal relations adversely. Nonetheless, in order for Baltasar to reach maturity, he must strike out on his own, severing the ties with his father as well as with his two Buenos Aires friends—a double crossing of the threshold, in the terms of Joseph Campbell's *The Hero with a Thousand Faces* (1949). Wandering alone over the entire continent and as far north as Mexico, Baltasar meets up with six archetypal mentors (an unusually large number)—from his childhood tutor, ex-Jesuit Julián Ríos, to the Mexican priest Anselmo Quintana—who help him, not only to experience certain ritual passages such as his sexual initiation and the test of physical bravery, but also to clarify and refine his political and philosophical ideas.

First, he meets the historical rebel priest Ildefonso de las Muñecas, one of the *caudillos* of the *republiquetas* 'small republics' of Alto Perú, who calls Baltasar *"pucelo"* (76), the masculine equivalent of the term "maiden" often associated with Joan of Arc. He facilitates Baltasar's sexual initiation by introducing him to one of the old Indian virgins of Lake Titicaca.

Next, the famous Simón Rodríguez, Bolívar's ex-mentor, serves as his guide in the archetypal descent into the underworld. After passing through a trapdoor in the basement of the local government building, they wind their way along a narrow mountain path that provides them with views of varying terrains, of flamingo eggs sprinkled over a lake, and of a herd of spitting llamas. After a hailstorm scatters the birds and the animals, they find themselves inside a dark cavern where there suddenly appears a vision of an entire city bathed in light, which is both the vision of El Dorado, the Indian city of gold, and the vision of the future. In that magic light, clearly linked to the French Enlightenment (the inspiration for the wars of independence) and possibly to Jerusalem, Baltasar begins to have doubts about his love for Ofelia and his faith in both Rousseau and reason: " . . . Union with nature is not necessarily the recipe for happiness; do not return to the beginning, do not search for an impossible harmony, appreciate all the differences that you may find. . . . Do not believe that we were happy at the beginning. Don't let it occur to you either that we'll be happy at the end" (90).

In the following months, Baltasar passes the archetypal test of manliness by participating in all the guerrilla activities of another historical *caudillo,* Miguel Lanza. Baltasar Bustos becomes Lanza's younger brother, substituting for the two real brothers who have died in the struggle for independence. Lanza's older brother was hanged in La Paz's main square in a preview of the 1946 lamppost upside-down hanging of deposed president Gualberto Villarroel, while the younger brother died in an archetypal grueling, hand-to-hand, single combat with a Spanish captain, which is reminiscent of the Arturo Cova–Narciso Barrera combat in *La vorágine* as well as of the fatal Galileo Gall–Rufino combat in Vargas Llosa's *La guerra del fin del mundo*.

After experiencing firsthand the violence of guerrilla warfare on the side of the *montoneros,* the enlightened Buenos Aires citizen begins to question his revolutionary passion—"have we made a mistake? was my father right? could we have avoided this bloodshed through compromise, patience, tenacity?" (107)—questions that imply the denunciation of the wars of independence. Fuentes may actually be wondering whether Spanish America would have been better off today if it had not severed its ties with Spain.

In spite of Baltasar's increasing maturity and in spite of his father's death, he still has three more encounters with archetypal mentors. In Lima, he meets his old Jesuit tutor, Julián Ríos, who continues to guide him. In keeping with the novel's defense of Spanish culture, Ríos asks, "Would the South American patriots understand that without that [colonial] past, they would never be what they longed to be: paradigms of modernity?" (134).

In Venezuela, Baltasar encounters the fifth mentor, an old mulatto general who lives in the future. He knows that Bolívar will die alone and that San Martín will be forced into exile. His stories go beyond the immediate future, projecting a pessimistic vision of nineteenth- and perhaps twentieth-century Spanish America, with a reference that is at least partially specific to Mexico:

> Each time he would tell more stories of unknown events, wars against the French and the Yankees, military coups, torture, exile, an unending story of failures and of unfulfilled dreams, everything put off, everything frustrated, pure hopes, nothing is ever completed, and perhaps it is better that way because here, when everything comes to an end, it's usually a bad end. . . . (184).

The last of the six archetypal mentors is the apocryphal Mexican priest Anselmo Quintana. Within an epiphanic[17] setting, Father Anselmo confesses on a Thursday to Baltasar, whom he identifies with Jesus because "in Maracaibo he cared for the fallen woman and the wounded enemy" (215). This identification strengthens the linkage between the protagonist and his New Testament namesake, one of the Three Wise Men: the black Baltasar. Father Anselmo affirms his faith in God, rejects Descartes' absolute rationalism,[18] and strongly recommends to Baltasar both complexity and faithfulness to his cultural heritage, with certain overtones of José Vasconcelos's *La raza cósmica* 'The Cosmic Race' (1925):

> Do not deliver your allegiance to any ruler, to any secular government, to any philosophy, to any military or economic power without your conditions, your reservations, your qualifications, your wild imagination capable of deforming every truth under the sun. . . .
> What I'm asking of you, my son, is that we not sacrifice anything, not the magic of the Indians, nor the theology of the Christians, nor the reason of our contemporary Europeans; let us rather join together every last bit of what we are in order to continue being and ultimately to be something better. (223–224)

With this advice, Baltasar completes his archetypal voyage, returns to his point of departure, and begins to act because, as he tells his two Buenos Aires friends, "there is still a big distance between the years I have lived and those remaining. I am telling you in advance. I am not going to live them in peace. Neither I, nor Argentina, nor the whole American continent . . ." (239). In other words, in spite of his maturity, Baltasar has not lost his enthusiasm, and if he should lose it, as Marcos Vargas does in Gallegos's *Canaima,* the archetypal cycle will begin again with his adopted son. In dialogic contrast with Baltasar's enthusiasm, this son never stops playing "blindman's buff, alone, with his eyes covered" (240), a leitmotif that may symbolize a negative vision of Spanish American history.

Whereas the male protagonist in *La campaña* evolves through the archetypal voyage of the hero, the female characters are often associated with the anthropophagus Terrible Mother,[19] in the tradition of Circe and the *criollista* Zoraida Ayram (from José Eustasio Rivera's *La vorágine*) and Doña Bárbara (from Rómulo Gallegos's novel of the same name). While crossing the pampas, the still virgin Baltasar, devotee of Rousseau, would like to consummate his spiritual marriage with the great, fertile Argentine plains, the positive image of the archetypal Great Mother, but the presence of the chattering merchants in the stagecoach prevent him from doing so (40). However, once he arrives at his father's ranch, he is besieged by a negative vision of his idealized Ofelia, who is equated with the unproductive, "impenetrable" (50) Andes. In the vision, naked, she offers her back to him "and then the woman turned around and did not give him her dreamed-of sex but rather her feared face: she was a Gorgon, she accused him with eyes as white as marble, she converted him into a stone of injustice, she hated him . . ." (50). He encounters a similar hatred in the eyes of his father's gauchos—"other Medusas" (50)—who resent his urban manners. The negative aspect of Ofelia is reaffirmed by her gift to her husband: a walking cane with a marble handle in the form of Medusa's bust, featuring "her fixed and terrifying look and her hard breasts . . . the old nipples of the atrocious mythological figure" (118). When Ofelia uses her sex to kill both insurgent and royalist officers, she is equated with the one-breasted Amazons and their queen Penthesilea (175, 179).

On the other hand, in keeping with the dialogic nature of *La campaña*, Fuentes gives a positive portrayal of Baltasar's sister and mother, perhaps consciously in reply to those critics who have accused him of representing women in a negative, ambiguous, and wrong way.[20] Although Baltasar does not receive any affection from his embittered sister, "who was born a spinster, a frustrated nun . . ." (45), Fuentes seems to justify her attitude. She resents Baltasar for his revolutionary ideas, which have deprived her and her father of their refuge: "the colonial regime . . . the crown . . . the church" (45). Fuentes also indicates his understanding of her envy of her brother's freedom—"Oh, how I too would love to go far away" (54)—by giving her the name Sabina, evoking the Roman rape of the Sabine women. Sabina also strikes a blow for feminism by denouncing her father's engendering many illegitimate children and telling him that she only hopes that at least one of them is the fruit of her mother's marital infidelity (66).[21] When her father responds calmly and tells her that she seems *"hechizada"* 'bewitched'(66), her reply is also in keeping with the post-1970 feminist era: "—That's right, father. The world has bewitched me" (66). With the death of her father, Sabina becomes the owner of the ranch, faced with the dilemma of dying in solitude or mating with the barbarous gauchos (114). Her role as a rural Argentine woman is hardly an improvement over that of her nearsighted mother, whom Fuentes has earlier equated with the archetypal ant and spider:

> Bent over and blind, José Antonio Bustos's wife stopped speaking to other human beings, who stood up straight in the distance, in order to maintain long monologues only with the ants on her more lucid days, and on her fantasy-filled days, with the spiders, who approached her, swinging in front of her staring eyes, tempting her, making her laugh with their silvery ascents and descents, forcing her to imagine things, to invent stories, wishing at times that she were entangled in those damp, sticky threads until she became a prisoner

in the center of a web as perfectly woven as the textiles which, in her husband's workshops, were transformed into the ponchos and the skirts and the gaucho dress. (46)

Since archetypal models are based on the philosophy that all human beings in all periods of time and in all geographical settings are basically similar, they are at odds with the philosophy projected in *La campaña*: the rejection of absolutes, the plea for flexibility, and the importance of changing circumstances—all of which are related to our third code.

3. The Dialogic, Carnivalesque, Bakhtinian Novel

Exemplifying the symbiotic relationship between novelistic praxis and literary theory, the recent proliferation of dialogic and carnivalesque novels coincides with the delayed but enthusiastic recognition accorded to the theories of Mikhail Bakhtin. Since Fuentes has called him "perhaps the greatest theorist of the novel in our century" ("Defend Fiction," 11), it is not at all surprising that dialogic and carnivalesque elements should abound in *La campaña*.

On the theoretical level, Baltasar rejects his earlier faith in reason, in progress, and in ultimate human happiness by recalling his revelation experienced with Simón Rodríguez in the land of El Dorado,

> where light was necessary because everything was so dark and therefore they could see with their eyes closed and they could develop their dreams at the thresholds of their eyelids notifying him, Baltasar Bustos, that for every reasonable act there is an unreasonable act without which reason would stop being reasonable: a dream that both denies and affirms reason simultaneously. That for each law there is an exception which makes it partial and tolerable. (217)

In his physical and mental traits as well as in his philosophy, Baltasar embodies the dialogic. Although he is usually referred to as being fat, he loses many pounds while fighting at the side of guerrilla chief Miguel Lanza (137), regains them while in Lima and Santiago de Chile—"hopelessly blind but fat by choice, relinquishing his hard, lean physique earned in the Inquisivi campaign with a diet of sweet cakes, custards, candied egg yolks and *polvorones*,[22] obeying the order to return to his natural nature, fat and gentle, losing the pride of his slender virility" (156)—loses them again during the crossing of the Andes with San Martín (173), and will undoubtedly regain them in the future.

Since most of the novel deals with Baltasar's archetypal apprenticeship, he is generally portrayed as being naive, but in his search for his sixth and last mentor, Anselmo Quintana, he proves his cleverness. Baltasar identifies Quintana by noticing that he is the only one in the military camp who hesitates in making a choice between two bottles of wine and also the only one without a hat, since his white hood would have given him away (206). Baltasar's reading material is also dialogic: the romantic Rousseau who "asked us to give in to our passions in order to regain our souls, and the early Church father San Crisóstomo who condemned ideal love that was never consummated because it led to inflamed passions" (20).

The conversion of Baltasar into a dialogic character is heralded by his repeated admiration for people unlike himself: "—My danger is that I admire everything that I am not" (97); "—I admire everything that I am not, you know. Force, realism, cruelty" (100). On his father's ranch, he is fascinated by his "atrocious twin . . . a dirty Baltasar, bearded, hungry, although bloated like a dead cow" (51). While fighting alongside Miguel Lanza in Alto Perú, Baltasar meets another "twin," his namesake, Lanza's Indian assistant, whose family name Cárdenas links the *porteño* to Mexico. A dark-skinned Indian, Baltasar Cárdenas is also referred to as *negro* (97). Although Baltasar Bustos has earlier preached to the Indians about the ideals of the independence movement, in his first mortal combat against the enemy he realizes that he is killing his royalist Indian foe, not for being a royalist, but for being an Indian: "for being weak, poor, different . . ." (108).

Baltasar later asks his father's corpse, "Can we simultaneously be everything that we have been and everything that we want to be?" (113). Fuentes's ultimate reply is clearly positive, as he describes Baltasar's double personality in the latter's final reencounter with Ofelia and her son: " . . . Baltasar, suspended physically between his two personalities; the fat and nearsighted youth and the slender and long-haired combatant; the frivolous Bohemian of the Buenos Aires balconies and the participant in the Alto Perú guerrilla campaigns; the frequenter of the Lima salons and the frequenter of the feverish Maracaibo brothels . . ." (227).

Baltasar's two Enlightenment friends, Dorrego and the narrator Varela, are also presented dialogically. Staunch proponents of Argentine independence, they are first presented in a very positive light. However, their adherence to Unitarian ideals is somewhat marred by their constant accommodation to political change (actually subverting the novel's advocacy of flexibility) and by their decision to remain in Buenos Aires while Baltasar risks his life fighting against the Spaniards:

Varela y Dorrego, playing with our clocks in Buenos Aires, adjusting them as we adjusted our political lives, accommodating ourselves to Alvear's leadership when Posadas resigned, without daring to pose the question, what are we doing here while our younger brother Baltasar Bustos, the weakest of the three, the most physically awkward, the most intellectual also, is risking his life in the mountains fighting against the Spaniards? (124)

By the final chapter of the novel, Dorrego and Varela have, perhaps, lost their revolutionary credibility: "We soon became disillusioned with revolutionary politics and returned to our inherited habits: he, a land-owner; I, a printer. . . . But now, Rivadavia was rekindling our hopes . . ." (235).

Still another example of Bakhtin's concept of the dialogic, fused in this case with the carnivalesque, is the characterization of Ofelia, as exemplified in the ambivalent meaning of her name. Fuentes seems to have selected *Ofelia* for two reasons. In the first place, it immediately evokes Shakespeare's *Hamlet,* a work that is synonymous with the theme of indecision, which is totally in keeping with the ideological message of *La campaña*: beware of absolute ideals. On the other hand, although the etymology of *Ofelia* could be from either the Greek word for 'serpent' or the Latin word for 'sheep',[23] Fuentes prefers to give it the meaning of 'fidelity'. On a superficial plane, Ofelia is unfaithful to her husband, who is appropriately named the Marqués de Cabra; "*cabra,*" meaning 'goat,' is the symbol for a cuckold known all over the Spanish-speaking world.

On a more complex plane, Shakespeare's "sweet Ofelia" (122) wears her hair "guillotine style" (21) and sports a red ribbon around her neck, indicating perhaps her revolutionary sympathies. However, Ofelia is transformed into the Biblical Judith when rumor has it that she has killed insurgent Colonel Martín Echagüe "while they were mak-ing love" (147). They say that she is responsible for the death of other revolutionary officers, but also of a royalist general (179). In keeping with Bakhtin's theory of the dialogic and with Borges's idea that it is impossible to discover the true reality, the Orizaba priest Father An-selmo Quintana assures Baltasar that Ofelia "has been the most faithful secret agent of the revolutionary war for independence in America" (228) and that she has used a chain of songs to maintain contact be-tween him, Bolívar, and San Martín. When Baltasar returns to Buenos Aires, he questions Father Quintana's statement, but narrator Varela, the Diderot devotee, assures the reader that Father Anselmo is absolutely right because Ofelia would pass on to him useful information "for the cause" (239) night after night while they made love—which is to say that the narrator himself was betraying his "younger brother" by allowing him to fall platonically in love with an adulteress.

The betrayal theme is also an integral part of the political campaign: Baltasar betrays the guerrilla leader Miguel Lanza by violating his pledge to fight alongside him to the bitter end; Bolívar and San Martín are both betrayed (183); and, according to Father Anselmo, "in this New Spain, there is no more certain solution than betrayal. Cortés betrayed Montezuma, the Tlaxcalans betrayed the Aztecs, Ordaz and Alvarado betrayed Cortés . . ." (211). Of course, Fuentes had previously used the betrayal theme to portray Mexican history, particularly in *La muerte de Artemio Cruz*.

As for the carnivalesque, many of the examples come under the next code, intertextuality. However, it is appropriate to point out that this element is particularly featured in Chapter 7, which takes place in the tropical port of Maracaibo. Nonetheless, in keeping with the dialogic, the carnivalesque coexists in this chapter with the grim representation of the destruction wreaked by the war,[24] with overtones of Arturo Uslar Pietri's *Las lanzas coloradas* and Erich Maria Remarque's *All Quiet on the Western Front* (1929).

4. The Intertextual Novel

Since the 1960s, the Boom writers have either joined together or competed with one another in cultivating certain types of novels. For example, in the August 1967 Caracas conference that consecrated the Boom, it was widely announced that several of the writers, including Carlos Fuentes, were collaborating in the composition of one novel about the archetypal Latin American dictator. The project was never carried out, but it may well have contributed to the engendering of such outstanding works as Roa Bastos's *Yo el Supremo* (1974), Carpentier's *El recurso del método* (1974), and García Márquez's *El otoño del patriarca* (1975). A few years later, Fuentes, García Márquez, and Vargas Llosa each published a somewhat parodic thriller or detective story: respectively, *La cabeza de la hidra* 'Hydra Head' (1978), *Crónica de una muerte anunciada* 'Chronicle of a Death Foretold' (1981), and *¿Quién mató a Palomino Molero?* 'Who Killed Palomino Molero?' (1986). Most recently, the same three authors have published historical novels: Vargas Llosa, *La guerra del fin del mundo* (1981); García Márquez, *El general en su laberinto* (1989); and Fuentes, *La campaña* (1990).

Although all three novels are very different from one another, the linkage between *La campaña* and *El general en su laberinto* is quite clear. In the last chapter of *La campaña*, Varela, the Buenos Aires narrator, asserts that he has in his hands "a life of the liberator Simón Bolívar, whose manuscript, spotted by the rain and tied with tricolor ribbons, was sent to me from Barranquilla, as best he could, by an author named Aureliano García" (234). In some ways, *La campaña* might be considered the counterpart of *El general en su laberinto*. In contrast to "the melancholy image of a Bolívar sick and defeated like his dream of Spanish American unity and civil liberty in our nations" (234), *La campaña* is much more panoramic, or muralistic, and puts the spotlight on José de San Martín as the model liberator. Energetic, pragmatic, a good strategist, and a man of great personal integrity, San Martín organizes the Army of the Andes, and only after winning the War of Independence will he proclaim "the ideals of the Enlightenment" (159), in order not to scare off the wealthy *criollos*. He insists that "in order to achieve justice, theories and individuals are not enough; what is needed is to create permanent institutions" (159). He also warns against the danger of militarism: "if we triumph, we will have actually been defeated if we turn over power to the strong man, to the military leader blessed with good fortune" (160).

In addition to the interplay with *El general en su laberinto*, the last chapter of *La campaña* interacts with Aureliano Babilonia's deciphering of Melquíades's manuscript in the last chapter of *Cien años de soledad*. According to Fuentes's narrator, "Baltasar knew that another chronicle of those years—the one I am holding in my hands at this moment and some day, you, reader, will too—had been written by himself with his continual letters to 'Dorrego and Varela,' which was beginning to make us sound like a trade name" (234). Baltasar's letters also falsely identify *La campaña* as an epistolary novel, establishing still another tie to Rousseau, as the author of the epistolary *La nouvelle Héloise*, "the biggest best-seller in the history of Spanish America" (234). When Baltasar asks the old man in the Venezuelan Andes where the war is being fought, the reply "What war? What are you talking about?" (181) recalls the episode in *Cien años de soledad* when nobody believes José Arcadio Segundo's story about the massacre of the three thousand banana workers. Similarly, no one in the village has ever heard of Bolívar, Páez, or Sucre. Fuentes, however, goes one step beyond García Márquez and converts the scene into a musical comedy burlesque (reminiscent of Leonard Bernstein's "What a day, what a day, for an auto-da-fé" in *Candide*) when the group of children surround Baltasar and sing in chorus, *"What war, what war?"* (181).

Not only is *La campaña* linked to García Márquez, but also the entire novel could be analyzed with an intertextuality code extending from medieval Spanish literature up through the Latin American New Historical Novel. Combining the Arcipreste de Hita's *"De las propiedades que las dueñas chicas han"* 'On the attractions that petite women have' from *El libro de buen amor* (ca. 1343) with the trysting scene from the anonymous *La Celestina* (1500), Fuentes describes with a thinly disguised smile Baltasar's rendezvous, not with his exalted and beloved Ofelia, but with another equally beautiful Chilean, the actress Gabriela Cóo: "One afternoon they met, our Younger Brother and the Diminutive Damsel, without making an appointment, they just met. He jumped over the wall at the exact moment that she was opening the gate that separated the two properties" (153). Baltasar has fallen in love with her while observing her rehearse her role in Rousseau's short tragedy *The Discovery of America.*

In view of Fuentes's well-known admiration for Cervantes, the latter's presence is hardly unexpected in a novel that stresses the continuity of Spanish America's cultural heritage. Baltasar, because of his rash decisiveness and his voracious reading of the eighteenth-century *philosophes,* is called "the Quijote of the Enlightenment" (26). He later views the arrival on mule of the rebel priest Ildefonso de las Muñecas as a "Cervantesque apparition" (76). Guerrilla leader Miguel Lanza's decision to fight to the death earns him the title of *"héroe numantino"* (107), from Cervantes's play about the Romans' siege of Numancia. What is even more ingenious is the intertextual fusion between *Don Quijote* and a recent novel by the Puerto Rican Luis Rafael Sánchez, *La importancia de llamarse Daniel Santos* 'The Importance of Being Named Daniel Santos' (1989). Just as Don Quijote and Sancho Panza are surprised to discover in the second part of the novel that their earlier adventures have already been recorded and published, Baltasar is surprised, as he draws near to the Caribbean, to hear his search for Ofelia set to music in a variety of rhythms—the *cumbia* in Buenaventura, the *tamborito* in Panamá, the *merengue,* the *zamba,* the Peruvian *valsecito, cueca,* and *vidalita* (172–173, 177), and the Mexican *corrido* (216)—suggesting a linkage to the Luis Rafael Sánchez novel, in which the protagonist is a well-traveled popular singer.

As a reply to the celebration of his heroic deeds in song, Baltasar exclaims four times, referring to himself with a tone of contempt, "Some hero . . . fat, long-haired, and near-sighted" (172). In other words, he is a most unlikely hero—unlikely as a romantic hero and unlikely as a revolutionary hero. His nearsightedness never abandons him. From the first to the last chapter, he is characterized as nearsighted or blind and as using eyeglasses—with the latter indicated by the three different words preferred respectively in Mexico, the Caribbean, and Spain: *anteojos, espejuelos,* and *gafas.* When he throws his glasses into the Guayas River in Guayaquil, Ecuador, the reader cannot help but identify him with Vargas Llosa's nearsighted but thin newspaperman in *La guerra del fin del mundo.*[25]

In an intertextual reading of a New Historical Novel, Jorge Luis Borges could hardly be missing. At one point Baltasar marvels at how the details of his daily life, such as washing down a snack of mountain cheese and Andean bread with pineapple rum (180), have been predestined by popular songs. This observation leads to a rather clear allusion to Borges's "Tema del traidor y del héroe," in which literary works prefigure historical events:

> He thought, as he chewed, of Homer, the Cid, and Shakespeare; their epic dramas were already written before they were lived: Achilles and Ximena, Helen and the hunchback Richard were really only carrying out the poet's stage directions, acting out what was already written. The inversion of the image was called "history": the credulous faith that the action took place first and then was put into words. It was the illusion, but he no longer let himself be deceived. (181)

A variety of other contemporaries of Fuentes are also present in *La campaña.*[26] The rather unusual phrase *"al filo del sol"* 'at the edge of the sun' (180) is a playful recognition of Mexico's first important modern novel, Agustín Yáñez's *Al filo del agua* 'The Edge of the Storm'. Similarly, a willingness to reconsider his earlier harsh judgment of the *criollista* novels may be reflected in Fuentes's description of Miguel Lanza as *"el cabecilla feroz"* 'the ferocious rebel leader' (151), a variation of the title of Mexican Rafael Muñoz's 1928 novel, *El feroz cabecilla.* The description of Anselmo Quintana's face as *"el rostro de una vieja pelota de cuero pateada"* 'the face of an old, kicked-around, leather soccer ball' (219) may be a tribute to one of José Revueltas's last short stories, the dialogic "Hegel y yo."[27]

What is perhaps most amazing about Fuentes's intertextuality is his familiarity with the most recent novels. His reference to the collaboration of the Aztecs' Indian enemies with the Spaniards—"without them, the Aztecs would have eaten Cortés and his five hundred Spaniards for lunch" (197–198)—is a tribute to Argentine Abel Posse's similar phrase in *Los perros del Paraíso* (1983)—"My lord, it would be best if we ate the white-faces for lunch, before they have us for supper" (34). The description of the masked ball in Lima is reminiscent of the masked ball in Mexican Fernando del Paso's *Noticias del imperio* (1987). The singing of a castrated young male during the ball (126) is a recognition of Argentine César Aira's *Canto castrato* (1984).

Fuentes's intertextuality also extends to the past, to Bolívar's famous 1815 Jamaica letter (his Jamaican exile is actually mentioned on page 139), in which he comments on the most suitable form of government for each of the new republics. When Baltasar and his father discuss the future of this richly endowed land of Argentina, the latter is more pessimistic than his son: "—I'd be more cautious. A country where all you have to do is spit to make the earth flourish, can be a lazy country, sleepy, arrogant, smug, lacking in self-criticism . . ." (56).

In addition to all his allusions to Spanish, Spanish American, and Mexican literary works, Carlos Fuentes indulges in some references to his own works—a form of self-intertextuality. The Veracruz coffee plantation owner Menchaca is undoubtedly related to Artemio Cruz's father in *La muerte de Artemio Cruz*. In that same novel, the relationship between Artemio's future wife Catalina and her father Gamaliel Bernal in Puebla prefigures somewhat the relationship between Baltasar's father and the latter's daughter Sabina. By the same token, Fuentes's biting parody of the upper-class Mexicans' ultrapolite language in *La región más transparente*—"*¡Don Asusórdenes y doña Estaessucasa, Míster Besosuspies y Miss Damelasnalgas!*" 'Don Atyourservice and Doña Makeyourselfathome, Mr. Ikissyourfeet and Miss Givemeyourass!' (449)—is an anticipation of his reproduction of the "prolonged courteous speech of Lima" (122) in *La campaña*.

Fuentes also plays with the lyrics of Mexican popular songs in *La campaña*. The description of Orizaba as *"olía a tierra mojada"* 'smelling of moist earth' (199) is an allusion to the song *"Guadalajara"* (*"hueles a pura tierra mojada"*), whereas the description of Gabriela Cóo at the very end of the novel *"con sus ojos negros bajo esas famosas cejas fuertes"* 'with her dark eyes below those famous thick brows' (241) is a variation on the lyrics of *"Malagueña salerosa"* (*"¡Qué bonitos ojos tienes debajo de esas dos cejas!"*). These allusions to popular songs also lead up nicely to the next code to be discussed, popular literature. Of course, the purpose of identifying all these intertextual elements is not to reveal influences but rather to indicate how *La campaña* is aesthetically enriched with the presence of so many other Spanish and Spanish American literary works (and songs), which also contributes to one of the novel's principal themes: the unity of Hispanic culture.

5. The Parody of the Popular Historical Novel

Ever since the genre of the historical novel was created by Sir Walter Scott in the early nineteenth century, it has maintained its popularity. The large majority of historical novels, not only in Spanish America but also in Europe and the United States, reflect the authors' commercial aspirations. Although some of them may be driven by a sincere desire to enrich their fellow citizens' knowledge of history or even the desire to create a literary work of art, they also tend to be strongly motivated by hopes for a best-seller. Such hopes tend to restrict the novel's complexity and artistic sophistication. The general formula for these works is the fusion of a love story and a dramatic historical event, with emphasis on the plot.[28] Carlos Alberto Montaner's 1987 novel, which combines the late nineteenth-century movement for Cuban independence, the international anarchist movement, the labor movement in the United States, and Jewish and Italian immigration to the United States, is actually entitled *Trama* 'Plot.' The characters in these popular historical novels or historical romances tend to be relatively one-dimensional and do not evolve significantly; dialogue abounds, while description is relatively scarce; time and space are precisely recorded; and the language employed by the usually omniscient narrator is relatively simple.

In keeping with postmodernism's supposed elimination of the barriers between serious and popular literature, *La campaña* follows the above formula, especially in its frame. In the novel's very first paragraph, the narrator informs the reader concisely that on the night of May 24, 1810, in Buenos Aires, Baltasar Bustos, in a gesture of racial equality, kidnapped the recently born child of the Marquesa de Cabra, replacing him in his cradle with the baby son of a black prostitute. A few pages later, the narrator tells us how Baltasar fell in love at first sight with the Marquesa Ofelia Salamanca as he spied on her from her balcony while rehearsing the kidnapping. He continues to adore her throughout the entire novel, but Fuentes alters the formulaic ending. *La campaña* does not end with the death of the idealized, beloved Ofelia, but rather with the unexpected appearance of the other Chilean beauty, Gabriela Cóo. Fuentes completes his parody of the popular historical novel with an unexpected happy ending: with Ofelia dead, Baltasar is free to marry Gabriela and raise his adopted son, the same boy he had kidnapped ten years earlier.

6. The New Historical Novel

The entire preceding analysis indicates that *La campaña*, like *Terra nostra* and *Gringo viejo,* qualifies as a New Historical Novel. In the same tradition as Carpentier's *El arpa y la sombra,* Posse's *Los perros del Paraíso,* del Paso's *Noticias del imperio,* and several other 1979– 1992 novels, *La campaña* contains most of the six ingredients identified in Chapter 1 in reverse order (all six of which are not required):

a. *The Bakhtinian concepts of the dialogic, the carnivalesque, parody, and heteroglossia.* The masked ball in Lima, the social gatherings in Santiago de Chile, and the Maracaibo brothel scenes, among others, provide the novel with a carnivalesque tone, which balances to a certain extent the grim realities of the wars of independence and of Spanish American history in general. This portrayal of reality as being simultaneously grim and hilarious is only one of many examples of the dialogic view of the world projected in *La campaña.* There are several examples of parody, but except for the *criollista* regionalisms, there is very little heteroglossia.

b. *Intertextuality.* The allusions to the novels of García Márquez and to a host of other works, including Fuentes's own *La muerte de Artemio Cruz,* contribute greatly to the carnivalesque aspect of *La campaña.*

c. *Metafiction, or self-conscious narrative.* Metafiction is relatively inconspicuous in *La campaña* because the book is conceived as a parody of the popular, best-selling historical novel, and as such the philosophical meanderings of *Tristram Shandy, Noticias del imperio,* and *Cristóbal Nonato* would be out of place. Other than the narrator Varela's periodic allusions to Baltasar's letters, perhaps the only example of metafiction occurs—most unexpectedly—at the beginning of the third and final section of Chapter 5: "All that remains to finish this chapter are a couple of documents" (139).

d. *The historical protagonist.* Although the protagonist Baltasar Bustos and his two Buenos Aires friends are entirely fictitious, there are at least four historical figures, of varying importance, who play significant roles in the novel: San Martín, Simón Rodríguez, and the guerrilla leaders of the autonomous *"republiquetas"* (74) of Alto Perú, Miguel Lanza and Father Ildefonso de las Muñecas.

e. *The conscious distortion of history through omissions, exaggerations, anachronisms, and the creation of apocryphal historical characters.* The latter is exemplified in the fictitious heroic and archetypal insurgent priest from the state of Veracruz who, paradoxically, has certain characteristics that clearly identify him with the historical Santa Anna.

f. *The subordination of the mimetic reproduction of a certain historical period to the development of more transcendent concepts.* This is probably the single most important trait that distinguishes the New Historical Novel from the traditional historical novel. In *La campaña*, although the specific wars of independence are described and denounced, the primary goal of the novel is not to re-create the world of 1810–1821 but rather to show the disastrous results of a passionate adherence to any ideology, not only in the early nineteenth century but also in the late twentieth century. The triple message is as follows:

(1) All dogmatic ideologies must be questioned constantly. The model must be, not Voltaire or Rousseau, but rather "Diderot's smiling mask: the conviction that everything changes constantly and offers us in every moment of our existence a menu from which to choose" (25).

(2) The various ingredients of the Spanish American cultural heritage must be appreciated, integrated, and maintained.

(3) In spite of all the destruction of the wars of independence and other violent historical encounters, we must maintain our enthusiasm, our hope for creating a better world.[29]

In accordance with Bakhtin's concept of the dialogic, this chapter has two possible endings:

Although Fuentes is to be admired for his final optimism, the events in *La campaña* hardly justify it. Anselmo Quintana's words to Baltasar may prove to be more prophetic: "Then those who fight for money and

Although the events of *La campaña* hardly justify its final optimism, the latter does coincide with the closing message of the very first of the New Historical Novels, Carpentier's *El reino de este mundo*, which therefore makes an appropriate ending for this book: " . . . A man never knows for whom he suffers and hopes. He suffers and hopes and toils for people he will never know, and power will arrive. That's what I fear, that will be the failure of the nation" (226).

who, in turn, will suffer and hope and toil for others who will not be happy either, for man always seeks a happiness far beyond that which is meted out to him. But man's greatness consists of the very fact of wanting to be better than he is" (185).

Notes

Prependix. Chronology of the Latin American Historical Novel, 1949–1992

1. Some of the following papers are shorter versions of the chapters in this book: "La guerra contra el fanatismo de Mario Vargas Llosa" (paper delivered at the triannual meeting of the Asociación Internacional de Hispanistas, Barcelona, August 22, 1989), subsequently published in *Cuadernos Americanos*, 4, no. 28 (July–August, 1991), 50–62; "La nueva novela histórica y *Las historias prohibidas del Pulgarcito* de Roque Dalton" (paper delivered at the Simposio de Críticos Centroamericanistas, Guatemala City, August 8, 1989), not included in this book; "Dos novelas seductoras: La culta y la popular o Genoveva e Inés" (paper delivered at the biannual meeting of the Asociación Norteamericana de Colombianistas, University of Kansas, November 10, 1989), not included in this book; "*Noticias del imperio:* Boom or Post-boom?" (paper delivered at Translating Latin America: An Interdisciplinary Conference on Culture as Text, SUNY—Binghamton, April 20, 1990), subsequently published under the title of "*Noticias del imperio* y la nueva novela histórica" in my book *Narrativa mexicana desde "Los de abajo" hasta "Noticias del imperio"; "Los perros del Paraíso* y la nueva novela colombina" (paper delivered at the Congreso Internacional del Centro de Estudios de Literaturas y Civilizaciones del Río de la Plata: Discurso historiográfico y discurso ficcional, University of Regensburg, Germany, July 3, 1990); "*Los perros del Paraíso,* the Denunciation of Power"

(paper delivered at the annual meeting of the Modern Language Association, San Francisco, December 28, 1991), subsequently published in *Hispania;* "*La campaña:* Crónica de una guerra denunciada" (paper delivered at the Tercer Encuentro de Mexicanistas, U.N.A.M., Mexico City, April 3, 1991; at Stanford University, April 30, 1991; at the University of California, Irvine, May 29, 1991; and at the Universidad Central de Venezuela, Caracas, July 12, 1991), subsequently published in *Universidad de México.*

2. Erico Verissimo's *O continente* (1949) is the first volume of the trilogy *O tempo e o vento.* The other volumes, *O retrato* (1955) and *O arquipélago* (1960–1962), are not included in this list because the events narrated transpired during the author's lifetime.

Chapter 1. Latin America's New Historical Novel

1. The following articles criticize, in varying degrees, Borges and the "Boom" novelists for their artistic complexities (i.e., "narcissism") and their lack of revolutionary commitment: Jaime Alazraki, "Borges, entre la modernidad y la postmodernidad"; Jean Franco, "Si me permiten hablar: La lucha por el poder interpretativo"; Juan Manuel Marcos, "La narrativa de Mempo Giardinelli," "Mempo Giardinelli in the Wake of Utopia," and his reviews of *De amor y de sombra* by Isabel Allende and *Andando el tiempo* by Eraclio Zepeda; Marta Morello-Frosch, "Biografías fictivas: Formas de resistencia y reflexión en la narrativa argentina reciente."

2. As far as I know, the first critics to perceive the emergence of the trend of the New Historical Novel were Uruguayan Angel Rama in 1981, Bronxite Seymour Menton in 1982, Mexican Juan José Barrientos from 1983 on, Venezuelan Alexis Márquez Rodríguez in 1984, and Mexican José Emilio Pacheco in 1985. Rama, in the prologue to his 1981 anthology *Novísimos narradores hispanoamericanos en "Marcha," 1964–1980,* praises Carlos Fuentes's *Terra nostra* and Roa Bastos's *Yo el Supremo* for having broken out of the romantic mold for historical novels. However, he mistakenly identifies Alejo Carpentier's novels with their romantic antecedents and does not draw a clear line between novels that portray the present (Haroldo Conti's *Mascaró,* 1975, and Fernando del Paso's *Palinuro de México,* 1975) and those that portray the past (Abel Posse's *Daimón,* 1978). On May 4, 1982, I gave a talk entitled "Antonio Benítez, la nueva novela histórica y los juicios de valor" (Antonio Benítez, the New Historical Novel and Value Judgments) at the annual conference of the Instituto Internacional de Literatura Iberoamericana in San Juan, Puerto Rico. I compared Benítez's two novels, *El mar de las lentejas* (1979) and *Paso de los vientos* 'Strait of the Winds,' the latter incomplete and still unpublished. Beginning in 1983, Barrientos published a series of carefully researched thematic studies on Padre Miguel Hidalgo, Christopher Columbus, and Lope de Aguirre, featuring respectively Jorge Ibargüengoitia's *Los pasos de López,* Abel Posse's *Los perros del Paraíso,* and Miguel Otero Silva's *Lope de Aguirre, príncipe de*

la libertad, along with their historical, literary, and cinematographic antecedents. In his 1983 study "El grito de Ajetreo: Anotaciones a la novela de Ibargüengoitia sobre Hidalgo," he actually refers to the *"nueva novela histórica hispanoamericana"* (20) and notes the liberties that the authors take with historical facts. Alexis Márquez, in his 1984 review of *La luna de Fausto* by Francisco Herrera Luque, stated that "today we are experiencing a real boom in the new historical novel in Spanish America" (174). Pacheco, in a much shorter piece published in *Proceso* in May 1985, observed the resurgence of the historical novel in 1985 and related it to the successful 1978 television series *I, Claudius,* based on Robert Graves's 1934 novel, and Marguerite Yourcenar's *Memoirs of Hadrian* (1951). None of these four critics, however, attempted to draw distinctions between the *new* historical novel and the traditional one.

Fernando Aínsa's September 1991 article "La nueva novela histórica," published in *Plural* and, in extended form, in *Cuadernos Americanos,* recognizes the existence of a *moda* and identifies ten different characteristics, but without defining the term *historical novel.* The same issue of *Cuadernos Americanos* contains five other studies on specific historical novels, including a shorter version of my own study of Vargas Llosa's *La guerra del fin del mundo.*

3. See John Beverley, "La ideología de la música posmoderna y la política de izquierda," 58. Beverley's article is based on Jean-François Lyotard's *La condition postmoderne* (1984).

4. The Spanish American novel in general, more than the European and U.S. novels, has been characterized since its inception in 1816—with Fernández de Lizardi's *El periquillo sarniento*—by its obsession with sociohistorical rather than psychological problems. In 1985, José Emilio Pacheco, in his introduction to a volume containing four nineteenth-century Mexican novels, wrote that "the novel since its origins has been the privatization of history . . . the history of private life, the history of people who have no history . . . and in that sense every novel is an historical novel" (v–vi).

5. Among the countries where romantic historical fiction developed, Chile should also be mentioned, for José Victorino Lastarria's two historical short stories "Rosa" (1848) and "El alférez Alonso Díaz de Guzmán" (1848), both of which could have been expanded into full-length novels.

6. In addition, the psychological novels of Brazilian Machado de Assis, *Memórias de Bras Cubas* (1880), *Dom Casmurro* (1890), and *Quincas Borba* (1891) were exceptional in all of Latin America for their sophistication and were a far cry from the romantic historical novels and the realistic *costumbrista* novels.

7. In addition to Ricardo Palma's six series of *Tradiciones peruanas,* there are actually five other series of *Tradiciones* with different titles, published between 1889 and 1911: *Ropa vieja* (1889), *Ropa apolillada* (1891), *Cachivaches y tradiciones y artículos históricos* (1899–1900), *Tradiciones en salsa verde* (1901), and *Apéndice a mis últimas tradiciones* (1911).

8. Carmen Vásquez, in her 1991 *Cuadernos Americanos* article, docu-

ments the existence of several Negro slaves in eighteenth-century Haiti named Noel, suggesting that there may be some historical basis to the figure Ti Noel.

9. Toussaint l'Ouverture appears only briefly and anonymously as the carpenter who is carving in wood the figures of a nativity scene, although in real life Toussaint l'Ouverture was not a carpenter—see Verity Smith's "Ausencia de Toussaint: Interpretación y falseamiento de la historia en *El reino de este mundo*" (1979). Carmen Vásquez, in her 1991 *Cuadernos Hispanoamericanos* article, states that Carpentier was very familiar with Victor Schoelcher's classic study *Vie de Toussaint Louverture* (1889).

10. See Menton, *Prose Fiction of the Cuban Revolution*, 44–46.

11. Raquel Aguilu de Murphy refers to the protagonist's arrival in Venice during Carnival as *"el gran carnaval de la Epifanía"* (164) and relates it to Bakhtin's definition of *carnival* in his *Rabelais and His World*.

12. Carpentier, *El arpa y la sombra*, 102. This translation and others in this chapter, unless otherwise indicated, are mine.

13. The ironical importance of the non-novelist Borges as a dominant inspirational figure in the New Historical Novel is reinforced by his presence in Umberto Eco's best-selling Italian NHN, *The Name of the Rose* (1980).

14. On Columbus's philatelic presence in the Dominican Republic, see *Scott Standard Postage Stamp Catalogue*, 774, 793, 804, C247, C264, C282; C377–379; C388–390; 916–919, 951–954, 980–984; 1002–1006.

15. In Carlos Fuentes's *Terra nostra* (1975), one of the two Spanish sailors who land in the New World asks, upon seeing Indians for the first time, "—Are they discovering us . . . or are we discovering them?" (384).

16. Although explicitly indebted to José Luis Martínez's biography, Vicente Leñero's play *La noche de Hernán Cortés* (which first appeared in June–July 1992) presents in a highly experimental production a more dialogic view of Cortés, who at times even bears a resemblance to Don Quijote.

17. The only novelistic genre capable of competing somewhat with the NHN is the testimonial or nonfictional novel. Although its antecedents go back as far as Ricardo Pozas's *Juan Pérez Jolote* (1948), Carolina de Jesus's *Quarto de despejo* 'Child of the Dark' (1960), and Oscar Lewis's *Five Families* (1959) and *Children of Sánchez* (1961), its heyday was in the 1970s and early 1980s, with Elena Poniatowska's *La noche de Tlatelolco* 'The Night of Tlatelolco' (1971), Rodolfo Walsh's *Operación Masacre* 'Operation Massacre' (1972), Roque Dalton's *Miguel Mármol* (1972), Vicente Leñero's *Los periodistas* 'The Newspapermen' (1978), Omar Cabezas Lacayo's *La montaña es algo más que una inmensa estepa verde* 'The Mountains Are Something More than an Immense Green Expanse' (1982), and Elizabeth Burgos Debray's *Me llamo Rigoberta Menchú* 'My Name Is Rigoberta Menchú' (1983). However, in the 1980s, the production of these testimonial works clearly declined, paralleling the decline of the revolutionary guerrilla movements throughout Latin America. Even at its height, the testimonial novel never attained the high productivity, the great

variety, and the outstanding artistic quality of the New Historical Novel. As a possible indication that the testimonial novel is being replaced by the NHN, Elena Poniatowska published the historical novel entitled *Tinísima,* based on the life of Tina Modotti, in late July 1992.

18. In spite of his anti-imperialism, Todorov is taken to task by Rolena Adorno in an essay included in the 1989 University of Minnesota publication *1492–1992: Re/Discovering Colonial Writing.* Expressing an activist Marxist attitude, she accuses Todorov of silencing "the speech of the dominated subject" (205) and favoring the leitmotif of his "concern for totalitarian regimes with implicit reference to the Soviet state" (204). She indicates that Michel de Certeau, in *Heterologies: Discourses on the Other* (1986), facilitates the reader's ability to listen to the discourse of the other by examining "native and peasant activism organized in the mid–1970s" and by inviting "his readers to participate in information sharing and active support work" (206).

19. In his 1950 thematic study of the American historical novel, Ernest Leisy stated: "Whatever the mode, the historical novel today is the most popular form of American fiction" (vii).

20. In an example of "round-trip" intertextuality, Jorge of Burgos appears parenthetically in the Argentine novel *Ansay* (1984) by Martín Caparrós (225).

21. Ciplijauskaité's study is a much more serious one than James Mandrell's attempt to generalize about historical novels written by women on the basis of three works, Elena Garro's *Los recuerdos del porvenir* 'Recollections of Things to Come' (1963), Elsa Morante's *La Storia: Romanzo* 'History: A Novel' (1974), and Isabel Allende's *La casa de los espíritus* 'The House of Spirits' (1982).

Chapter 2. Mario Vargas Llosa's War on Fanaticism

1. The verb *ver* 'to see' is used anaphorically in the same ironic sense in Gabriel García Márquez's *El otoño del patriarca.* See my article *"Ver para no creer: 'El otoño del patriarca'"* in *Caribe* and reprinted in my book *La novela colombiana: Planetas y satélites.* Over thirty years earlier, Jorge Luis Borges used the same verb anaphorically in his stories "La muerte y la brújula" 'Death and the Compass' and "El sur" 'The South'. See *Ficciones* (English version), 137, 170.

Quotes in Spanish are from *La guerra del fin del mundo* (1981). Quotes in English are from *The War of the End of the World,* translated by Helen R. Lane (1984).

2. In a 1986 interview with Ricardo Setti, Vargas Llosa expresses his preference for Borges of all Latin American writers because of his great originality, his imagination, his culture, and his precise, concise language (17). See also Vargas Llosa's lecture at Syracuse University, "An Invitation to Borges's Fiction" in Mario Vargas Llosa, *A Writer's Reality,* 1–20. His respect for García Már-

quez as a novelist has been well known since their famous August 1967 meeting in Caracas and the publication in 1971 of his very detailed study *García Márquez: Historia de un deicidio,* their subsequent falling-out notwithstanding.

3. Like so many Latin American intellectuals, Vargas Llosa enthusiastically supported the Cuban Revolution in its early years, but he consistently maintained the intellectual's right and duty to criticize socialism for the purpose of improving it. However, from 1967 on, he has been persona non grata to the Cuban government for his public polemic with Haydée Santamaría, director of the *Casa de las Américas,* and for his critical positions regarding the Soviet invasion of Czechoslovakia in August 1968 and the Padilla Case between 1968 and 1971. See Menton, *Prose Fiction of the Cuban Revolution* (146, 153–156) and Vargas Llosa's "The Author's Favorite of His Novels" and "Transforming a Lie into Truth" in *A Writer's Reality.*

4. In a 1986 interview with Raymond L. Williams, Vargas Llosa refers to the Shining Path as "abstract violence, blind terror" (Williams interview, 205). See also Mario Vargas Llosa, "Inquest in the Andes."

5. Among the significant studies published about the novel, Raymond Souza's comes closest to foregrounding the importance of fanaticism. He recognizes the relationship between the novel and the Peruvian guerrillas of the Shining Path (69), and he points out the novel's condemnation of fanaticism and the positive evolution of the Baron, but he does not identify the condemnation of fanaticism as the structural axis of the entire novel. Angel Rama discusses at great length the novel's ideology without alluding to its application to present-day Peru. José Miguel Oviedo, in his 1982 *Eco* study, identifies many of the novel's positive features but neglects to comment on the key role of the Barón de Cañabrava. Alfred Mac Adam raises the question of why Vargas Llosa, whose previous works all deal with Peru, became interested in a late-nineteenth-century uprising in northeastern Brazil, but, instead of answering his own question, concentrates on the intertextual nature of the theme of the writer and the epic struggle. Raymond Leslie Williams comments on fanaticism as "one factor that motivates characters . . . although it is not the predominant one" (*Mario Vargas Llosa,* 150). Jorge Ruffinelli, after warmly praising the novel's artistry, criticizes its ideological position, but without recognizing the significance of the Barón de Cañabrava: the novel "never succeeds in giving a broad, comprehensive view of what is a movement of liberation in search of its own freedom and autonomy" (*"Vargas Llosa,"* 108).

6. Another similarity between the two opposing fanatics, the Consejero and the Colonel, is that they are both named Antonio. However, whereas the Consejero's full name is prominently revealed in the last sentence of the novel's very first section—"his Christian name was Antonio Vicente and his last name Mendes Maciel" (6)—Colonel Moreira César's first name is never mentioned in the novel, although it does appear in *Os sertões* and in Cunninghame Graham's *A Brazilian Mystic* (166). Vargas Llosa may have omitted it thinking that the additional symmetry was too much of a coincidence for a novel.

7. In the New Testament, Caifás (or Caiaphas in English) is the High Priest who interrogated Jesus and ordered his execution.

8. Although the relationship between the two women is never explicitly identified as being lesbian, the author does not leave much room for doubt. The Baron recalls how jealous he was in the early years of their marriage, and how adamant Estela was about not firing Sebastiana: "if Sebastiana left, she was leaving too" (309). The Baron considers himself more flexible than his landowner friend Adalberto de Gumúcio: "And he wondered if Adalberto would have permitted in his home as intimate a relationship as that between Estela and Sebastiana" (310). Before the rape scene, the Baron recalls that Sebastiana resented the fact that Estela had treated Jurema with considerable affection (502). During the actual rape, the Baron says to his wife, "'I always wanted to share her with you, my darling'" (540).

9. The term *focalizer* comes from Mieke Bal, *Narratology: Introduction to the Theory of Narrative*.

10. Although Cunninghame Graham presents a much more negative view of the Consejero and his followers than does Vargas Llosa, he too can not help but feel a certain sympathy for them: "When all is said, it is impossible not to sympathize to some extent with the misguided sectaries, for all they wanted was to live the life they had been accustomed to, and sing their litanies. Clearly Antonio Conselheiro had no views on any subject under heaven outside his own district. His dreams were fixed upon a better world, and his chief care to fit his followers for the change that he believed was to take place so soon" (173).

11. Antonio's threat to kill his wife in this situation is even more shocking considering that he earlier felt pity for the charging infantrymen against whom he was firing: "How could he possibly feel pity for men who are trying to destroy Belo Monte? Yes, at this moment, as he sees them fall to the ground, hears them moan, and aims at them and kills them, he does not hate them: he can sense their spiritual wretchedness, their sinful human nature, he knows they are victims, blind, stupid instruments, prisoners caught fast in the snares of the Evil One" (470).

12. The episode of Queluz's supposed heroics is reminiscent of Artemio Cruz's first "heroic" feat in Carlos Fuentes's 1962 novel *La muerte de Artemio Cruz*.

13. For Vargas Llosa's use of newspapermen as characters in several of his novels, see Carlos Meneses, "La visión del periodista, tema recurrente en Mario Vargas Llosa."

14. The fact that previously the reporter's glasses flew off and did not break (303) may be an intertextual allusion to Julio Cortázar's vignette about dropping eyeglasses in *Historias de cronopios y famas* 'Cronopios and Famas' (1962). In any case, it reinforces the illogical-world theme.

15. The illogical-world theme is introduced in the very first chapter of the novel in the biographical segment on Antonio el Beatito: "If there had been such a thing as logic in this world, he should never have gone on living" (9).

16. Vargas Llosa's fascination with the writer as a central character is also evident in his novels *La tía Julia y el escribidor* (1979) and *Historia de Mayta* (1984) and in his play *La señorita de Tacna* (1981).

17. The narrator subtly pokes fun at his own hero, the questioning reporter who seeks different points of view, when—after his ink runs out, his last quill pen breaks, and his roll of notes disappears—he finds himself in a semi-dream state, and nonetheless the phrase "he is certain" (337, 338, 340) is repeated almost anaphorically.

18. Vargas Llosa has often expressed his fondness for the novels of chivalry and in 1969 published an edition of *Tirant lo Blanc.*

19. Like a traditional symphony, the novel is divided into four parts, which reflect the four different military expeditions sent against Canudos; the four principal fanatics; the four Antonios in Canudos (Consejero, Beatito, Vilanova, and the Fogueteiro). The four-part symphonic structure is also constantly reinforced by groups of four parallel names, words, and phrases: "the inhabitants of Tucano, Soure, Amparo, and Pombal had heard his words" (6); "he had palpated yellow, black, red, and white craniums" (15); "armed with every sort of weapon capable of cutting, piercing, perforating, tearing out" (16); "he had noticed that the Street Commander's eyes were gleaming, his cheeks glistening, his chin trembling, his chest heaving" (557). The number four traditionally symbolizes totality: the four cardinal points, the four seasons of the year, the four elements of the pre-Aristotelian world, the four Gospels, and the closed square, as in the name of Maria Quadrado who was raped . . . four times.

20. See Isaiah 65:17 and 66:22.

21. The unidentified invaders appeared earlier in two short stories by Veiga, "The Factory on the Other Side of the Hill" (1959) and "The Misplaced Machine" (1968), and in three short novels, *The Three Trials of Manirema* (1966), *Shadows of Bearded Kings* (1972), and *The Sins of the Tribe* (1976).

Chapter 3. Abel Posse's Denunciation of Power

1. Published in 1983, *Los perros del Paraíso* received the Rómulo Gallegos Prize in 1987 for the best Spanish American novel of the preceding five years. Previous winners were Mario Vargas Llosa, Gabriel García Márquez, Carlos Fuentes, and Fernando del Paso. Quotes in Spanish are from *Los perros del Paraíso* (1987); quotes in English are from *The Dogs of Paradise,* translated by Margaret Sayers Peden (1989).

2. See René Jara and Hernán Vidal, eds., *Ficción y política: La narrativa argentina durante el proceso militar* (1987). Neither Posse nor his novels are mentioned in any of the six papers that were presented at the University of Minnesota in March 1986. In one of them, Marta Morello-Frosch's *"Biografías fictivas: Formas de resistencia y reflexión en la narrativa argentina reciente,"* the fictionalized biographies by Ricardo Piglia, Carlos Dámaso Martínez, Andrés Rivera, and Jorge Manzur are considered to be ideologically—and per-

haps morally—superior to the carnivalesque works by the unmentioned Posse and others: *"La práctica también da por tierra con la ficción 'carnavalesca' de la novela latinoamericana precedente, esa polifonía de voces que signaban con la hipoglosia más aberrante, un vacío central de significado"* (70) 'The trend also lays to rest the carnivalesque fiction of the preceding group of Latin American novels, that polyphony of words that, with the most aberrant hypoglossia, subscribed to a basic absence of meaning' (my translation). In the University of Maryland meeting of December 2–4, 1984, Posse was not mentioned either. See Saúl Sosnowski, *Represión y reconstrucción de una cultura: El caso argentino* (1988).

3. The possible key to Posse's ideology may be found in his later novel *Los demonios ocultos* 'The Hidden Demons' (1987), where his protagonist/spokesman Lorca states clearly that he is an anarchist: "Soy anarquista. Creo que desde 1968 me quedó un repudio total por los estados y el infierno que crean desde sus razones y sinrazones" (226) 'I am an anarchist. I think that since 1968 I have felt a total repudiation of governments and the hell they create through their reasoning and lack thereof' (my translation).

4. In Carlos Fuentes's novella *Aura,* a doorknocker in the shape of a dog's head signals the entrance into the Inferno.

5. Dogs appear throughout the novel, usually as symbols of ferocity and lust. This leitmotif builds to a crescendo in Part 4, which begins with the description of Spain as an empire, "the first world power" (232), juxtaposed with the description of Isabella's "bitch Diana, who could not resist the attraction of Fernando's hunting dogs, penned and howling in sexual frustration" (232). In the New World, the dogs, "usually German shepherds . . . came to have such importance that some of these zealous guardians of Christian order were the subject of biographies. The chronicler Oviedo, for example, extolled the moral influence of one Becerillo in these words: 'He was a ferocious canine defender of the Catholic faith and of sexual morality; he tore apart more than two hundred Indian idolators, sodomites, and other abominable offenders' " (282). Colonel Roldán, who carries out the first *golpe militar* in the New World, "organized a canine commission, guardian of public morality and censorship. In this, too, he was a precursor" (282, n. 3).

6. Posse's 1987 novel *Los demonios ocultos* begins with a description of the death of Eva Perón on July 26, 1952.

7. Another example of intertextual discourse in the novel is the Homeric description of dawn, imitated in the sixteenth-century Spanish chivalric novels and parodied in Cervantes's seventeenth-century *Don Quijote:* "As the dawn of August 3d, 1492, crept near, its rosy fingers unbuttoned the Jesuitical cassock of night. More than a day was dawning" (16). And, in a literal example of polyglossia, the narrator parodies a poetic Portuguese description of moonlight on the sea: *"Rielar de la luna sobre el mar. Destellos de plata antigua. Luar de la luna ruando el mar"* (134) 'Glimmer of the moon upon the sea. Shimmer of antique silver. Moonshimmer on silverglimmer' (177).

8. In a review of *Los perros del Paraíso* published by Line Karoubi in *Le Matin* of Paris, Posse confirms the homology: *"J'ai cherché . . . à recréer par le roman l'homologie profonde entre deux situations historiques: celle de la conquête originelle de l'Amérique et notre situation coloniale actuelle"* 'I have sought . . . to re-create through the novel the profound homology between two historical situations: that of the original conquest of America and our present colonial situation.' The literary antecedent of Posse's homology may be found in the juxtaposing of the American cruiser and Columbus's three caravels in Gabriel García Márquez's *El otoño del patriarca* (46).

9. Tzvetan Todorov, whose 1982 *The Conquest of America: The Question of the Other* is quite critical of Columbus on moralistic grounds, makes a cameo appearance in Posse's novel as a landsknecht (a European mercenary foot soldier of the sixteenth century) who witnesses some of the Spaniards' atrocities (283).

10. At the 1990 annual meeting of the Modern Language Association in Chicago, Eugenio D. Matibag questioned the existence of Caribbean cannibalism in his unpublished paper "Self-Consuming Fictions: The Dialectics of Cannibalism in Recent Caribbean Narratives."

11. Posse utilizes the cannibal image again in *Los demonios ocultos* in the protagonist's reference to the Trotskyite terrorists and the military government of 1976: *"—El que devora caníbales, también se vuelve caníbal"* (187) 'he who devours cannibals also becomes a cannibal'.

12. The discovery of Europe by the Indians, in 1392, is later "confirmed" in the dialogue between Beatriz de Bobadilla and Columbus. The admiral himself explains why the Indians desisted in their invasion, with a good example of the delightful anachronisms that sparkle throughout the novel: "'Who *would* be interested in a world increasingly more perverted by democracy and public education?'" (175).

13. *Los perros del Paraíso*, 79. Christopher Columbus's actual *Libro de las profecías* contains several passages from the Old Testament prophet Isaiah: "For the islands wait for me, and the ships of the sea in the beginning: that I may bring thy sons from afar" (Isaiah 60:9a); "And I will set a sign among them, and I will send of them that shall be saved, to the Gentiles into the sea, into Africa and Lydia, them that draw the bow: into Italy and Greece, to the islands afar off, to them that have not heard of me and have not seen my glory" (Isaiah 66:19a). See the 1991 *en face* edition of *The Libro de las profecías of Christopher Columbus*, 251. Isaiah's prophecy is also included in the Brazilian novel *A estranha nação de Rafael Mendes* (1983) by Moacyr Scliar: *"As ilhas me esperarão; e as naves de Tarshish trarão teus filhos; e com êles a prata e o ouro, para honra do Eterno"* 'The islands will await me; and the ships of Tarshish will bring your children; and with them the silver and the gold, for the honor of the Eternal' (113).

14. *"Bolivianazo"* is a neologism referring to the record number of coups d'état suffered by Bolivia. The translation 'military takeover' loses the allusion to Bolivia.

15. In Parts 1 and 2, approximately equal numbers of pages are devoted to Columbus and Isabella, but the latter does not appear at all in Part 3 and appears only briefly in Part 4.

16. *Los perros del Paraíso*, 75. The narrator again questions the pervasiveness of phallocracy in describing the tyranny exercised by Beatriz de Bobadilla: "The sad case with Núñez de Castañeda: overly confident in his ephemeral phallocracy, he was crushed by the deadly repression, the instinctive vengeance, of the spider who devours her mate" (185). The archetypal equation between spiders and anthropophagous women is reaffirmed in the description of the terrestrial Paradise: "Velvety spiders so silky they could have been born in María Félix's hair" (252).

17. The original Spanish, *"de poder a poder"* (48) 'power to power', better reflects the main theme of the novel: the denunciation of power.

18. The identification of Nietzsche with Rousseau's tiger reflects the former's obsession with the beast of prey as a prototype for the superman.

19. *Los perros del Paraíso*, 157−158. Pascal and Kafka are also introduced parenthetically, as being opposed to happiness: "Meditation, the arts that elevate and delight (no Pascalites, no Kafkaizing)" (258).

20. *Los perros del Paraíso*, 300. As indicated in note 2, Posse and *Los perros del Paraíso* have been ignored by leftist critics in Argentina and the U.S. What is even more amazing is that some non-leftist critics who have reviewed or analyzed the novel have not dared to offend the Left by commenting on the portrayal of Marx or even mentioning his presence in the novel.

21. A further indication of Posse's fascination with Nietzsche appears in his later novel *Los demonios ocultos* (1987) in the more mimetic description of Nietzsche's kissing the horse's snout in Turin on January 3, 1889, as the ultimate sign of his increasing insanity (131). In *Los perros del Paraíso*, the scene is portrayed more ambiguously: " . . . He had come from the duchy of Turin, pursued by the fearsome Guard of Savoy, accused of bestiality after having been found, *in fraganti*, embracing a horse" (19).

22. Groupings of four include "the four corners of the civilized world" (40); "four years of civil war" (119); during Columbus's visit to Beatriz de Bobadilla, the "four beautiful young girls" he is attended by (172) and "the four maidservants" he is bathed by (183); the four priests, "Buil, Valverde, Colángelo, and Pane" (260); Columbus's "brothers, children, nephews, and cousins" (260); Padre Squarcialuppi "followed by four seminarians" (263); and the four years, rather than four days, spent in Paradise (288).

23. These four elements also constitute one of the structures of *Cien años de soledad,* but not explicitly.

24. Although the Renaissance is usually considered a positive development by most historians, in this dialogic novel it also heralds the rise of international or multinational capitalism, from the fifteenth-century Italian city-states, to the nineteenth-century Lübeck from Thomas Mann's 1901 novel *Buddenbrooks*

(7), to the twentieth-century Central American operations of the United Fruit Company (298).

25. *The Dogs of Paradise,* 163, 190. The vulgar comparison that follows this quotation about Columbus's ability to float is a reference to World War I and plays with the false cognates *belga* 'Belgian' and *bélica* 'war-time' (which the translator failed to capture): *"Sumerge la cabeza en la bañera y flota boca abajo, como muerto. Sólo emerge su culo fofo y blanco como el trasero de una monja belga ahogada en un canal de Flandes después de una violación bélica"* (143) 'Colón submerges his head in the tub and floats face downward, like a dead man. All that is visible is an arse as soft and white as the buttocks of a Belgian nun raped by soldiers and drowned in a Flemish canal' (190).

Chapter 4. The Instant Canonization of a Bakhtinian Symphony

1. Sara Sefchovich calls *Noticias del imperio,* "on the basis of its prose, the best novel in all of Mexican literature" (166). For other positive reviews, see those by Fabienne Bradu, Juan Bruce-Novoa, and Peter N. Thomas. For an opposing point of view, see Adolfo Castañón's review in *Vuelta.*

2. Napoleon III, who appears in the novel, may be inherently a carnival-esque figure, as suggested by the title of John Bierman's 1988 biography of Napoleon III, *Napoleon III and His Carnival Empire.*

3. The sentence " 'No, Benito: history will absolve you' " (626) in this section is a clear allusion to Fidel Castro's famous speech at his 1953 trial for the attack on the Moncada Barracks, one of the many examples of the novel's intertextuality.

4. The arguments over Juárez—whether he was hero or villain—continued through the first half of the twentieth century. For example, his monument in Mexico City was periodically painted black by the *sinarquistas* and other right-wing groups in the 1940s.

5. Joseph-Arthur de Gobineau's *Essay on the Inequality of Human Races,* published in France in 1854, is mentioned toward the beginning of Chapter 2 (32) and in other parts of the novel and was utilized by the European imperial powers for decades as the "scientific" justification for their taking on "the white man's burden."

Chapter 5. The Bolívar Quartette, or Varieties of Historical Fiction

1. In the appendix to *El general en su laberinto,* entitled *Gratitudes,* the author states, "During two long years I submerged myself in the quicksands of a torrential documentation, contradictory and often false, ranging from Daniel Florencio O'Leary's 34 volumes to the most unexpected newspaper clippings" (272). The two other García Márquez novels that bear the greatest resemblance to the New Historical Novel are *Cien años de soledad* and *El otoño del patriarca,* but I have reluctantly excluded them as historical novels because, al-

though the action takes place primarily in the past, both novels include a time period experienced directly by the author.

The quotations in this chapter are from *El general en su laberinto* (Madrid: Mondadori, 1989). The translations are mine.

2. As far as I know, all the literary critics are in agreement on the superior aesthetic quality of *El general en su laberinto*. See articles by Mary E. Davis, Roberto González Echevarría, George R. McMurray, Julio Ortega, José Miguel Oviedo (*"García Márquez"*), Michael Palencia-Roth, and Federico Patán.

3. Robert D. Spector, Review of *Protocols of Reading* by Robert Scholes.

4. Critics' dependency on the comparative approach could not be more clearly expressed than it is by the narrator of Robert Graves's *I, Claudius* (1934), the television adaptation of which in the late 1970s contributed to the surge of interest in the historical novel: "It was the first sword-fight I had been permitted to attend. . . . It was my luck that the fight was the best that had ever been exhibited at the amphitheater. As it was my first, however, I could not appreciate its excellence, having no background of previous displays to use for purposes of comparison" (128).

5. Bolívar had an exaggerated fear of rats, as is seen in Denzil Romero's *La carujada* 'The Carujo Epic' (1990).

6. In Julio Cortázar's novel *Libro de Manuel* (1973), *"la joda"* 'the screwery' is the code name for the plan of a group of revolutionary Latin American expatriates in Paris to kidnap a VIP. *Joda* is the imperative form of the verb *joder* 'to fuck'.

7. Asturias received the Nobel Prize in 1967 to a great extent because his anti-imperialistic banana trilogy coincided with worldwide opposition to U.S. intervention in Vietnam.

8. In 1991, Venezuelan Eduardo Casanova published a novel about the Sucre assassination, *La noche de Abel*. The novel consists mainly of a series of dialogues between Sucre and the biblical Abel, in which fragments of Sucre's life are interwoven with philosophizing about human beings.

9. In 1990 Denzil Romero published *La carujada*, a novel about Pedro Carujo conceived in epic tones, as indicated in the title. Although Romero has written two New Historical Novels about Francisco de Miranda, *La tragedia del generalísimo* (1983) and *Gran tour* (1987), in addition to an erotic novel starring Manuela Sáenz, *La esposa del doctor Thorne* (1988), *La carujada*, like *El general en su laberinto*, sticks too closely to the historical version of its protagonist to be considered a New Historical Novel. It is, nonetheless, an interesting novel, featuring an exuberant, neo-baroque style, which at times becomes excessive.

10. Of Bolívar's amatory episodes, Michael Palencia-Roth writes, "almost all of them [were] invented by García Márquez (e.g., the charming Miranda Lindsay) but some not (Manuela Sáenz and Anita Lenoit)" (57).

11. The term *autointertextual* is used by Edward Hood in the title of his 1990 dissertation: "La repetición autointertextual en la narrativa de Gabriel

García Márquez" 'Self-intertextuality in the Fiction of Gabriel García Márquez'. José Miguel Oviedo ("García Márquez," 24–25) also points out the self-
intertextuality between *El general en su laberinto* and *El coronel no tiene quien
le escriba* 'Nobody Writes to the Colonel' (1961), *El otoño del patriarca*, *Crónica de una muerte anunciada*, and *El amor en los tiempos del cólera* 'Love in
the Time of the Cholera' (1985). George McMurray, in addition to indicating
the specific episodes and characters that *El general* shares with the previous
novels, also comments on the techniques of foreshadowing and hyperbole.

12. In the July–December 1990 issue of *Review: Latin American Literature and Arts*, Alvaro Mutis called "El último rostro" a novella and asserted
that he began to work "on a novel about Bolívar's last days" (64) in 1963.

13. In general, short stories are less suitable than novels for historical
themes. In Julio Ortega's 1989 anthology *El muro y la intemperie: El nuevo
cuento latinoamericano*, of the sixty-one stories, only two fall into the historical
category: "Seva" by Puerto Rican Luis López Nieves and "Maroma con pira-
tas" by Peruvian Jorge Velasco Mackenzie.

14. Bolívar has been a favorite subject of novelists, dating back to Arturo
Uslar Pietri's anti-war *Las lanzas coloradas* (1931), and possibly earlier. In the
1949–1992 period covered by this book, three other singular Bolívar novels
were published: Ecuadoran Demetrio Aguilera Malta's *La caballeresa del sol*
'The Sun Lady' (1964), starring Manuela Sáenz, which was the first of a series
of unabashedly popular historical novels; Venezuelan Ramón González Paredes's
Simón Bolívar, la angustia del sueño 'Simón Bolívar, the Anguish of the Dream'
(1982), a very long (681-page) and detailed account of Bolívar's life starting
with his final arrival in Santa Marta and narrated in first person by the Liberator
himself (the author asserts that he studied Bolívar's style for ten years in preparation for writing the novel); and Venezuelan Manuel Trujillo's *El gran dispensador* 'The Great Dispenser' (1983), the first third of which is devoted to the
autobiography of a Spanish *pícaro* who participates in the Conquest of Venezuela, while the other two-thirds are devoted to Bolívar's evocation of different
moments in his life, with allusions to Salvador de Madariaga's biography.

15. The phenomenon of the best-seller has been much more prevalent in
the United States in the past decades than in Latin America because of the huge
size of the literate but not culturally elite middle class in the U.S. On the other
hand, the relatively small reading public in Latin America has traditionally been
associated with the culturally elite.

16. In the epilogue to *Sinfonía desde el Nuevo Mundo*, Germán Espinosa
asserts that he wrote the novel in less than two months and that it was intended
as a film script (155–156).

17. Jean Franco hailed the demise of "High Culture" at the "Translating
Latin America" Conference at SUNY–Binghamton on April 19, 1990, and at
previous conferences going back to at least the meeting of the Asociación Internacional de Hispanistas at Brown University in 1983. In October 1990 the Museum of Modern Art in New York presented an exhibit entitled "High and Low:

Modern Art and Popular Culture." See the *Los Angeles Times,* Calendar Section, October 28, 1990, pp. 3, 4, 93.

18. See my paper "Dos novelas seductoras," cited in Prependix, note 1.

Chapter 6. Bending the Rules, or The Art of Subversion

1. The name Renzi may have been chosen as a tribute to the possibly historical labor leader Renzi who accompanied the Patagonian strikers in 1922 and fought in the International Brigades during the Spanish Civil War, according to Pedro Orgambide's short story "Un poeta en el asilo" published in the volume *La mulata y el guerrero* (1986). However, the historical (?) Renzi is not mentioned in several books on Argentine labor history that I have consulted.

2. A *matrioshka* is a set of Russian dolls that fit inside of each other. As an example of the quick changes of narrators, in the second part, Tardewski tells Renzi how Marconi told him about a woman who praised his (Marconi's) sonnets: *"En cuanto a ella, se apasionaba por la literatura desde siempre, pero no se sentía capaz de dedicarse a escribir porque, dijo la mujer, contó Marconi, me dice Tardewski: ¿Sobre qué puede un escritor construir su obra si no es sobre su propia vida?"* 'In regard to her, she had always had a passion for literature, but she didn't feel capable of devoting herself to writing because, said the woman, Marconi related, Tardewski tells me: What can a writer base her work on if not her own life?' (203).

The quotations in this chapter are from Ricardo Piglia's *Respiración artificial* (1980). The translations are mine.

3. For another example of Piglia's obsession with Roberto Arlt, see Ellen McCracken's recent article "Metaplagiarism and the Critic's Role as Detective: Ricardo Piglia's Reinvention of Roberto Arlt," *PMLA,* 106, no. 5 (October 1991), 1071–1082.

4. Morello-Frosch, *"Biografías fictivas,"* 70. See Chapter 3, note 2 for complete quotation.

5. Brazilian novelist and critic Silviano Santiago alluded in 1990 to Brazilian authors' contempt for the theorists: *"Los grandes escritores del país en general tienden a despreciar completamente la discusión teórica académica en virtud de una jerga, según ellos, impenetrable"* 'The great writers of the country in general tend to regard with complete contempt the academic theoretical discussion because of its jargon, which is, according to them, impenetrable' (55).

6. For example, Maggi writes to Renzi about Luciano, "On seeing him, one had the tendency to be metaphoric and he himself reflected metaphorically" (24).

7. The Ezeiza message may have inspired Tomás Eloy Martínez's *La novela de Perón* (1985) which, somewhat like *Respiración artificial,* uses a family saga (Perón's) in order to explain the violence of the novelistic present, the Ezeiza massacre of June 1973.

8. On February 9, 1992, *New York Times* correspondent Nathaniel C.

Nash reported that "Argentina's decision to open previously secret files on Nazis who fled here after World War II has caused embarrassment to the Government and anxiety among old-line Peronists."

Chapter 7. Over Two Thousand Years of Exile and Marginality—the Jewish Latin American Historical Novel

1. For more details on Jewish immigration to Latin America, see Judith Laikin Elkin's *Jews of the Latin American Republics*, 56.

2. Nora Glickman, in her 1977 Ph.D. dissertation, "The Image of the Jew in Brazilian and Argentine Literature," gives the origin of the phrase "Wandering Jew" as follows: "The origin of the Wandering Jew is the Jerusalem bystander who taunted Jesus on the way to Calvary for his crucifixion. Jesus stopped to rest a moment, but the shoemaker in righteous zeal, told him to move on. Jesus replied: 'Thou shalt wander without rest in death until the last day' (186). The legendary "Wandering Jew" became internationally famous as a result of Eugene Sue's serial novel *Le Juif errant* (1844–1845), and he even appears in García Márquez's *Cien años de soledad*.

3. Among the novels based on the history of the Jews across the centuries, probably the best of all is Frenchman André Schwarz-Bart's *Le dernier des justes* 'The Last of the Just' (1959), still not sufficiently appreciated in literary circles in spite of having won the prestigious Goncourt Prize. Although it is principally a novel of the Holocaust, *Le dernier des justes* actually begins with the Maccabean suicide of Rabbi Yom Tov Levi in York in 1185. The novel then proceeds to trace briefly, in a concise, Borgesian style, the tragic history of several generations of the *"Lamed-Vov"* 'Thirty-six' Just Men, before focusing in greater depth on the odyssey of the Levy family, which begins in a small town in nineteenth-century Poland and ends with their extermination in the Nazi concentration camps.

Marek Halter's *La Mémoire d'Abraham* 'The Book of Abraham' (1983) is a more straightforward, less artistically wrought family saga of the Jews, starting with the flight from Jerusalem in 70 A.D. and ending in the Warsaw uprising of 1943, with each generation receiving almost equal time, whether it be in Alexandria, Toledo, Constantinople, Amsterdam, or Strasbourg.

4. Pedro Orgambide's *Aventuras de Edmund Ziller* is not mentioned by any of the scholars who have written on the phenomenon of the New Historical Novel, and the MLA computerized bibliography revealed only one real study of the novel, by Saúl Sosnowski, published in the Mexican journal *La Semana de Bellas Artes*, which does not have a wide circulation outside of Mexico. The only other item that appeared in the bibliography was a review by Francisco Hinojosa in the Mexican journal *Nexos* (1978). Orgambide's literary works in general are not analyzed in Leonardo Senkman's rather complete *La identidad judía en la literatura argentina* (1983) or in Saúl Sosnowski's *La orilla inminente: Escritores judíos argentinos* (1987).

The translations of the quotations from all the novels in this chapter are mine. The original editions are listed in the Bibliography.

5. *Encomenderos* were landowners who received groups of Indians to help them work the land.

6. John Reed (1887–1920) was a U.S. revolutionary writer and activist who covered the Mexican Revolution in 1914. He helped form the Communist Party in the U.S., became a close friend of Lenin, and witnessed the 1917 Bolshevik Revolution in Russia.

7. During the summer of 1955, I conversed frequently with Monteforte Toledo in Guatemala City, where he had founded and was directing the anti-imperialist weekly newspaper *Lunes* that was critical of the government of Carlos Castillo Armas. At the same time, he was writing *Una manera de morir,* which, according to him, would offend many of his leftist friends, particularly José Revueltas. In June 1956, Monteforte was sequestered from his home and, along with some other critics of Castillo Armas, was driven to the Honduran border and left there without money or passport. He made his way to Costa Rica, where President José Figueres helped him get a passport which allowed him to settle in Mexico. When I arrived in Guatemala City in late June 1956, Monteforte's Mexican wife told me that she and her baggage had been so thoroughly searched at the Guatemala City Airport that she had twice missed her plane to Mexico. She was afraid that the only manuscript of *Una manera de morir* would be confiscated. Since I was planning to travel by land to Costa Rica in August, I offered to take the manuscript and deliver it to Monteforte. I did so, and the next year it was published in Mexico by the Fondo de Cultura Económica. However, to my knowledge, it was not reviewed. Since Monteforte began to write for the leftist weekly *Siempre,* and later received an appointment as a social sciences researcher at the Universidad Nacional Autónoma de México and identified with all the revolutionary causes in Latin America, he did not make any special effort to publicize the novel. To this day, it remains one of Latin American literature's best-kept secrets. Orgambide lived in Mexico from 1974 to 1984 and is surely acquainted with Monteforte.

8. Dr. Francisco Maldonado de Silva is also the protagonist of two fine traditional historical novels: *Camisa limpia* (1989) by the Chilean Guillermo Blanco (1926) and *La gesta del marrano* (1991) by the Argentinean Marcos Aguinis (1935).

9. In addition to Borges's short story entitled "Tres versiones de Judas" and Orgambide's two interpretations (the Jesus who goes to India and the one who is reincarnated as the gaucho Buenaventura), there are at least four other versions of Jesus in post–1975 NHNs and other historical novels. In *Terra nostra* (1975) by Carlos Fuentes, the Christian version of Jesus's crucifixion (694–698) is complemented by an apocryphal one: it was not Jesus but his disciple Simon of Cyrene who was crucified, while Jesus lived in hiding in Alexandria for many years before going to Rome, where he witnessed Nero's persecutions of his followers (202–203, 217–219). Fuentes emphasizes Jesus's

Jewishness. On the other hand, in *La piedra que era Cristo* (1984) by Venezue-lan Marxist Miguel Otero Silva, the Christian Jesus is clearly separated from the negatively portrayed Hebrews, Israelites, and Jews, and the novel ends on a revolutionary note: " . . . *Vivirá por siempre en la música del agua, . . . en la paz de los pueblos, en la rebelión de los oprimidos, sí, en la rebelión de los oprimidos, en el amor sin lágrimas*' ' . . . He will live forever in the music of the water, . . . in the peace among nations, in the rebellion of the oppressed, yes, in the rebellion of the oppressed, in love without tears' (162).

In Colombian Germán Espinosa's *El signo del pez* 'The Sign of the Fish' (1987), the figure of Jesus is fused with that of Saul/Paul, with most of the novel devoted to the latter, who spends most of his time trying to reconcile Jewish beliefs with Hellenism. By sheer coincidence, the same year, Mexican Gerardo Laveaga published *Valeria* (1987) which portrays Ieshúa (Jesus) as a renegade Zealot who would like to restore the former glory of the Jews by cultivating the friendship of the Romans. His lover Valeria is the daughter of an important Roman official during the reign of Tiberius. After actually living in Rome, Ieshúa returns to Israel where he wanders in the desert and begins to preach as the Messiah.

10. A variation of Habacuc's name, Abacuc, is used by Elena Garro in *Recuerdos del porvenir* for the heroic legendary leader of the *Cristeros*.

11. According to the Jewish religion, children are not named after living relatives.

12. Chess games recur throughout the novel, often as a means of settling a dispute, but also as a game. The cartographer's son and his friend Afonso Sanches maintain their morale in the Inquisition dungeon by playing chess with imaginary pieces on an imaginary board (116), which is reminiscent of the new rules for chess proposed by Tardewski in *Respiración artificial,* and still another testimony to the influence of Borges in the post-Boom novels.

13. In April 1991 in Mexico City, Angelina Muñiz told me that her own family and others in Spain had continued to practice Judaism secretly from the fifteenth century through the Franco regime.

14. Since the theme of *Tierra adentro* is the journey to the Promised Land, a better title for the novel, in Spanish or English, might have been *Artzah,* a Hebrew word meaning 'to the Land' or 'to the land of Israel'.

The other two novels by Angelina Muñiz are *Morada interior* 'Interior Dwelling' (1972) about the Spanish mystic Santa Teresa and *La guerra del unicornio* 'The War of the Unicorn' (1983), set vaguely in the fourteenth cen-tury and featuring the friendship between the Christian, Muslim, and Jewish protagonists.

15. El Greco and Velázquez are the only historical figures mentioned in the novel, and they are mentioned only in conjunction with the knights, the mystics, and the *pícaros* 'rogues' in order to describe the Spaniard's national charac-ter (50).

16. The other Latin American historical or partially historical novels about

the experiences of European Jewish immigrants in the late nineteenth and early twentieth centuries are *O ciclo das águas* 'The Cycle of the Water' (1977) by Brazilian Moacyr Scliar; *Nada que perder* 'Nothing to Lose' (1981) by Argentine Andrés Rivera; *Hacer la América* 'To Build Your America' (1984) by Argentine Pedro Orgambide; and *El rumor del astracán* 'The Murmur of Astrakhan' (1991) by Colombian Azriel Bibliowicz.

Chapter 8. *La campaña* by Carlos Fuentes

1. Fuentes affirms his fascination with numerology in *Terra nostra* in the section entitled *"Dos hablan de tres"* 'Two speak about three', where he spends three pages explaining the symbolic meanings of numbers 2 to 11 (535–537).

2. In *Terra nostra*, Fuentes laments that Erasmism did not become the foundation for Spanish American culture (774).

3. Fuentes, *Valiente mundo nuevo* (1990), 272. All translations from *Valiente mundo nuevo* and *La campaña* are mine.

4. Carlos Saura is the name of the internationally known Spanish film director of the 1980s and 1990s.

5. *La campaña*, 195. The quotations are taken from *La campaña*'s first edition in Spanish (Madrid: Mondadori), published toward the end of 1990. The German edition actually appeared a few weeks earlier (Hamburg: Hoffmann und Campe Verlag, 1990). The first Spanish American edition was published in December 1990 by the Mexican publisher Fondo de Cultura Económica . . . in Buenos Aires!

6. In *Valiente mundo nuevo*, Fuentes reveals his fascination with the figure of Santa Anna: "How can a novelist invent fictitious characters capable of surpassing our historical characters? . . . Who can invent a more picturesque character than Antonio López de Santa Anna, the Mexican dictator who held the office of president of the republic eleven times between 1833 and 1855, even staging coups d'état against himself: a womanizer, cock-fight enthusiast, and gambler . . ." (194).

7. The six historical caudillos are José Vicente Camargo, Miguel Lanza, Juan Antonio Alvarez de Arenales, *el padre* Ildefonso de las Muñecas, Ignacio Warnes, and Manuel Ascencio Padilla with his wife (74).

8. In *"En busca de la nación: La novela hispanoamericana del siglo veinte"* 'In Search of the Nation: The Twentieth-Century Spanish American Novel,' my 1954 paper presented at the annual meeting of the Modern Language Association, I pointed out that the principal goal of the *criollista* authors was the search for national identity through a synthesis of their nations' different geographical regions, historical periods, and ethnic groups, with their respective dialects. If we consider Rómulo Gallegos's complete works as a paradigmatic compendium of all of those aspects of Venezuela, then there were certain authors who tried to capture the totality of their nations in a single novel: Jorge Icaza's *Cholos* (1938) for Ecuador, Ciro Alegría's *El mundo es*

ancho y ajeno 'Broad and Alien is the World' (1941) for Peru, José Revueltas's *El luto humano* 'The Stone Knife' (1943) for Mexico, and Mario Monteforte Toledo's *Entre la piedra y la cruz* 'Between the Stone and the Cross' (1948) for Guatemala. Furthermore, in a 1985 paper entitled "La obertura nacional" 'The National Overture,' I analyzed a series of prose fiction works that captured the totality of their nations with a kind of operatic overture, in the same vein as but not necessarily influenced by John Dos Passos's prologue (1938) and epilogue (1936) to *U.S.A.*: Miguel Angel Asturias's *Leyendas de Guatemala* 'Legends of Guatemala' (1930), Rómulo Gallegos's *Canaima* (1934), Eduardo Mallea's *La ciudad junto al río inmóvil* 'The City on the Motionless River' (1936), and, in the post-*criollista* era, *La región más transparente* 'Where the Air Is Clear' (1958) by Fuentes himself and *De donde son los cantantes* 'From Cuba with a Song' (1967) by Severo Sarduy.

9. I say Fuentes is "perhaps" parodying the *criollista* novels because the parody seems to be fused with a genuine fascination with these names on the part of a sixty-two-year-old nostalgic author who was born in Panama, spent the years of his adolescence in Chile and Argentina, and has traveled extensively over the entire continent. In his essay on Rómulo Gallegos in *Valiente mundo nuevo,* Fuentes equates the Venezuelan novelist with the sixteenth-century chroniclers: "For Gallegos the first step in emerging out of anonymity is to baptize nature itself, naming it. The author is carrying out here a primary function which prolongs that of the discoverers and heralds that of the narrators who are conscious of the creative power of names. With the same urgency, with the same power of a Columbus, a Vespucci, or an Oviedo, here we have Gallegos baptizing: 'Amanadoma, Yavita, Pimíchin, the Casiquiare, the Atabapo, the Guainía!' " (111–112). In *La campaña*, Baltasar's first teacher, Julián Ríos, had taught him the importance of names: "'There must be a reason why the fascination with proper names engendered the first treatise of literary criticism, which is Plato's *Cratylus*' " (188).

10. *La campaña,* 13. Although the Voltairian Dorrego is the greatest clock-lover of the three friends, Baltasar's idol Rousseau was the son of a Swiss clockmaker.

11. Fuentes's fascination with the different aspects of time is also present in *Valiente mundo nuevo,* in the chapter on José Lezama Lima's *Paradiso* (238). In Fuentes's short novel *Aura* (1971), once Felipe Montero enters the fantastic/infernal house on Donceles Street, his watch is no longer of any use: "You will not look at your watch again, that useless object that falsely measures a time suitable for human vanity, those little hands that tediously mark the long hours invented to falsify true time, the time that runs with the insulting, mortal velocity that no clock can measure" (57).

In his essay on Carpentier's *Los pasos perdidos* 'The Lost Steps' in *Valiente mundo nuevo,* Fuentes notes that "Fray Pedro speaks of the 'power of walking through time, forwards and backwards.' This is not a mirage: it is simply the reality of another culture, of a different culture. . . . The other culture is the other time. And since there are many cultures, there will also be many times. Certainly as possibilities—but only on the condition that we recognize their sources, and that we not deform them *ad usum ideologicum* in order to serve the progressive time of the Western world, but rather enrich Western time with a variety which is that of the civilizations in their times—foreseen by Carpentier, by Vico, by Lévi-Strauss, by Marcel Mauss, by Nietzsche . . ." (127–128).

12. *Zambos* are half-breeds of Indian and Negro parentage, *cambujos* are of Indian and Chinese parentage, and *tentenelaires* are of quadroon and mulatto parentage.

13. *La campaña*, 45. Reinforcing the importance of the number 6 in the novel, on the same page as the reference to the sixth sense, the word *"necesitaba"* 'he needed' is repeated anaphorically six times.

14. Used in the Argentine context, the word "perhaps" is a clear indication of the intertextual presence of Jorge Luis Borges.

15. See the Fall 1990 issue of the journal *Encounters,* published by The Spain '92 Foundation and the Latin American Institute of the University of New Mexico, for more information on the television documentaries.

16. Fuentes's familiarity and fascination with Jungian archetypes are evident in his essay *"Juan Rulfo: El tiempo del mito"* in *Valiente mundo nuevo,* 145–168.

17. I use the word *epiphanic* because Fuentes himself, in *Valiente mundo nuevo,* speaks of epiphanies (although in a somewhat different vein), referring to Proust, Lezama Lima, and Joyce: "In speaking about Lezama and *Paradiso,* I attach to the word "epiphany" the same value that James Joyce gave it in *Stephen Hero:* 'By epiphany, I meant a sudden spiritual display emerging from the midst of the most commonplace conversations and gestures as well as from the most memorable intellectual situations. I thought that it was incumbent on the literati to record those epiphanies with the utmost care since they represent the most delicate and the most fleeting moments' " (218).

18. In *Terra nostra*, the authorial voice recognizes that he has previously misread Descartes, and he now realizes that Descartes must be tempered with Pascal (774).

19. For an excellent study of the concept of the Great Mother in its positive and negative aspects, consult Erich Neumann, *The Great Mother: An Analysis of the Archetype.*

20. See Will H. Corral, "Gringo viejo/ruso joven o la recuperación dialógica en Fuentes" (130, n. 17).

21. Fuentes's greater understanding of the woman's perspective in his more recent fiction is also evident in Harriet Winslow's ambiguous relationship with her father in *Gringo viejo,* which is quite different from the relationship between Catalina and her father Don Gamaliel Bernal in *La muerte de Artemio Cruz.*

22. *Polvorones* are Mexican wedding cookies: small, soft, round cookies made of flour, butter, sugar, and ground pecans that crumble instantly when put in one's mouth.

23. According to Charlotte Yonge, *History of Christian Names,* Ofelia comes from the Greek word for 'serpent' (346). Harry A. Long, however, in *Personal and Family Names* ([1883]1968), maintains that Ophelia means 'shepherdess' (105) and that it comes from the Latin word for 'sheep', *ovis* (240).

24. According to Arturo Uslar Pietri's *Bolívar hoy,* "one third of the Venezuelan population perished, directly or indirectly, in the war. The prosperity attained at the end of the eighteenth century disappeared. . . . The peasants became soldiers and fought in the swamps of Guayaquil or the high plateaus of Titicaca. The former foreman was now a general or a magistrate. The returning soldiers were not ready to return to the fields. They were preparing violent coups against the authorities or they were marauding in the wilderness like bandits" (26).

25. In an April 1991 conversation with me in Mexico City, Fuentes indicated that another source for the Baltasar Bustos character is the fat and near-sighted Pierre Besukhov in Tolstoy's *War and Peace.*

26. Throughout the pages of *Valiente mundo nuevo,* Fuentes reveals an astonishing familiarity with a great variety of Spanish American novelists, including the most recent ones.

27. See Menton, "En busca del cuento dialógico" in *Narrativa mexicana desde "Los de abajo" hasta "Noticias del imperio,"* 121–129.

28. In a review of Colleen McCullough's 1990 novel *The First Man in Rome,* Robert James writes that it "succeeds as a piece of fiction in entertaining, through intrigue, romance and adventure, but it also shows McCullough's ability to present archaic culture in a palatable, accessible form" (L6).

29. The same message of hope in the face of terrible reality is included in Fuentes's lecture on *El otoño del patriarca* in *Valiente mundo nuevo:* "From the autumn of the patriarch we proceed to the false spring of the technocrat. We have not yet passed through the winters of development without justice, nor through the infernos of debt, inflation, and stagnation of every kind. The true democratic spring will have to pass through these tests. We cannot tolerate another illusion of well-being for the few while we postpone well-being for the majority. Many lessons have been learned. The new model for development, political democracy plus social justice, will be demanding for all the participants in our political life: whether they come from the Right or the Left. It will impose obligations on all of us. It will require an effort unprecedented in our history. There will be no modernity that does not take into account the cultural totality of our countries. There will be no modernity by decree. Nobody believes any longer in an ideal country divorced from the real country" (206).

Bibliography

Adorno, Rolena. "Arms, Letters and the Native Historian." In René Jara and Nicholas Spadaccini, eds., *1492–1992: Re/Discovering Colonial Writing*. Minneapolis: Prisma Institute, 1989.

Aguinis, Marcos. *La gesta del marrano*. Buenos Aires: Planeta, 1991.

Aínsa, Fernando. "La nueva novela histórica latinoamericana." *Plural,* 240 (September 1991), 82–85.

———. "La reescritura de la historia en la nueva narrativa latinoamericana." *Cuadernos Americanos,* nueva época 4, no. 28 (July–August 1991), 13–31.

Aira, César. *Canto castrato*. Buenos Aires: Javier Vergara, 1984.

———. *Moreira*. Buenos Aires: Achával Solo, 1975.

Alazraki, Jaime. "Borges, entre la modernidad y la postmodernidad." *Revista Hispánica Moderna,* 41, 2 (December 1988), 175–179.

Alter, Robert. *Partial Magic: The Novel as a Self-Conscious Genre*. Berkeley: University of California Press, 1975.

Alter, Robert, and Frank Kermode, eds. *The Literary Guide to the Bible*. Cambridge: Harvard University Press, 1987.

Anderson Imbert, Enrique. "Notas sobre la novela histórica en el siglo XIX." In Arturo Torres-Rioseco, ed., *La novela iberoamericana*, 1–24. Albuquerque: University of New Mexico Press, 1952.

Antillano, Laura. *Solitaria solidaria*. Caracas: Planeta, 1990.

Arenas, Reinaldo. *La loma del ángel*. Miami: Mariel, 1987.

————. *El mundo alucinante.* Mexico City: Diógenes, 1969.

Aridjis, Homero. *Memorias del Nuevo Mundo.* Mexico City: Diana, 1988.

————. *1492: Vida y tiempos de Juan Cabezón de Castilla.* Mexico City: Siglo XXI, 1985.

Baccino Ponce de Léon, Napoleón. *Maluco, la novela de los descubridores.* Havana: Casa de las Américas, 1989.

Bakhtin, M. M. *The Dialogic Imagination: Four Essays.* Translated by Caryl Emerson and Michael Holquist. Austin: University of Texas Press, 1986.

Bal, Mieke. *Narratology: Introduction to the Theory of Narrative.* Translated by Christine van Boheemen. Toronto: University of Toronto Press, 1985.

Balderston, Daniel. "Latent Meanings in Ricardo Piglia's *Respiración artificial* and Luis Gusman's *En el corazón de junio.*" *Revista Canadiense de Estudios Hispánicos,* 12, no. 2 (Winter 1988), 207–219.

————, ed. *The Historical Novel in Latin America.* Gaithersburg, Md.: Ediciones Hispamérica, 1986.

Barrientos, Juan José. "Aguirre y la rebelión de los marañones." *Cuadernos Americanos,* nueva época 4, no. 8 (March–April 1988), 92–115.

————. "América, ese paraíso perdido." *Omnia* (Mexico City), June 1986, 69–75.

————. "Colón, personaje novelesco." *Cuadernos Hispanoamericanos,* 437 (November 1986), 45–62.

————. "El grito de Ajetreo: Anotaciones a la novela de Ibargüengoitia sobre Hidalgo." *Revista de la Universidad de México,* July 1983, 15–23.

Barth, John. *The Sot-Weed Factor.* New York: Bantam Books, 1975.

Benítez Rojo, Antonio. *El mar de las lentejas.* Havana: Letras Cubanas, 1979.

Bensoussan, Albert. "Celui qui croyait au Paradis." *La Quinzaine Littéraire,* June 16, 1986.

Bertrand, Marc. "Roman contemporain et histoire." *The French Review,* 16, no. 1 (October 1982), 77–86.

Beverley, John. "La ideología de la música posmoderna y la política de izquierda." *Nuevo Texto Crítico,* 6 (July 1990), 58.

Bibliowicz, Azriel. *El rumor del astracán.* Bogotá: Planeta, 1991.

Bierman, John. *Napoleon III and His Carnival Empire.* New York: St. Martin's Press, 1988.

Blanco, Guillermo. *Camisa limpia.* Santiago, Chile: Pehuén, 1989.

Bolinger, Dwight. *Language, the Loaded Weapon: The Use and Abuse of Language Today.* London: Longman, 1980.

Bona, Dominique. "Abel Posse: Un rêve de conquête." *Le Figaro,* May 26, 1986.

Borges, Jorge Luis. *Ficciones*. Buenos Aires: Emecé, 1968.
———. *Ficciones*. [English version.] New York: Grove Press, 1962.
———. *Labyrinths*. Edited by Donald A. Yates and James E. Irby. New York: New Directions, 1964.
Bradu, Fabienne. Review of *Noticias del imperio* by Fernando del Paso. *Vuelta*, 139 (May 1988), 48–50.
Bruce-Novoa, Juan. "*Noticias del imperio* o la historia apasionada." *Literatura mexicana*, 1, no. 2 (1990), 421–438.
Bryce Echenique, Alfredo. "Una gran novela histórica." *El País* (Madrid), June 26, 1983.
Burgess, Anthony. *Napoleon Symphony*. London: Cape, 1974.
Burns, E. Bradford. "Bartolomé Mitre: The Historian as Novelist, the Novel as History." *Inter-American Review of Bibliography*, 22, no. 2 (1982), 155–166.
Campbell, Joseph. *The Hero with a Thousand Faces*. New York: Pantheon Books, 1949.
Campos, Jorge. "Nueva relación entre la novela y la historia: Abel Posse y Denzil Romero." *Insula*, no. 440–441 (July–August, 1983), 19.
Caparrós, Martín. *Ansay ó los infortunios de la gloria*. Buenos Aires: Ada Korn, 1984.
Carpentier, Alejo. *El arpa y la sombra*. Mexico City: Siglo XXI, 1979.
———. *Concierto barroco*. Mexico City: Siglo XXI, 1974.
———. *La consagración de la primavera*. Mexico City: Siglo XXI, 1978.
———. *Guerra del tiempo* ("El camino de Santiago," "Viaje a la semilla," "Semejante a la noche," and "El acoso"). Mexico City: Compañía General de Ediciones, 1958.
———. *The Harp and the Shadow*. Translated by Thomas Christensen and Carol Christensen. San Francisco: Mercury House, 1990.
———. *The Kingdom of This World*. Translated by Harriet de Onís. New York: Collier Books, 1970.
———. *El recurso del método*. Mexico City: Siglo XXI, 1974.
———. *El reino de este mundo*. Santiago, Chile: Orbe, 1972.
———. *El siglo de las luces*. Mexico City: Compañía General de Ediciones, 1965.
Casanova, Eduardo. *La noche de Abel*. Caracas: Monte Avila, 1991.
Castañón, Adolfo. Review of *Noticias del imperio* by Fernando del Paso. *Vuelta*, 142 (September 1988), 32–33.
Chamberlin, Roy B., and Herman Feldman. *The Dartmouth Bible*. Boston: Houghton Mifflin, 1950.
Ciplijauskaité, Biruté. *La novela femenina contemporánea (1970–1985): Hacia una tipología de la narración en primera persona*. Barcelona: Anthropos, 1988.

Cla, André. "La Renaissance: Deux bourlingeurs des mers." *L'Evènement du Jeudi,* October 7, 1986.

Cobo Borda, Juan Gustavo. "Empresas y tribulaciones de Maqroll 'el gaviero.'" *Quimera,* 3 (March–April 1990), 50–54.

Coleman, Alexander. "*The Dogs of Paradise.*" *New York Times Book Review,* March 18, 1990, 22.

Columbus, Christopher. *The 'Libro de las profecías' of Christopher Columbus.* Translated and annotated by Delno C. West and August Kling. Gainesville: University of Florida Press, 1991.

Corral, Will H. "Gringo viejo/ruso joven o la recuperación dialógica en Fuentes." *Cuadernos Americanos 4,* no. 6 (1987), 121–137.

Cowart, David. *History and the Contemporary Novel.* Carbondale: Southern Illinois University Press, 1989.

Cruz Kronfly, Fernando. *La ceniza del libertador.* Bogotá: Planeta, 1987.

Cunninghame Graham, Robert B. *A Brazilian Mystic: Being the Life and Miracles of Antônio Conselheiro.* New York: Dodd, Mead, 1920.

Da Cunha, Euclides. *Os sertões.* 1902. Reprint. São Paulo: Editora Cultrix, 1973.

Davis, Mary E. "Sophocles, García Márquez and the Labyrinth of Power." *Revista Hispánica Moderna,* 44, no. 1 (June 1991), 108–123.

Day, Mark R. Review of Moacyr Scliar's *The Strange Nation of Rafael Mendes. Los Angeles Times,* January 24, 1988, Book Review Section, 2, 9.

Del Paso, Fernando. *José Trigo.* Mexico City: Siglo XXI, 1966.

———. *Noticias del imperio.* Mexico City: Diana, 1987.

———. "La novela que no olvidé." *Revista de Bellas Artes,* 3 (1983), 46–49.

———. *Palinuro de México.* Madrid: Alfaguara, 1977.

Dershowitz, Alan M. *Chutzpah.* Boston: Little, Brown, 1991.

Di Benedetto, Antonio. *Zama.* Buenos Aires: Centro Editor de América Latina, 1967.

Domecq, Brianda. *La insólita historia de la Santa de Cabora.* Mexico City: Planeta, 1990.

Doctorow, E. L. *Ragtime.* New York: Random House, 1975.

Eagleton, Terry. *Saints and Scholars.* London: Verso, 1987.

Eco, Umberto. *The Name of the Rose.* Translated by William Weaver. San Diego: Harcourt Brace Jovanovich, 1983.

———. *Il nome della rosa.* Milan: Bompiani, 1980.

———. *Postscript to "The Name of the Rose."* New York: Harcourt Brace Jovanovich, 1984.

Elkin, Judith Laikin. *Jews of the Latin American Republics.* Chapel Hill: University of North Carolina Press, 1980.

Elkin, Judith Laikin, and Gilbert W. Merkx, eds. *The Jewish Presence in Latin America*. Boston: Allen and Unwin, 1987.

Espinosa, Germán. *El signo del pez*. Bogotá: Planeta, 1987.

———. *Sinfonía desde el Nuevo Mundo*. Bogotá: Planeta, 1990.

———. *La tejedora de coronas*. Bogotá: Pluma, 1982.

Feierstein, Ricardo. *Cien años de narrativa judeo-argentina, 1889–1989*. Buenos Aires: Editorial Milá, 1990.

Filer, Malva E. "*Los perros del Paraíso* y la nueva novela histórica." In Keith McDuffie and Rose Minc, eds., *Homenaje a Alfredo A. Roggiano*, 395–405. Pittsburgh: Instituto Internacional de Literatura Iberoamericana, 1990.

Fleishman, Avrom. *The English Historical Novel: Walter Scott to Virginia Woolf*. Baltimore: Johns Hopkins Press, 1971.

Franco, Jean. "Si me permiten hablar: La lucha por el poder interpretativo." *Casa de las Américas*, 171 (November–December 1988), 88–94.

Fuentes, Carlos. *Aura*. 6th ed. Mexico City: Alacena, 1971.

———. *La campaña*. Madrid: Mondadori, 1990.

———. "Defend Fiction, and You Defend Truth." *Los Angeles Times*, February 24, 1989, sec. 2, p. 11.

———. "Latin America's Alternative: An Ibero-American Federation." *New Perspectives Quarterly*, 8, no. 1 (Winter 1991), 15–17.

———. *La muerte de Artemio Cruz*. 1962. Reprint. Mexico City: Fondo de Cultura Económica, 1973.

———. *La nueva novela hispanoamericana*. Mexico City: Joaquín Mortiz, 1969.

———. *La región más transparente*. 3rd ed. Mexico City: Fondo de Cultura Económica, 1960.

———. *Terra nostra*. 2nd ed. Mexico City: Joaquín Mortiz, 1976.

———. *Valiente mundo nuevo*. Madrid: Mondadori, 1990.

Gallo, Marta. "Intrascendencia textual en *Respiración artificial* de Ricardo Piglia." *Nueva Revista de Filología Hispánica*, 35, no. 2 (1987), 819–834.

Gamboa, Federico. *Suprema ley*. Mexico City: Eusebio Gómez de la Puente, 1920.

García Márquez, Gabriel. *El amor en los tiempos del cólera*. Mexico City: Diana, 1985.

———. *Cien años de soledad*. Buenos Aires: Sudamericana, 1967.

———. *Crónica de una muerte anunciada*. Bogotá: La Oveja Negra, 1981.

———. *El general en su laberinto*. Madrid: Mondadori, 1989.

———. *One Hundred Years of Solitude*. Translated by Gregory Rabassa. New York: Harper and Row, 1970.

———. *El otoño del patriarca*. Barcelona: Plaza y Janés, 1975.

Gateau, Jean-Charles. "Christophe Colomb parmi les séraphins." *La Tribune à Genève,* June 28, 1986.

Genette, Gérard. *Figures: Essais.* Paris: Editions Du Seuil, 1966.

Gilbert, Catherine. "Une chronique étrangère." *Humanité Dimanche,* May 23, 1986.

Glickman, Nora. "The Image of the Jew in Brazilian and Argentine Literature." Ph.D. dissertation, New York University, 1977.

Glissant, Edouard. *La case du commandeur.* Paris: Editions Du Seuil, 1981.

González Echevarría, Roberto. "García Márquez y la voz de Bolívar." *Cuadernos Americanos,* nueva época 4, no. 28 (July–August 1991), 63–76.

———. "Sarduy, the Boom, and the Post-Boom." In Yvette E. Miller and Raymond Leslie Williams, eds., *The Boom in Retrospect: A Reconsideration.* Special issue of *Latin American Literary Review,* 15, no. 29 (January–June 1987), 57–72.

González Paredes, Ramón. *Simón Bolívar, la angustia del sueño.* Caracas: Producciones Gráficas Reverón, 1982.

Graves, Robert. *I, Claudius.* New York: Modern Library, 1934.

Henderson, Harry B., III. *Versions of the Past: The Historical Imagination in American Fiction.* New York: Oxford University Press, 1974.

Herrera Luque, Francisco. *Los cuatro reyes de la baraja.* Caracas: Grijalbo Mondadori, 1991.

Hinojosa, Francisco. Review of *Aventuras de Edmund Ziller en tierras del nuevo mundo,* by Pedro Orgambide. *Nexos,* 5 (March 1978), 25.

Hoffmann, Léon-François. *Le roman haitien: Idéologie et structure.* Sherbrooke, Canada: Editions Naaman, 1982.

Holquist, Michael, and Vadim Liapunov. *Art and Answerability: Early Philosophical Essays by M. M. Bakhtin.* Austin, Tex.: University of Texas Press, 1990.

Hood, Edward. "La repetición autointertextual en la narrativa de Gabriel García Márquez." Ph.D. dissertation, University of California, Irvine, 1990.

Hughson, Lois. *From Biography to History: The Historical Imagination and American Fiction, 1880–1940.* Charlottesville: University Press of Virginia, 1988.

Hutcheon, Linda. *The Politics of Postmodernism.* London and New York: Routledge & Kegan Paul, 1989.

Ibargoyen, Saúl. *Noche de espadas.* Montevideo: Signos, 1989.

Ibargüengoitia, Jorge. *Los pasos de López.* Mexico City: Océano, 1982.

"Isabelle et Christophe." *Elle,* June 16, 1986.

James, Robert. Review of *The First Man in Rome* by Colleen McCullough. *Santa Ana Register,* October 28, 1990, L5.

Jara, René, and Nicholas Spadaccini, eds. *1492–1992: Re/Discovering Colonial Writing*. Minneapolis: Prisma Institute, 1989.

Jara, René, and Hernán Vidal, eds. *Ficción y política: La narrativa argentina durante el proceso militar*. Buenos Aires: Alianza Editorial; Minneapolis: University of Minnesota, Institute for the Study of Ideologies and Literature, 1987.

Jiménez, Maritza. "Abel Posse ganó Premio Rómulo Gallegos." *El Nacional* (Caracas), July 26, 1987.

Jordan, Constance. Introduction to "Cluster on Reader-Response Criticism." *PMLA*, 106, no. 5 (October 1991), 1037–1039.

Karoubi, Line. "Les chasseurs de paradis." *Le Matin*, April 22, 1986.

Kestergat, Jean. "Colomb, prototype de l'homme latino-américain." *La Libre Belgique*, June 26, 1986.

Krieger, Murray. "Fiction, History, and Empirical Reality." *Critical Inquiry*, 1, no. 2 (December 1974), 335–360.

Kristeva, Julia. *The Kristeva Reader*. Edited by Toril Moi. Oxford: Basil Blackwell, 1986.

"La libertad no es sólo un delirio literario." Entrevista con Abel Posse. *Papeles para el Diálogo* (Caracas), 1 (1988), 30–37.

Larreta, Antonio. *Volavérunt*. Barcelona: Planeta, 1980.

Laveaga, Gerardo. *Valeria*. Mexico City: Diana, 1987.

Legido, Juan Carlos. *Los papeles de los Ayarza*. Montevideo: Proyección, 1988.

Leisy, Ernest E. *The American Historical Novel*. Norman: University of Oklahoma Press, 1950.

Lindenberger, Herbert. *Historical Drama: The Relation of Literature and Reality*. Chicago: University of Chicago Press, 1975.

Lindstrom, Naomi. *Jewish Issues in Argentine Literature from Gerchunoff to Szichman*. Columbia: University of Missouri Press, 1989.

Lóizaga, Patricio. "Abel Posse: El escritor es el último samurai." *Cultura* (Buenos Aires), 7, no. 34 (1990), 7–10.

Long, Harry. *Personal and Family Names; A Popular Monograph on the Origin and History of the Nomenclature of the Present and Former Times*. London: Hamilton, Adams, 1883. Reprint. Detroit: Gail Research Co., 1968.

Lukács, Georg. *La novela histórica*. Translated into Spanish by Manuel Sacristán. Barcelona: Grijalbo, 1976.

Mac Adam, Alfred. "Euclides da Cunha y Mario Vargas Llosa: Meditaciones intertextuales." *Revista Iberoamericana*, 126 (January–March, 1984), 157–164.

Mandrell, James. "The Prophetic Voice in Garro, Morante, and Allende." *Comparative Literature*, 42, no. 3 (Summer 1990), 227–246.

Maranhão, Haroldo. *Memorial do fim (A morte de Machado de Assis)*. São Paulo: Marco Zero, 1991.

Marcos, Juan Manuel. "Mempo Giardinelli in the Wake of Utopia." *Hispania*, 70 (May 1987), 240–249.

———. "La narrativa de Mempo Giardinelli." *Escritura* (Caracas), 8, no. 16 (July–December 1983), 217–222.

———. Review of *Andando el tiempo* by Eraclio Zepeda. *Revista Iberoamericana*, 130–131 (January–June 1985), 406–411.

———. Review of *De amor y de sombra* by Isabel Allende. *Revista Iberoamericana*, 137 (October–December 1986), 1086–1090.

Marlowe, Stephen. *The Memoirs of Christopher Columbus*. London: Jonathan Cape, 1987.

Márquez Rodríguez, Alexis. "Abel Posse: La reinvención de la historia." *Papel Literario* (Caracas), August 2, 1987.

———. *Arturo Uslar Pietri y la nueva novela histórica hispanoamericana: A propósito de "La isla de Robinson."* Caracas: Contraloría General de la República, 1986.

———. Review of *La luna de Fausto* by Francisco Herrera Luque. *Casa de las Américas*, 144 (May–June 1984), 174.

Martínez, Gregorio. *Crónica de músicos y diablos*. Hanover, N.H.: Ediciones del Norte, 1991.

Martínez, Herminio. *Diario maldito de Nuño de Guzmán*. Mexico City: Diana, 1990.

———. *Las puertas del mundo: Una autobiografía hipócrita del Almirante*. Mexico City: Diana, 1992.

Martínez, Tomás Eloy. *La novela de Perón*. Buenos Aires: Legasa, 1985.

Mattos, Tomás de. *¡Bernabé, Bernabé!* Montevideo: Banda Oriental, 1988.

McCracken, Ellen. "Metaplagiarism and the Critic's Role as Detective: Ricardo Piglia's Reinvention of Roberto Arlt." *PMLA*, 106, no. 5 (October 1991), 1071–1082.

McEwan, Neil. *Perspective in British Historical Fiction Today*. London: MacMillan, 1987.

McGrady, Donald. *La novela histórica en Colombia, 1844–1959*. Bogotá: Editorial Kelly, 1962.

McHale, Brian. *Postmodernist Fiction*. New York: Methuen, 1987.

McMurray, George R. "*El general en su laberinto*: Historia y ficción." *Revista de Estudios Colombianos*, 7 (1989), 39–44.

Meneses, Carlos. "La visión del periodista, tema recurrente en Mario Vargas Llosa." *Revista Iberoamericana*, no. 123–124 (April–September, 1983), 523–529.

Menton, Seymour. "*La campaña*: Crónica de una guerra denunciada." *Universidad de México*, 46, no. 485 (June 1991), 5–11.

———. "In Search of a Nation: The Twentieth-Century Spanish American Novel." *Hispania*, 38, no. 4 (December 1955), 432–442.

———. *Narrativa mexicana desde "Los de abajo" hasta "Noticias del imperio."* Tlaxcala, Mexico: Universidad Autónoma de Tlaxcala, 1991.

———. *La novela colombiana: Planetas y satélites.* Bogotá: Plaza y Janés, 1978.

———. "La obertura nacional: Asturias, Gallegos, Mallea, Dos Passos, Yáñez, Fuentes y Sarduy." *Revista Iberoamericana*, 51, no. 130–131 (June 1985), 151–166.

———. "*Los perros del Paraíso*, the Denunciation of Power." *Hispania*, 75, no. 4 (October 1992), 930–940.

———. *Prose Fiction of the Cuban Revolution.* Austin: University of Texas Press, 1975.

———. "Teorizando sobre la teoría." *El Café Literario* (Bogotá), 2, no. 12 (November–December 1979), 35ff.

———. "Theorizing on Theory." *Hispania*, 63, no. 1 (March 1980), 69–70. Reprint. *Journal of Literary Theory*, 4 (1983), 20–22.

———. "*Ver para no creer*: '*El otoño del patriarca*'." *Caribe*, 1, no. 1 (1976).

Mercader, Martha. *Juanamanuela, mucha mujer.* Barcelona: Planeta, 1983.

Mestre, J.-Ph. "Abel Posse: La découverte de l'Amérique." *Le Progrès*, n.d. [1986].

Mier, Fray Servando Teresa de. *Memorias.* [Ca. 1820]. Reprint. Prologue by Alfonso Reyes. Madrid: América, 1917.

Molina, Silvia. *Ascensión Tun.* Mexico City: Martín Casillas, 1981.

———. *La familia vino del norte.* Mexico City: Océano, 1987.

Morales Pradilla, Próspero. *Los pecados de Inés de Hinojosa.* Bogotá: Plaza y Janés, 1986.

Morello-Frosch, Marta. "Biografías fictivas: Formas de resistencia y reflexión en la narrative argentina reciente." In René Jara and Hernán Vidal, eds., *Ficción y política: La narrativa argentina durante el proceso militar*, 60–70. Buenos Aires: Alianza Editorial; Minneapolis: University of Minnesota, Institute for the Study of Ideologies and Literature, 1987.

———. "Ficción e historia en *Respiración artificial* de Ricardo Piglia." *Discurso Literario*, 1, no. 2 (Spring 1984), 243–245.

Morson, Gary Saul, ed. *Literature and History: Theoretical Problems and Russian Case Studies.* Stanford: Stanford University Press, 1986.

Morson, Gary Saul, and Caryl Emerson. *Rethinking Bakhtin: Extensions and Challenges.* Evanston, Ill.: Northwestern University Press, 1989.

Moya Palencia, Mario. *El México de Egerton, 1831–1842.* Mexico City: Miguel Angel Porrúa, 1991.

Muñiz, Angelina. Interview. *Gaceta UNAM*, 2, no. 28 (April 5, 1984), 18, 25.

―――. *La guerra del Unicornio*. Mexico City: Artífice, 1983.

―――. *Morada interior*. Mexico City: Joaquín Mortiz, 1972.

―――. *Tierra adentro*. Mexico City: Joaquín Mortiz, 1977.

Murphy, Raquel Aguilu de. "Proceso transformacional del personaje del amo en *Concierto barroco*." *Revista Iberoamericana*, 57, no. 154 (January–March 1991), 161–170.

Mutis, Alvaro. "Bolívar and García Márquez." *Review: Latin American Literature and Arts*, 43 (July–December 1990), 64–65.

―――. "El último rostro." In *Obra literaria*, vol. 2, 101–118. Bogotá: Procultura, 1985.

Nadel, Ira Bruce. *Biography: Fiction, Fact and Form*. London: MacMillan, 1984.

Neumann, Erich. *The Great Mother: An Analysis of the Archetype*. Translated by Ralph Manheim. Princeton, N.J.: Princeton University Press, 1970.

Newman, Kathleen Elizabeth. "The Argentine Political Novel: Determinations in Discourse." Ph.D. dissertation, Stanford University, 1983.

Nye, Robert. *Falstaff: Being the Acta Domini Johannis Fastolfe, or Life and Valiant Deeds of Sir John Faustof, or The Hundred Days War, as told by Sir John Fastolf, K.G., to his Secretaries William Worcester, Stephn Scrope, ...* London: Hamilton, 1976.

Ocampo, Aurora M., and Ernesto Prado Velázquez. *Diccionario de escritores mexicanos*. Mexico City: Universidad Nacional Autónoma de México, 1967.

Orgambide, Pedro. *El arrabal del mundo*. Buenos Aires: Bruguera, 1983.

―――. *Aventuras de Edmund Ziller en tierras del nuevo mundo*. Mexico City: Grijalbo, 1977.

―――. *Hacer la América*. Buenos Aires: Bruguera, 1984.

―――. *Los inquisidores*. Buenos Aires: Sudamericana, 1967.

―――. *La mulata y el guerrero*. Buenos Aires: Ediciones del Sol, 1986.

Ortega, Julio. "El lector en su laberinto." *Casa de las Américas*, 176 (September–October 1989), 144–151.

―――. *El muro y la intemperie: El nuevo cuento latinoamericano*. Hanover, N.H.: Ediciones del Norte, 1989.

Ortega y Medina, Juan A. *La idea colombina del descubrimiento desde México (1836–1986)*. Mexico City: Universidad Nacional Autónoma de México, 1987.

Otero Silva, Miguel. *Lope de Aguirre, príncipe de la libertad*. Barcelona: Seix Barral, 1979.

―――. *La piedra que era Cristo*. Bogotá: Oveja Negra, 1984.

Oviedo, José Miguel. "Chronology." *Review: Latin American Literature and Arts,* 14 (Spring 1975), 6–11.

———. "García Márquez en el laberinto de la soledad." *Revista de Estudios Colombianos,* 7 (1989), 18–26.

———. "Vargas Llosa en Canudos: Versión clásica de un clásico." *Eco,* 246 (April 1982), 641–664.

———. "Vargas Llosa in Canudos." *World Literature Today,* 60, no. 1 (Winter 1986), 51–54.

Pacheco, José Emilio. "Historia y novela: Todos nuestros ayeres." *Proceso,* 444 (May 6, 1985), 50–51.

———, ed. *La novela histórica y de folletín.* Mexico City: Promexa, 1985.

Palencia-Roth, Michael. "Gabriel García Márquez: Labyrinths of Love and History." *World Literature Today,* 65, no. 1 (Winter 1991), 54–58.

Patán, Federico. "Una novela de postrimerías." *Revista de Estudios Colombianos,* 7 (1989), 45–47.

Peyre, Henri. *French Novelists of Today.* New York: Oxford University Press, 1967.

Piglia, Ricardo. *Respiración artificial.* Buenos Aires: Pomaire, 1980.

Poniatowska, Elena. *Tinísima.* Mexico City: Era, 1992.

Posse, Abel. *Daimón.* Buenos Aires: Emecé, 1989.

———. *Los demonios ocultos.* Buenos Aires: Emecé, 1987.

———. *The Dogs of Paradise.* Translated by Margaret Sayers Peden. New York: Atheneum, 1989.

———. *El largo atardecer del caminante.* Buenos Aires: Emecé, 1992; Barcelona: Plaza y Janés, 1992.

———. *Momento de morir.* Buenos Aires: Emecé, 1979.

———. *Los perros del Paraíso.* Barcelona: Plaza y Janés, 1987.

Promis, José. "Balance de la novela en Chile: 1973–1990." *Hispamérica,* 19, no. 55 (1990), 15–26.

Rama, Angel. "*La guerra del fin del mundo,* una obra maestra del fanatismo artístico." *Eco,* 246 (April 1982), 600–640.

———. *Novísimos narradores hispanoamericanos en "Marcha," 1964–1980.* Mexico City: Marcha, 1981.

Ramírez, Sergio. *Castigo divino.* Madrid: Mondadori, 1988.

Ramos, Luis Arturo. *Este era un gato . . . .* Mexico City: Grijalbo, 1987.

Read, J. Lloyd. *The Mexican Historical Novel, 1826–1910.* New York: Instituto de las Españas en los Estados Unidos, 1939.

Reed, Ishmael. *Mumbo Jumbo.* Garden City, N.Y.: Doubleday, 1972.

Reyes, Alfonso. *La experiencia literaria.* Vol. 14 of *Obras completas.* Mexico City: Fondo de Cultura Económica, 1962.

Rivera, Andrés. *Nada que perder.* Buenos Aires: Centro Editor de América Latina, 1981.

Roa Bastos, Augusto. *Vigilia del Almirante*. Madrid: Alfaguara, 1992.

———. *Yo el Supremo*. Bogotá: Oveja Negra, 1985.

Rodríguez Juliá, Edgardo. *La noche oscura del Niño Avilés*. Río Piedras: Ediciones Huracán, 1984.

———. *La renuncia del héroe Baltasar*. San Juan: Antillana, 1974.

Rodríguez Monegal, Emir. "Carnaval/Antropofagia/Parodia." *Revista Iberoamericana*, 45, no. 108–109 (July–December 1979), 401–412.

Romero, Denzil. *La carujada*. Caracas: Planeta, 1990.

———. *La esposa del doctor Thorne*. Barcelona: Tusquets, 1988.

———. *Grand tour: Epítasis*. Caracas: Alfadil; Barcelona: Laia, 1987.

———. *La tragedia del generalísimo*. Barcelona: Argos Vergara, 1983.

Ruffinelli, Jorge. "Uruguay: Dictadura y re-democratización. Un informe sobre la literatura 1973–1989." *Nuevo Texto Crítico*, 5 (1990), 37–66.

———. "Vargas Llosa: Dios y el diablo en la tierra del sol." In Jorge Ruffinelli, ed., *La escritura invisible*, 98–109. Xalapa: Universidad Veracruzana, 1986.

Saer, Juan José. *El entenado*. Mexico City: Folios, 1983.

———. *La ocasión*. Barcelona: Destino, 1988.

Santiago, Silviano. "El estado actual de los estudios literarios en Brasil." *Hispamérica*, 56/57 (1990), 47–56.

———. *Em liberdade: Diário de Graciliano Ramos*. Rio de Janeiro: Paz e Terra, 1981.

Saramago, José. *Baltasar and Blimunda*. Translated by Giovanni Pontiero. San Diego: Harcourt Brace Jovanovich, 1987.

Sarduy, Severo. *Escrito sobre un cuerpo*. Buenos Aires: Sudamericana, 1969.

Scanlan, Margaret. *Traces of Another Time: History and Politics in Postwar British Fiction*. Princeton: Princeton University Press, 1990.

Schabert, Ina. *Der historische roman in England und Amerika*. Darmstadt: Wissenschaftliche Buchgesellschaft, 1981.

Schwarz-Bart, André. *Le dernier des justes*. Paris: Editions Du Seuil, 1959.

———. *The Last of the Just*. Translated by Stephen Becker. New York: Atheneum, 1960.

Scliar, Moacir. *O ciclo das águas*. Porto Alegre: Globo, 1977.

———. *A estranha nação de Rafael Mendes*. Porto Alegre: L&PM Editores, 1983.

Scott Standard Postage Stamp Catalogue: 1990. New York: Scott Publishing Co., 1990.

Sefchovich, Sara. *México, país de ideas, país de novelas: Una sociología de la literatura mexicana*. Mexico City: Editorial Grijalbo, 1987.

Senkman, Leonardo. *La identidad judía en la literatura argentina*. Buenos Aires: Ediciones Pardes, 1983.

Setti, Ricardo A. *Conversas com Vargas Llosa*. São Paulo: Editora Brasiliense, 1986.

Simón, Francisco. *Martes triste*. Santiago: Bruguera, 1985.

Sklodowska, Elzbieta. *La parodia en la nueva novela hispanoamericana (1960–1985)*. Purdue University Monographs in Romance Languages. Amsterdam and Philadelphia: John Benjamins, 1991.

———. "El (re)descubrimiento de América: La parodia en la novela histórica." *Romance Quarterly*, 37, no. 3 (1990), 345–352.

Smith, Verity. "Ausencia de Toussaint: Interpretación y falseamiento de la historia en *El reino de este mundo*." In *Historia y ficción en la narrativa hispanoamericana*, 275–284. Caracas: Monte Avila, 1984.

Solares, Ignacio. *Madero, el otro*. Mexico City: Joaquín Mortiz, 1989.

———. *La noche de Angeles*. Mexico City: Diana, 1991.

Sosnowski, Saúl. *La orilla inminente: Escritores judíos argentinos*. Buenos Aires: Legasa, 1987.

———. "¿Quién es Edmund Ziller?" *La Semana de Bellas Artes*, 8 (January 1978), 8–11.

———. *Represión y reconstrucción de una cultura: El caso argentino*. Buenos Aires: EUDEBA, 1988.

Souza, Raymond D. *La historia en la novela hispanoamericana moderna*. Bogotá: Tercer Mundo Editores, 1988.

Spector, Robert D. Review of *Protocols of Reading* by Robert Scholes. *World Literature Today*, 64, no. 3 (Summer 1990), 539–540.

Süskind, Patrick. *Perfume: The Story of a Murderer*. Translated by John E. Wooks. New York: Pocket Books, 1987.

Taibo, Paco Ignacio, II. *La lejanía del tesoro*. Mexico City: Planeta–Joaquín Mortiz, 1992.

Thomas, Peter N. Review of *Noticias del imperio* by Fernando del Paso. *Chasqui*, 20, no. 1 (May 1991), 152–153.

Thorne, Carlos. *Papá Lucas*. Buenos Aires: La Flor, 1987.

Todorov, Tzvetan. *The Conquest of America: The Question of the Other*. Translated by Richard Howard. New York: Harper and Row, 1984.

Trujillo, Manuel. *El gran dispensador*. Caracas: CADAFE, 1983.

Turner, Joseph W. "The Kinds of Historical Fiction: An Essay in Definition and Methodology." *Genre*, 12, no. 3 (Fall 1979), 333–355.

Uslar Pietri, Arturo. *Bolívar hoy*. Caracas: Monte Avila, 1990.

———. *La isla de Robinson*. Barcelona: Seix Barral, 1981.

———. *Las lanzas coloradas*. Madrid: Zeus, 1931.

———. *La visita en el tiempo*. Bogotá: Norma, 1990.

Vargas Llosa, Mario. *La guerra del fin del mundo*. Barcelona: Plaza y Janés, 1981.

———. "Inquest in the Andes." *New York Times Magazine*, July 31, 1983, 18–23, 33ff.

————. *The War of the End of the World*. Translated by Helen R. Lane. New York: Farrar Straus Giroux, 1984.

————. *A Writer's Reality*. Edited by Myron I. Lichtblau. Syracuse: Syracuse University Press, 1991.

Vásquez, Carmen. "*El reino de este mundo* y la función de la historia en la concepción de lo real maravilloso." *Cuadernos Hispanoamericanos*, 28 (July–August 1991), 90–114.

Veiga, José J. *A casca da serpente*. Rio de Janeiro: Bertrand Brasil, 1989.

Verissimo, Erico. *O tempo e o vento*. Vol. 1, *O continente*. Porto Alegre: Globo, 1949.

————. *O tempo e o vento*. Vol. 2, *O retrato*. Porto Alegre: Globo, 1951.

————. *O tempo e o vento*. Vol. 3, *O arquipélago*. Porto Alegre: Globo, 1961.

Vidal, Hernán, ed. *Fascismo y experiencia literaria: Reflexiones para una recanonización*. Minneapolis: Institute for the Study of Ideologies and Literature, 1985.

Von Hagen, Victor W. *The Four Seasons of Manuela: A Biography*. New York: Duell, Sloan and Pearce; Boston: Little, Brown and Company, 1952.

Wesseling, Elisabeth. *Writing History as a Prophet: Postmodernist Innovations of the Historical Novel*. Amsterdam and Philadelphia: John Benjamins, 1991.

White, Hayden. *Metahistory: The Historical Imagination in Nineteenth-Century Europe* (1973). Baltimore: Johns Hopkins Press, 1987.

Williams, Raymond Leslie. "The Boom Twenty Years Later: An Interview with Mario Vargas Llosa." In Yvette E. Miller and Raymond L. Williams, ed., *The Boom in Retrospect: A Reconsideration*, 201–206. Special issue of *Latin American Literary Review*, 15, no. 29 (January–June 1987).

————. *Mario Vargas Llosa*. New York: Ungar, 1986.

Woolf, Virginia. *Orlando: A Biography*. New York: Harcourt Brace Jovanovich, 1956.

Yonge, Charlotte. *History of Christian Names*. London: MacMillan, 1884. Reprint. Detroit: Gale Research, 1966.

Zamudio Zamora, José. *La novela histórica en Chile*. Santiago: Ediciones Flor Nacional, 1949.

Index

Lightning Source UK Ltd.
Milton Keynes UK
UKHW011835030221
378186UK00001B/46